FIELD COMMAND

FIELD COMMAND

Charles "Sid" Heal

Lantern Books | New York
A DIVISION OF BOOKLIGHT INC.

2012
Lantern Books
128 Second Place
Brooklyn, NY 11231
www.lanternbooks.com

Printed in the United States of America

Heal, Sid.
Field command / Charles "Sid" Heal.
p. cm.
ISBN 978-1-59056-344-1 (pbk. : alk. paper) — ISBN 978-1-59056-355-7 (ebook)
1. Law enforcement. 2. Tactics. 3. Crisis management. I. Title.
HV7921. H427 2011
363.2'3—dc23

2011050492

CONTENTS

As with my other books, this one is also dedicated to Linda, my bride of more than forty years who has stood with me through five children, 41 years in the USMCR, 33 years in law enforcement, four tours of combat in four different theaters, and too many stitches, crutches, bandages, slings and broken bones to mention. She has blessed me with years of laughter and five great kids who picked five great sons and daughters-in-law. Our reward has been our family, not the least of which is our nine grandchildren.

"Many women do noble things, but you surpass them all."

—PROVERBS 31:29 (NIV)

ACKNOWLEDGEMENTS

Like *Sound Doctrine*, this book is a reflection of mentors who have not only assisted me in understanding the factors and influences in play during tactical operations but have actually shaped my thinking. When it came time to write a more comprehensive text I unhesitatingly sought the insight and guidance from the two who most helped me with the previous text, Larry Richards and Tim Anderson. Tragically, Larry Richards suffered a fatal stroke a few weeks before I began this manuscript. Larry and I had served together in Iraq in 2003 where he earned a Bronze Star. We both returned home and were retired; me as a CWO-5 and Larry as a "full-bird" Colonel. Both of us rejoined the Los Angeles Sheriff's Department and continued our careers. Although he hid it well, Larry had developed a heart condition and retired from the LASD shortly after me. On July 14th, 2010, Larry suffered a massive stroke and died a few days later. His sense of humor, wit and clarity of thought are greatly missed.

Colonel T.G. "Tim" Anderson, USMCR (retired) has thrice been my reporting senior officer in the Marine Corps; the first as a captain and brigade platoon commander in the mid-1970s, then as a Lieutenant Colonel and the Commanding Officer of 3rd ANGLICO[1] in the mid-1980s and finally as a Colonel and Chief of Staff of 1st MACE.[2] He is both a Vietnam veteran and a graduate

1 ANGLICO is an acronym which stands for Air-Naval Gunfire Liaison Company. There are currently five ANGLICO units in the world, two of which (3rd and 4th) are in the USMCR. In the simplest terms, their dual mission is to serve as liaisons to allied militaries of the United States and as airborne, amphibious forward observers to plan and coordinate fire support.

2 MACE is an acronym which stands for Marine Air-Ground Task Force Augmentation Command Element. In the simplest terms, their mission is to assist the 1st Marine Expeditionary Force in planning, coordinating and implementing combat missions.

of Army War College. Likewise, our police careers have paralleled, he with the LAPD and me with the LASD. We've both spent our early years in law enforcement working the streets of south central Los Angeles, in SWAT and other "high adventure" assignments. Since 2008 we've taught together throughout the United States. We have been life-long friends and I have immeasurably profited from both his guidance and example.

R.K. Miller is another Marine Vietnam veteran who got out and became a police officer. He served for 30 years eventually retiring as a Lieutenant with the Huntington Beach (Calif.) Police Department. During his police career he worked in SWAT and other tactical assignments for more than 17 years. R.K. continues to serve as a reserve police officer in his home town. He is in much demand as a trainer in law enforcement tactical subjects throughout the United States and currently is in charge of a local SWAT Academy. He is also a well-known author in police professional magazines and a featured columnist for *Law Officer Magazine*. If there are any mistakes left in the manuscript it is because I didn't take some of RK's comments seriously enough.

The manuscript was well underway when I sought a "sanity check" on the chapter focused on time as a dimension of battlespace. USMCR Colonel Stanton S. "Stan" Coerr is another Marine who has gained a reputation for understanding and applying tactical science and was my SALT Team[3] leader in the last war. He also holds degrees from Duke, Harvard and the Naval War College and is a published author in military professional journals. When he finished describing some of the more esoteric concepts for maneuvering in time he volunteered to become a reader/editor. After explaining what he was letting himself in for I sent him the entire manuscript completed to that point and over the next several months he painstakingly edited the entire final draft.

---

3 SALT is an acronym that stands for "Supporting Arms Liaison Team." A SALT team (Yes, I know "team" is redundant but that is how the term is used in the Marine Corps) typically works at a battalion level and oversees at least two firepower control teams (FCT).

One of the advantages of being an avid reader is that I not only gain knowledge of a particular subject but I subconsciously (and sometimes consciously) critique how it is presented. Early on I sought and received the help and support of Chris Branuelas to illustrate some of the more difficult concepts. Despite a demanding assignment at the LASD Narcotics Bureau, where he works as a Lieutenant, Chris took time from what can only be described as a hectic schedule to interpret concepts into understandable graphics and illustrations. For months we exchanged emails, graphics, and photographs at all times of the day and night, weekends and holidays, not to mention numerous meetings to go over drafts and examples. Besides sprucing up my own ideas, he often suggested ways that elucidated abstractions and concepts far better than I could have even imagined.

Besides these four primary advisors, I received insight and guidance from a number of other subject matter experts who kept me on the straight and narrow. Robert Coram, (Yes, THAT Robert Coram, author of *John Boyd: The Fighter Pilot Who Changed the Art of War* and numerous others) assisted in the chapter on time, especially with the Boyd cycle. He was especially helpful in encapsulating the essence of the OODA Loop and making it understandable at an introductory level.

Dr. Robert J. Bunker has not only been a long-time friend, he has mentored me in multi-dimensional warfare and asymmetric strategies since 1996. He continues to serve as a consultant to both the military and law enforcement communities and is a founding member of the Los Angeles Terrorism Early Warning Group. He has been a Futurist in Residence at the FBI Academy as well as a college professor and author in his own right. The concepts described in the chapter on cyberspace have been derived directly from his teachings and writings.

Commander Daryl Evans and I have been colleagues in the Los Angeles Sheriff's Departments for decades but we became fast friends when he worked for me as a SWAT Commander at the Special Enforcement Bureau. In the midst of the most complex and dangerous operations with barricaded suspects, hostages, active shooters, and fleeing felons he was the pivot. Besides being a tactical scholar in his own right he has a humorous wit that enables him to strike right to the heart of the matter without offending. His ability to make the esoteric understandable has made him invaluable as a sounding board long after we went our separate ways.

Colonel John Alexander, and I first met in the mid-1990s and discovered we had been following similar career paths, albeit mine was "in trace" and far less noteworthy. His career in the US Army Special Forces sounds like something from a Tom Clancy novel. The fact that he is also a former police officer with a Ph.D. provides him with a practitioner's appreciation of the pragmatic and a scientist's perception of the possible. He quickly became both a friend and mentor and I routinely consult him for advice and direction.

Gordon Graham and I first met during the earliest part of our careers when we taught at the California Specialized Training Institute. He has become renowned for his practical insight and understanding of risk management and his sense of humor is exceeded only by his sense of justice. His "Five Pillars of Success" has become a standard in assessing and managing risk for the public safety services. We routinely correspond, sometimes exchanging information and sometimes commiserating the absurd. He's quite possibly the only police officer who has ever succeeded in making traffic investigations sound interesting.

Dennis "Denny" Beene and Captain (ret.) Richard "Odie" Odenthal were my partners at the LASD Emergency Operations Bureau. Together we worked through earthquakes, fires, storms, mudslides, floods, riots, parades, tournaments, and every other imaginable major event. I first met Odie while he was my Sergeant at Firestone Station and then later worked with him at the Emergency Operations Bureau. Likewise, Denny and I worked EOB together for years while he was the commander and I was his Operations Lieutenant. Denny is currently an Assistant Chief of California's Office of Emergency Services and was instrumental in establishing California's Standardized Emergency Management System (SEMS), a predecessor to the National Incident Management System (NIMS).

As my career progressed I was coached by a number of instructors, many of whom were from other departments and who not only taught me in formal sessions but became lifelong mentors when I was confronted by something beyond my abilities. They were especially helpful when I was struggling with something and needed encouragement as well as guidance. While they didn't directly participate in the writing of this text, it would be disingenuous to ignore their profound influence in my thinking and understanding of how domestic tactical operations and emergency responses unfold.

I was introduced to John Kolman, the founder of the National Tactical Officers Association after I was assigned to our Special Enforcement Bureau as a Sergeant/Team Leader in the mid-1980s. He was the first one who encouraged and coached me in writing on tactical subjects. To say he has been influential in both my thinking and success would be an understatement.

Mike Hillmann and Ron McCarthy from LAPD were already well-known in the law enforcement community about the time I was learning to drive. Over the years I've felt like an adopted son as they identified pitfalls and kept me on solid ground.

Steve Ijames and I became fast friends during the early period of using flashbangs in domestic law enforcement applications and later with nonlethal options. As we both gained recognition it was interesting to note that we saw each other more often in other countries than when we were home. The Internet became our forum and we have continued to frequently exchange information long after we both retired.

In my early (and formative) years as the Commanding Officer of the LASD's Special Enforcement Bureau my champion was my reporting senior (then) Commander Marvin "Marv" Cavanaugh. To say the least, many of my ideas were "outside the box" and came as somewhat of a shock to those who thought they were throwing "Br'er Rabbit back into the briar patch." Marv became my guardian angel as I sought to change things that were not necessarily broken. I found out much later that he had been defending me in disputes at the executive level where I was the subject but not a participant. Many of our concerns have proven valid and late in 2001 he commented that "On June 4th you were an alarmist; on September 12th you were a prophet." [4]

Mike Grossman and I had known each other for nearly two-decades before we became friends while assigned as Lieutenants to the LASD's Technology Exploration Project. Even more interesting is that we are polar opposites in our approach from everything from management and problem solving to planning and decision making. We don't even have similar hobbies. That said, we complimented each other so well that each of us came to admire the differences that made the other successful. Together we made a formidable team. Mike obtained his MA in Security Studies (Homeland Security and Defense) from the Naval Postgraduate School in Monterey, CA and is now the Chief of the LASD's Office of Homeland Security.

Ken Hubbs is a Lieutenant with the San Diego Police Department and president of the California Association of Tactical Officers. He has long been a friend and mentor and has provided me with many one-liners as quotable insights. He is unremitting in his continual demand for safety in these hazardous undertakings and is a sought after trainer throughout the United States.

Last, but certainly not least are the thousands of students of tactical science who have not only provided the incentive to write this text but asked questions I should have asked myself. To the degree that these concepts are understandable can be largely attributed to their insistence of me providing them with understandable answers. This has not only served to help me distill the essence of each concept but to hone my own understanding. Ultimately, the success or failure of this book will be determined by how well I have succeeded in answering their questions.

---

4 June 4th, 2001 was the day I made public a three-year strategic plan that was focused on enabling the LASD SWAT teams to become the first domestic law enforcement agency in the nation to have a true counterterrorist capability. For those old enough to remember, this was not seen as "value added" before 9-11. Marv was eventually (and wisely) promoted to Assistant Sheriff.

FOREWORD

In my long career in the military, in academia, and in law enforcement training, I have never had the privilege, the honor, to hold in my hands a more important book than Sid Heal's *Field Command*. This book will influence and shape law enforcement tactics and leadership for generations to come. And we are in desperate need of this book, and the contribution it will make to the law enforcement community.

AN URGENT NEED FOR WARRIOR LEADERS IN THE LAW ENFORCEMENT COMMUNITY

If you are in a *war*, you are a *warrior*.

Is there a war on drugs? Is there a war on crime? Is there a war against terrorism? Is our nation at war? Are our armed forces fighting and dying across the globe to confront and contain a terrorist threat that murdered 3,000 of our citizens and could strike again at any time? Are you confronting and containing aggression as a peace officer at home, or as a law enforcement trainer or peacekeeper in some distant land? Then, you are a warrior.

In Lakewood, Washington, in 2009, a man walked into a coffee shop and murdered four police officers. This was the all-time record body count of police officers in a single incident by a single perpetrator in American history. Every piece of information that we have tells us that the killer had never met those four officers before in his life. So, why did he kill them? Because of the uniform they wear.

When people who don't know you try to kill you because of the uniform you wear, there is a word for that. What do they call it when people try to kill each other because of the uniform they wear? It's called war.

Thus, I say again: if you are in a *war*, you are a *warrior*. Do not be ashamed or afraid to use that word.

Today our military, our peacekeepers, and our peace officers are moving toward each other. Around the world, warriors in blue (police and other peace officers) and warriors in green (soldiers, marines and others in peacekeeping, counterterrorism, and counter-insurgency operations across the globe) find themselves facing very similar missions.

Increasingly, our police must face organized opponents armed with assault rifles and bombs. Indeed, they may very well face deliberate acts of war from international terrorists. In response, police have begun to carry assault rifles and call upon Special Weapons and Tactic (SWAT) teams.

Meanwhile, the military is finding that the use of artillery and air strikes in peacekeeping and counterterrorism missions can be potentially counterproductive, and that it can be more effective to use small teams on a 'beat' or checkpoint. In Bosnia and New York, Iraq and Los Angeles, and Afghanistan and Littleton, Colorado, the police are becoming more like the military in equipment, structure and tactics, while the military is becoming more like the police in equipment, missions and tactics.

In addition to the threat of domestic terrorism (such as the Oklahoma City bombing, which is the all-time record domestic terrorist act in U.S. history, and the slaughter at Columbine High School, which is the all-time record juvenile suspect mass murder in human history) and international terrorism (such as the 9/11 attack on the World Trade Center, which is now in the *Guinness Book of World Records* as the all-time record terrorist act), there has been an explosion of violent crime that has influenced this change in law enforcement agencies.

The murder rate is being held down by medical technology, and over any period of time the number of people who are murdered completely misrepresents and under-reports the full magnitude of the problem. Per capita aggravated assaults (a much better measure of the problem than the murder rate) in the U.S. increased almost sevenfold between 1957 and 1993. During the 1990s and the 2000s there was a slight downturn in crime rates, due largely to aggressive policing, the longest sustained economic boom in American history, and a fivefold increase in per capita incarceration rates since 1970. Still, the violent crime rate today is four times greater than in 1957.

In Canada, per capita assaults increased almost fourfold since 1964. Since 1977 the per capita serious assault rate (as reported by each nation to Interpol) is up nearly fivefold in Norway (which also experienced its own record-setting domestic terrorist attack, with 77 citizens murdered by a single attacker in a single day) and Greece, and it has increased approximately fourfold in Australia and New Zealand. During the same period, the per capita serious assault rate tripled in Sweden, Austria, and France, and it approximately doubled in Belgium, Denmark, England-Wales, Germany, France, Hungary, Netherlands, Scotland, and Switzerland. It is not just happening in traditional "Western" nations. Brazil, Mexico, and all of Latin America are seeing an explosion of violent crime, while nations like Japan and Singapore are also experiencing unprecedented increases in juvenile violent crime.

To respond to this extraordinary rise in violence, law enforcement agencies of the free world have trained and organized the finest peace officers the world has ever seen. Yet, in spite of ever better equipment, training, organization and tactics, American law enforcement fatalities in the line of duty went up by double-digits in every year since 2008. We know that if it were not for all the body armor (bulletproof vests) worn by our officers, law enforcement fatalities in the United States would easily be double or even triple what they are today. And, research tells us that if we had 1970's level of medical technology, the number of police officers murdered in the line of duty would be four times what it is today.

Our magnificent law enforcement warriors have risen to the challenge. The weak link thus far, the failure at this point in the process, is a lack of law enforcement leaders who are trained and prepared to lead these magnificent men and women in the face of this new challenge.

This is *not* to speak poorly of the incredible law enforcement leaders who are striving to their utmost to do the very best job that they can! It is not their fault if we fall short in this area. The art and science of field command, the leadership of warriors in a tactical environment, has developed across 5,000 years of recorded history. In the U.S., combat leadership has been nurtured and developed in a systematic scientific manner, passed on from generation to generation, at the U.S. Military Academy at West Point, since the very earliest days of our nation. The U.S. Naval Academy followed shortly thereafter. The Army War College at Carlyle Barracks has nurtured our leaders at higher ranks for well over a hundred years, and similar military schools have served our nation at all levels, from NCO academies to war colleges, often with over a century of their own institutional existence, experience and heritage to draw upon.

On the military side of the house, our nation's leadership builds upon countless institutions and centuries of experience and systematic education dating back literally across the millennia, learned at tragic cost in the unforgiving and fearsome forge of countless wars. On the law enforcement side of this equation there is a *desperate* and *urgent* need to apply this vast body of military doctrine and methodology to the specific needs of the law enforcement community.

SID HEAL: COMES THE MOMENT, COMES THE MAN

This daunting task, this Herculean challenge, to take the 5,000 year-old body of military doctrine, experience, science, and education, and transfer it to the law enforcement community, in a manner that is specifically tailored and appropriate for that community, has now been met, in this book, by a man who is uniquely experienced, prepared and equipped to accomplish this mission.

Sid Heal. A living legend. A man who has risen to assume leadership positions at the highest level in the warrior-elite of both the military and law enforcement community.

He served an amazing 41 years in the US Marine Corps Reserves, with four tours of combat in four different theaters, spanning the decades and spanning the globe, serving our nation at the place and hour of greatest need.

He simultaneously served in the Los Angeles Sheriff's Department for 33 years, and was ultimately selected to command the Special Enforcement Bureau, the premier assignment in the entire Department, leading a unit composed of our nation's most elite law enforcement officers: six full-time SWAT teams, the Canine Services Detail, and the Emergency Services Detail composed of certified paramedics who are also trained in SWAT operations, mountain and swift-water rescue. He has served and excelled, while operating and leading at the highest levels, for years on end, in an environment where daily, desperate, life-and-death events occurred that could have come straight out of Hollywood or TV scripts.

But, to my mind, Sid Heal's greatest achievement, his most lasting and profound contribution, has been as a law enforcement educator and a warrior-wordsmith. His book, *Sound Doctrine: A Tactical Primer* has been in print for over a decade, touching countless lives, and serving as a textbook and standard reference across the law enforcement community. And his "tactical science" classes to law enforcement leadership, teaching in this vital field, across the years, have influenced and educated a generation of leaders.

Now, the capstone of this singular lifetime of service can be found in this remarkable book. I sincerely believe that, with this book, Sid Heal has established himself as this generation's Clausewitz, our Sun Tzu, making a contribution that will impact lives for decades to come, laying a foundation of law enforcement science and scholarship, with simplicity and clarity that will echo down across the generations.

Well done, Sid. Semper Fi, Marine!

Dave Grossman
Lt. Col., USA (ret.)
author of *On Combat*
and *On Killing*
www.killology.com

PREFACE

It's hard to believe, but *Sound Doctrine: A Tactical Primer* has been in print for more than a decade. It is not only being used as the textbook for which it was intended but also for promotional examinations and is becoming cited more and more as a reference and resource. No one is more surprised and pleased by the success than I am. Notwithstanding, *Sound Doctrine* was never intended to be more than a primer—an introduction to the science that supports good planning and decision making during crisis situations.

A lot has happened to me personally in the last ten years also, not the least of which was being recalled to active duty for Operation Iraqi Freedom; my fourth tour of combat in as many theaters. I turned 53 in Al Amarah, Iraq, a few weeks after the youngest member of my team turned 19. The realization that I had spent my entire adult life in these activities was a startling revelation when he pointed out that he was a first-grader in school while I was there the last time (Operation Desert Storm) and that I was older than his father. Nor did it pass the Marine Corps unnoticed either as I was mandatorily retired with maximum years of service when I returned to the United States later that year.

Likewise, my career in the Los Angeles Sheriff's Department advanced and I was selected as the Commanding Officer of the Special Enforcement Bureau, the premier assignment in the entire Department (I'll admit to some bias here.) The unit is only about one-hundred people divided into three details that regularly work together in handling some of the most hazardous and complex assignments confronting law enforcement. The Special Enforcement Detail is comprised of six, full-time SWAT teams. The Emergency Services Detail is comprised of certified paramedics who are also trained in SWAT operations, mountain and swift-water rescue. Canine Services Detail is staffed with dog handlers who also function in SWAT and search operations. The people selected for these assignments represent less than one percent of the total Department applicant pool. Working in these assignments is the only time where the activities actually mimicked movie scripts and television. When I was eventually promoted to Commander and "out of billet" it was with a certain nostalgic melancholy that I realized that no other assignment would be as satisfying (or challenging) as this one. My law enforcement career was also coming to an end and I retired from the LASD in the spring of 2008. Since that time I've worked as a consultant, taught and written about the lessons learned, not to mention two bicycle trips across the United States and long hours playing with our nine grandchildren.

After the attacks of September 11th, 2001, American law enforcement was pulled into handling homeland security missions in protecting our communities against terrorists. It quickly became clear that the tools and thinking used in the war on crime are inadequate for the war on terrorism. For just one example, consider how effective the conventional surround and negotiate strategies used when confronting barricaded suspects would be against terrorists like those attacking the London Underground Railway trains in 2005 or those in Mumbai, India in 2008. In such cases these tactics would not only be ineffective, they would be counterproductive—actually exacerbating the situation by providing time and opportunity for terrorists to consolidate their gains, secure their positions and construct defenses.

Where before, using terms like "counterterrorism" and "law enforcement" in the same sentence was sure to attract criticism and scorn, domestic law enforcement counterterrorist assignments are now becoming common. No one wanted the additional missions but they quite naturally and reasonably have become the responsibility of the law enforcement community. As some smart general once noted, we have to fight the war we have—not the one we want.

Notwithstanding, some of the more staid administrators, concerned with propriety and appearance, insist that terrorism is simply a different form of criminal behavior and that their departments are quite capable of dealing with it, if and when it ever occurs in their own jurisdiction. They shun even the appearance of preparation lest they be accused of overreacting. On the other end of the spectrum are alarmists who emphatically advocate for increased firepower while naively ignoring the fact that it is no harder to kill terrorists than criminals. Bigger bullets, faster cyclic rates and heavier armor can certainly be an advantage but are not decisive in and of themselves.

Preparing to fight terrorist attacks calls for clear thinking and decisive action not more firepower. Only by understanding the underpinnings does it become clear that retooling rather than rearming is necessary. This is the setting which stimulated the effort to undertake a more comprehensive work on tactical science. "We will not solve the problems of the future with the same thinking that created them in the first place."[5]

Near the end of my police career I authored a course on tactical science and asked for help teaching it from two of my long-time mentors, Tim Anderson and Dick "Odie" Odenthal. Both of them are retired career police officers with extensive backgrounds in police tactical and emergency operations and both with broad military experience. In fact, Tim Anderson was my reporting senior on three different occasions and retired from the USMCR as a "full-bird" colonel, while Odie and I paralleled our careers in emergency management in the LASD where he eventually became the Commanding Officer of the LASD's Emergency Operations Bureau.

The course was entitled "Tactical Science" and we first taught it in December of 2004 and each December after that until 2007. By then, it was so popular that we began giving it twice a year and had to limit the class size. We had also recruited a number of outstanding former students to help teach. By 2008 we were teaching versions of the week-long course ten times a year throughout the United States and have had increasing demands for it since. *Sound Doctrine* has been used as the course text but with the

5 Attributed to Albert Einstein. Interestingly, he is also reported to have said, "Intellectuals solve problems, geniuses prevent them." Both of these thoughts emphasize the importance of a thorough understanding of the factors and influences in play.

depth of experience and knowledge of the instructors the course far exceeded what was written in both scope and depth—which in turn created a demand for a more comprehensive text.

To the best of my knowledge, *Field Command* is a first of its kind; a full-length tactical science textbook focused specifically on crisis situations faced by the law enforcement community. Greater in depth and scope than *Sound Doctrine*, the intent is to introduce and explain the concepts without elaborate and esoteric descriptions. The concepts and principles are taken from tactical texts and military field manuals and are presented as close to how they are used as possible. In some cases it was necessary to paraphrase from military jargon or esoteric explanations to a simpler and clearer version. When more than one definition was available the simplest was chosen. Accordingly, the application of these principles and precepts should not be construed too narrowly or only in the context in which they are explained. Likewise, the terminology remains unedited. No attempt has been made to assuage personal sensitivities or seek political correctness. To facilitate understanding, illustrations are abundant and not only clarify the text but amplify it with new insights and applications.

The book is divided into six sections, each of which focuses on a discrete aspect of a tactical operation or disaster response and follows the same simple to understand format as *Sound Doctrine* with each concept and principle bold-printed when first introduced. To facilitate an easier style of reading, no footnotes are used in the text. Instead, end notes are provided to explain and/or amplify concepts, ideas, and principles, and in many cases provide the historical background for when and how the insight came to light. The end notes are numbered sequentially throughout the book rather than restarted after each section or chapter so that each one has a unique identifying number. For the same reasons, a comprehensive index is provided to quickly locate terms and concepts, as well as a concept glossary which concisely describes the major concepts and principles discussed in the text.

As law enforcement adapts to the challenges of the 21st century the new role in combatting terrorism is at the forefront. Law enforcement's role in homeland security has greatly benefitted from the advances resulting from the military's efforts in homeland defense, not the least of which has been the technological advancements. Yet while law enforcement has become enraptured with technology that is not only needed but long overdue, it lags in understanding the science that supports sound tactical decisions and planning. No one would be impressed with a medical doctor who had all the latest X-rays, CAT scans, MRIs and lab tests but lacked the knowledge to determine the significance of what they reveal. So it is with tactical commanders who have all the latest equipment but only the vaguest notion of the factors and influences in play and are devoid of any understanding of what they mean. What is more, the consequences of ignorance in either profession are equally deadly.

It is somewhat ironic that in the most technologically advanced period in history the most conspicuous capability gap appears to be a lack of knowledge of tried and true scientific principles that can be dated back thousands of years. What is needed is a culture of examination and learning in which mistakes are culled and archaic practices and thinking are banished. The two most useful tools for this endeavor are hindsight and science. Even without any tactical acumen, failures become both apparent and irrefutable when examined in the harsh light of hindsight. Science enables understanding to be distilled. It is my hope that this book will provide a small step in that direction.

NOTE

I considered subtitling this book, "Tactical Science for the Alpha Sheepdog." The phrase is taken from a metaphor described by Lt. Col. Dave Grossman in his book, *On Combat*, as well as a number of articles and presentations.[6] He relates a discussion with a retired Vietnam veteran, who stated:

"Most of the people in our society are sheep. They are kind, gentle, productive creatures who can only hurt one another by acci-

6 One version of the article in its entirety is available online at: http://killology.com/sheep_dog.htm

dent. Then there are the wolves and the wolves feed on the sheep without mercy. Then there are sheepdogs and I'm a sheepdog. I live to protect the flock and confront the wolf."

In the animal world, an "alpha" is the leader of the group; the dominant one who controls the other members of the pride, pack, herd or flock; the one who fights for the rest. The pack or herd follows the alpha to hunting places and watering holes. The alpha, then, is often seen as deciding the fate of the group. The status of an alpha is not bestowed but earned, often through repeated bloody confrontations. Moreover, alpha status is not permanent. When an alpha grows weak and wanting it is ousted. The pack or herd simply cannot survive following a leader who is lacking and fails to fulfill the duties of this essential role. The similarities for teams of humans handling tactical operations and responding to disasters should not go unnoticed.

SECTION 1

SECTION 1

AT THE SCENE

. . . we do not know a truth without knowing its cause.[1]

—ARISTOTLE

ONE CONCEPT INHERENT IN EVERY SCIENCE IS CAUSALITY. IN short, this means that all consequences have causes. It has been the most fundamental tenet of science for thousands of years. The science that supports tactical decisions is no exception. In order to achieve a favorable outcome it stands to reason that those that produce favorable consequences should be encouraged, and conversely, those that produce unfavorable consequences should be discouraged. Notwithstanding, many tactical commanders have only the vaguest notion of the factors and influences in play during operations in which lives are at stake. This is almost never due to any fault or neglect on their own. Law enforcement training for tactical situations and disaster responses has been focused on what to do and how to do it, as if every situation had a particular skill set that affords a solution. This shallow understanding has led to catch phrases like, "Time is on our side," "We can wait him out," "We have nothing to lose by talking," or "The odds are in our favor." This is wishful thinking, at best. In reality, each situation is always somewhat unique. What is more, it is in a constant state of change and any solution must be adapted to fit the circumstances at any given time. Certainly, every skill set has some flexibility but without knowledge of why it works there is no way of distinguishing why a skill set that is successful in one instance is a recipe for disaster in another. Only with an understanding of why something is (or isn't) applicable and appropriate do any of these become valid.

This first section begins by citing some of the spectacular tactical failures that resulted in civil judgments, criminal charges and loss of public confidence. They were chosen because of their notoriety, not because they were exceptional. Albeit on a smaller scale, similar failures reoccur on a fairly regular basis. As the law enforcement community accepts the new role of defending their communities against terrorists it becomes starkly apparent that the tools and tactics used to fight the war on crime are woefully inadequate to fight the war on terrorism.

The second chapter is focused on the nature of the situations themselves. For the same reasons doctors study anatomy, tacticians need more than a passing understanding of what is actually transpiring and why it is important. This is particularly important when a crisis involves antagonists because force of some type is always involved. Accordingly, the chapter concludes with an overview of force, to include not only its characteristics but how it is applied and measured.

The third chapter describes the ad hoc organizations that are both crafted and evolve to handle a developing crisis. Without understanding how they work and why they develop any attempt at imposing order on a situation that is inherently disorderly will be met with obstruction and frustration. The "business as usual" methods and procedures that are efficient in the day to day operations of an agency can be highly ineffective in the chaotic circumstances that characterize crises. The chapter concludes by describing the natural seams within any organization and when it becomes necessary to split it into more manageable sections why division along these lines makes the most sense.

1. Aristotle, *Metaphysics*, Book II, Part 1, circa 350 B.C., Nearly everyone knows of Aristotle, the great philosopher and teacher. What many do not know is that he was also a tutor of Alexander the Great during his early teen years and influenced both his thinking and his love for knowledge. Alexander went on to become one of the greatest generals in history while Aristotle became renowned as both a philosopher and scientist. While there are many law enforcement tactical works describing what to do and how to do it, there are nearly none explaining why it is important. Hence, this quote by Aristotle is particularly fitting.

INTRODUCING THE PROBLEM

And what physicians say about disease is applicable here: that at the beginning a disease is easy to cure but difficult to diagnose; but as time passes, not having been treated or recognized at the outset, it becomes easy to diagnose but difficult to cure.

—NICCOLÒ MACHIAVELLI[2]

ASK JUST ABOUT ANYONE ABOUT LAW ENFORCEMENT TACTICAL fiascoes and they will be quick to cite the raid on the Branch Davidian Compound in Waco, Texas, or perhaps the "Ruby Ridge Standoff" with Randy Weaver and his family in Idaho. They may even describe the terrible fires in Philadelphia that burned more than sixty houses after local police attempted to serve arrest warrants on members of the MOVE group.[3] Some may describe an event in which their local police were involved, almost certainly a scenario alleging inappropriate force. Regardless of what is described, the scenarios almost always involve allegations of an overreaction of some type. In contrast, consider the following scenarios.

After attempting to serve arrest warrants on a bunch of radical farmers who, among other things, were accused of frauds and refusing to pay taxes, agents from the federal government surrounded their farm headquarters near Jordan, Montana, and pleaded with them to surrender. Fearing a repeat of the tragic events at Ruby Ridge, the operation continued for months and the media labeled the conspicuously timid efforts as "Weaver fever." When the suspects finally surrendered after 81 days, local citizens danced in the streets. The operation remains the longest police "siege" in U.S. history.

A year later, local police attempted to serve commitment papers on a 51 year-old widow and former nurse living in a house near Roby, Illinois, when relatives claimed she was mentally unstable. For nearly six weeks she single-handedly held off police. The so called "Roby Ridge Siege" cost the local authorities nearly a million dollars[4] and gained international attention as protestors picketed the site while neighbors paid her bills and attempted to sneak food to her.

Unlike their comparative equivalents, these incidents are clearly cases of under-reaction, but are they any less tactical fiascos? The ridicule and scorn used to describe them clearly indicates some of the sentiments of the community and serves to undermine the legitimate authority of our governments to enforce the laws. The greater question that emerges, however, is what *is* appropriate?

In point of fact, there is no perfect solution to these situations and therein lays the root of the problem. Because there is no one right answer some conclude that there is also no wrong answer; there are just some better than others. This reveals a sad, but true, state of affairs in that many law enforcement tacticians lack even the most rudimentary understanding of any supporting science for making sound tactical decisions and would be hard put to quote a single source, theory or doctrine to justify their decisions. Without an understanding of the factors and influences in play, tactical decisions must be based upon impressions, suppositions and conjectures. In the medical field these tacticians would be the functional equivalent of witch doctors. Tactical terms—like tempo, fog or friction—are no more unfamiliar to them than medical terms such as lavage, dermabrasion or hemodialysis. They simply apply what worked last time without any idea of why the preferred course of action in one situation can be a recipe for disaster in another. It is especially disheartening to have the noblest intentions disparaged by a plaintiff's "expert" who possesses all of the credentials and none of the knowledge to make effective and reliable tactical decisions. The fact that juries find them credible at all attests to law enforcement's superficial understanding of fundamental doctrinal concepts that have withstood the test of time and trial for hundreds, and in some cases, thousands of years.

Law enforcement tactical failures have long been a critical weakness that creates civil exposure, criminal liability and a loss of public confidence. Some law firms now specialize in suing police agencies and multi-million dollar judgments are becoming increasingly common. For example, one city in Pennsylvania was recently ordered to pay $4.8 million resulting from an abortive attempt to arrest a fleeing suspect[5] and; in another incident, a jury awarded 12.5 million dollars to the family of a California man shot to death during a SWAT raid.[6]

Notwithstanding the civil exposure, law enforcement officers are increasingly becoming subject to individual criminal liability. The charge of manslaughter against an FBI sharpshooter in the Ruby Ridge incident[7] serves as only one poignant example. Another, more well-known, example is the prosecution of four Los Angeles police officers and the successful conviction and imprisonment of two of them resulting from the notorious Rodney King incident. More recently, the indictment of six police officers from New Orleans involved in a shooting incident a few days after Hurricane Katrina[8] also serves as an example of this legal trend. One alarming incident concerned charges of involuntary manslaughter against the police chief and a lieutenant in Eureka, California after they were accused of showing poor judgment in their handling of a tactical situation involving a mentally disturbed woman. . . even though they were not present at the scene![9]

Despite the focus of attention and recognized vulnerability of police tactical operations, the law enforcement community has been slow to react to this problem. Today's tactical solutions are essentially past oriented. Preceding operations dictate tactics for future ones. Without a thorough understanding of fundamental tactical principles it is impossible to tell if an operation was successful because of the tactics used or if opportune circumstances simply allowed for a favorable outcome. In fact, fortuitous circumstances are frequently mistaken for tactical acumen. In the words of one law enforcement tactical instructor, "We confuse good luck with good tactics."[10]

Even many seasoned officers are unaware of this large body of science. Few think about underlying doctrinal tenets that not only assure more predictable and reliable outcomes but a greater chance for success. Likewise, there is no generally accepted terminology or understanding of fundamental concepts to aid in critiquing or describing tactical problems. Those that do exist, tend to be ambiguous and imprecise and require us to resort to personal images and metaphors rather than a much richer comprehension of "real world" tactics. Further, there is nearly no curriculum or institution that teaches such concepts. Training and courses that address these issues, even in the most general sense, are incredibly rare. In truth, they are all but nonexistent. A great irony lies in the fact that some of these principles have been documented from as far back as 500 BC.

As the war global war on terror is underway and law enforcement is shouldering the lion's share of the burden for guarding our communities from attack, it would seem judicious that commanders of tactical operations be fully immersed in the science from which to draw upon for prudent and perceptive tactical responses. Referring again to our medical analogy, a patient complaining of stomach pain expects a bona fide medical doctor to be able to tell the difference between indigestion and stomach cancer. Caught early enough and appropriately treated even potentially lethal illnesses are curable. Conversely, undergoing radiation, chemotherapy, or surgery only to discover that the problem was indigestion is just as repugnant. In the same manner, members of our communities have a right to expect law enforcement professionals to be capable of making a similar diagnosis in their specialty. This is especially true for a commander's ability to recognize when a tactical operation or emergency response is moving in unanticipated directions and expected outcomes become dubious. Accountants study math, doctors and nurses study medicine, and weather forecasters study meteorology, so why don't tacticians study tactical science? While the problem is pervasive throughout the ranks, it is most acute at the command level. Although a strong emphasis is placed on physical ability and prowess with weapons, the truth is that good tactics have saved more lives than good marksmanship.

Predominately, the problem seems to stem from a general lack of awareness that there actually is a system of knowledge covering general truths for reconciling tactical ends with supporting scientific principles. In all but the rare exception, officers desiring to advance in rank, especially to a command level, must demonstrate some basic knowledge of managing, budgeting, staffing, organizing, and planning. Those same officers, though, may not have the faintest inkling of logistics, intelligence, operations, or command and control. Is it any wonder that these people make great managers and poor commanders? It is a bitter irony, that because of their rank, these leaders are also the most likely to be called upon to handle the largest and most complex tactical operations. It is a gut-wrenching experience listening to a person who has gained respect and acclaim as an administrator, but who has minimal experience, and little knowledge or understanding of tactical science, criticizing an operation for which they have only minimal comprehension.

So what exactly is **tactical science**? In the simplest terms, it is the systematized body of knowledge covering the principles and doctrines associated with tactical operations and emergency responses. It reconciles scientific knowledge with practical ends. Unlike the "hard" sciences, such as chemistry, physics and mathematics, tactical science more closely resembles the "soft" sciences, like economics, sociology, and anthropology. This is because scientific truths cannot be determined to an absolute certainly but instead are limited to a range of likely probabilities. Nevertheless, doctrinal concepts such as objective, mass, maneuver, fog, friction, initiative and tempo go a long way towards elucidating the factors and influences involved in crafting reliable plans and making sound decisions in responding to emergency situations.

Likewise, tactical science is an "applied science" in that the major contribution is not merely identifying the principles and precepts in play, but rather in applying that knowledge to forecast and influence behaviors and outcomes to enhance a more satisfactory outcome. In this manner, law enforcement tacticians more closely resemble engineers than scientists. The problem, however, is that unlike the military services which teach these subjects as part of an officer's education, no such requirement exists for law enforcement leadership.

Most law enforcement tacticians practice strategy and tactics as a "skill set" rather than an intuitive application of doctrinal principles and precepts. Skills are far easier to teach and understand than knowledge. As long as the situation encountered resembles those for which these officers were trained they work just fine. A problem occurs; however, when some permutation results in a deviation from the norm and a commander attempts to impose a solution which has been successful in the past but is not suitable for the new problem. Failures in tactical operations occur when a plan collapses, and this happens because a commander fails to recognize the influence of some indispensable factor (like the loss of the element of surprise in the raid on the Branch Davidians in Waco, TX), or because the strategy was fundamentally flawed (as in attempts to surround and negotiate with the active shooters at Columbine High School.)

The advantage in understanding the science of tactics is in the value of relevant concepts. Unlike skills, concepts are context free. This means that while a skill is designed for a specific set of circumstances, a concept has nearly universal application. Thus, decisions and actions grounded in reliable concepts will provide an ability to recognize and adapt to changes. Like all sciences, tactical science is comprised of a number of concepts and prin-

$$2X = 4 \qquad \delta = \sqrt{\sum \frac{(x-\bar{x})^2}{N-1}}$$

FIGURE 1-1 EQUATION: Both of these equations are relatively simple. The first, however, is so simple that it can be solved intuitively and is one of the first problems presented when teaching algebra. The other is obviously more complex but still easily solved if the mathematician has learned the basics of algebra. So it is with tactical situations. Planners and decision makers who have not mastered the supporting science will be no less confused than a high school freshman encountering the formula for standard deviation for the first time.

ciples that provide insight and understanding far greater than is possible by uninformed observation. Without the clarity and comprehension of science even personal experience fails to reveal the insight necessary to identify mistakes, recognize deviations and anticipate opportunities. Tactical science allows good tactics to be distinguished from good fortune.

As skills differ from knowledge, so too does training differ from education: we train for the expected, while we educate for the unexpected. This is the difference between a set of skills and a frame of concepts. The military profession has long recognized the value of studying tactical science in order to educate officers, and has established institutions to do just that from West Point and Annapolis through the various senior-level service war colleges. All of these institutions strive to instill the importance of this science and to provide a forum for understanding and applying tactical principles that have been proven through the ages.

The military is highly self-critical, believing that clear-eyed analysis of mistakes will make officers into better leaders. The military begins training officers right out of high school (in the service academies), and it is expected that those officers will return to

TRAINING	EDUCATION
• Provides skills	• Provides knowledge
• Instills confidence	• Explains the importance
• Improves methods	• Improves understanding
• Fosters expertise and proficiency	• Fosters ingenuity and adaptability
Teaches how to do things better	**Teaches how to recognize the right things**

FIGURE 1-2 TRAINING V EDUCATION: Because contemporary law enforcement is so well-trained there is a tendency to confuse how well we do something with how much it contributes to a solution. Training and education are not synonyms, however. The essential skills for working in crisis conditions are myriad but relatively easily taught and learned. The knowledge and understanding of what is actually unfolding are far more complex and require an understanding of the factors and influences involved and how they interact.

formal instruction about every five years, and even when they are generals. Training, and education, never stop.

By contrast, no equivalent exists anywhere for law enforcement. Only through self-study do law enforcement officers—new ones and senior leaders alike—build a systematized internal framework of professional knowledge, and thereby leverage others' mistakes to build tactical savvy. Law enforcement and military leaders both face life and death responsibilities . . . they should also share structures for learning.

As law enforcement continues to ramp up for the war on terrorism it is more critical than ever to build upon a solid foundation of science. Law enforcement's new role in countering acts of terrorism will necessitate a thorough understanding of the inherent factors and influences involved in this uniquely demanding realm of conflict. It is flawed thinking in the extreme to believe that actions that work against criminals will be equally effective against terrorists.

It is vitally important that law enforcement planners and decision makers know how to conduct an operational analysis and terrain analysis; to maneuver in time as well as space; to recognize the significance of fighting in five dimensions; to recognize differences and implications of analysis and synthesis; to see symmetric and asymmetric strategies, plans that are loosely or closely coupled, and many other such tactical concepts. It is especially important to develop a capability for early recognition of operations that are moving away from the norm to prompt more scrutiny and apply corrective measures.

The concepts and principles in this book have been excerpted from texts and manuals where they are explained in detail. Rather than condensing the thoughts and ideas behind them to a more compact form, the process more closely resembles distillation, until only the essence is left. Understandably, many are far broader in concept and application than can be presented in a single text and the practitioner is encouraged to use vision and imagination rather than arbitrarily insist on narrow interpretations.

This book assumes no prior knowledge of tactical science or military or even law enforcement experience. Whenever practical, examples are provided using common every day activities and competitive games to increase understanding without distorting the meaning or significance. Among other things, readers will learn of the importance of envisioning an end state and planning to achieve it, the inherent factors involved in all crises, regardless of how they manifest themselves, as well as the importance of early recognition and preparation for opportunities.

Command personnel need to be thoroughly familiar with tactical concepts, principles, axioms and doctrine. Promotional examinations need to include material on tactical science. Professional associations, like the National Tactical Officers Association, need to be as important on a resume as the International Association of Chiefs of Police. Agencies need to recognize that the knowledge and skills for handling tactical operations are just as real and just as necessary as those for preparing budgets, managing personnel or organizing programs. They also need to invest as much in education for commanders as in training for the troops. It is time to recognize that the "art of war" is the application of the science. To do less is too horrible to consider in a profession that chastens its failures with death.

---

2. Niccolò di Bernardo Machiavelli, *The Prince*, circa 1532. Machiavelli was an Italian political philosopher during the Renaissance era. *The Prince* was only one of his works but is the best-known and is considered to be among the first books on modern philosophy. The book is generally cited when it was published but was certainly written before 1513. He is nearly as famous for another of his books, *The Art of War*, in which he talks about military science. The metaphor of a disease is particularly poignant in that it is as applicable today as it was 500 years ago, both in medical and tactical interventions.
3. The "MOVE Group" was a loosely-knit group of people advocating a "back-to-nature" lifestyle and an aversion to technology. During a failed operation to serve arrest warrants on members of the group a violent gun battle erupted as well as a fire which killed eleven people and destroyed more than 60 homes. The City of Philadelphia was ordered to pay more than $25 million in settlements.
4. Even the most conservative estimates start at $500,000 but Illinois State Police Director, Terry Gainer, placed the figure between $750,000 and $1,000,000!
5. Agresta v. Gillespie, 631 A.2d 772 (Pennsylvania Commonwealth)

6. "Jury Awards Millions After SWAT Raid," Associated Press, March 16, 1999, as reported in *CATO News*, Spring 1999, p. 26 also "Relatives of Man Killed in Police Raid Get $12.5 Million," *Los Angeles Times*, March 16, 1999, p. A16. The damages were reported to be twice the entire annual budget of the city.
7. The charges stemmed from an accidental shooting of a woman inside a house near Ruby Ridge, Idaho. The charges were brought by the State of Idaho alleging gross negligence in her death. The charges were eventually dismissed by a federal judge in Boise, Idaho.
8. The incident began after an officer radioed that police were taking fire from a bridge and that there were officers "down" under the bridge, which led some officers to interpret that police officers had been shot. Charges were filed after a two-year investigation by the federal government revealed that responding officers had shot an innocent person without cause and later attempted to cover it up.
9. This incident was widely reported and gained national attention. While the charges were eventually dismissed the incident remains controversial and is often cited by activists and on websites as an example of police misconduct.
10. Sergeant (now Lt.) Ken Hubbs, San Diego Police Department, during a training session with the National Tactical Officer's Association.

NATURE OF CRISES

Res in cardine est (The affair is hanging on the hinge)
—LATIN PROVERB[11]

TACTICAL OPERATIONS AND DISASTER RE-sponses come in all sizes, shapes, kinds, styles and varieties. Regardless of whether the operation involves a high-risk warrant service, evacuation, barricaded suspect or storm, it is some sort of a crisis. A **crisis** is an emotionally stressful event or situation involving an impending, abrupt and decisive change. While we all have a natural tendency to view a crisis as bad, a crisis is more precisely defined as a situation that can turn bad. Fundamental to the understanding is that these situations are inherently unstable and involve an abrupt and decisive change. For better or worse, things will not be the same afterwards. Thus, a crisis is best understood as a threat. Throughout our lives, each of us has experienced many types of crises. They are an inevitable part of life and involve our businesses, friends, family, or even our health. While crises tend to be relatively short-lived, they almost never get better by themselves. Even with our best efforts the outcome to a crisis is never entirely certain. We can, however, draw a conclusion: in a crisis, some type of intervention is necessary.

TYPES OF CRISES

In law enforcement crises consistently manifest themselves in three recurring varieties. The first type is those that occur during *natural* disasters such as earthquakes, hurricanes, tornadoes, floods or blizzards. Interventions may require evacuations, rescues, searches, and any combination thereof. The second type is those that are *technological* or *mechanical* in nature. Examples of this type include airplane crashes, traffic accidents, railroad derailments, hazardous materials spills, and so forth. While both natural and mechanical disasters can be very dramatic with tremendous damage and loss of life, the adverse effects of those that are technological in nature can be diminished, either by making the incident less likely to occur or providing protective measures to attenuate the effects when they do. This is because they involve factors such as fatigue, wear, corrosion, erosion, decomposition and so forth, and these can be estimated. Accordingly, actions such as preventative maintenance, overhauling, repairing, refurbishing or replacing, decrease both the likelihood of failure as well as diminishing the adverse effects when

TYPES OF CRISES	NATURAL	MECHANICAL	ADVERSARIAL (CONFLICT)
Characterized By	Nature is the causal agency	Human failure is the primary agent	The presence of one or more opposing wills
Typical Manifestations	Floods, forest fires, blizzards, earthquakes, hailstorms, hurricanes, avalanches, and tornadoes	Car collisions, train wrecks, plane crashes, bridge failures, and hazardous material spills	Riots, lootings, hostages, shootings, arsons, bombings, robberies, smuggling, and terrorism
Major Historical Examples	Earthquake in Japan—2011 Tsunami in the Indian Ocean—2004	British Petroleum oil spill—2010 Chernobyl nuclear accident—1986	Murders in Mumbai, India—2008 Beslan school hostages—2004

FIGURE 2-1 CRISES COMPARED: Depending on a person's perspective, the severity of a crisis may be measured by the number of casualties, the amount of damage, the size of the afflicted area, the magnitude of the response, the cost of recovery, or other criteria. There is no doubt; however, that the involvement of a human will actively opposing efforts to succeed increases the complexity.

they do occur. This point is easily illustrated with traffic collisions. Adherence to traffic laws reduces accidents but does not eliminate them. Seatbelts, airbags and "crush zones" in cars reduce injuries when traffic accidents happen.

The third kind of crisis results from those with malicious intent; that is they are deliberately caused by another person. This means they are *adversarial* in nature in that there are one or more suspects who must be captured or defeated in some manner. Examples include terrorists, snipers, barricaded suspects, hostage situations, fleeing felons, and so forth. This last type is a special type of crisis, called a conflict.

A **conflict** is any situation in which there is an irreconcilable clash between opposing human wills.[12] While a crisis may result from whims of nature, such as fires, floods, or earthquakes or mishaps from traffic accidents and airplane crashes, conflicts always involve an adversary who is actively engaged in thwarting the will of the tactical commander. Consequently, conflicts are far more dangerous and complex. It is a logical necessity that a suspect(s) must be defeated to succeed and *an implied objective inherent in these situations is to impose the will of the commander on the suspect.*

CHARACTERISTICS OF CRISES

All crises share five common characteristics. First, these situations are among the most confusing likely to be encountered by anyone. There is always a lack of reliable information, and what is available is always somewhat incomplete, confusing, ambiguous, and sometimes even conflicting. While it is true with all crises, it is especially critical in conflicts. This is because the very nature of conflict makes certainty impossible. The dynamic interplay between the will of the suspect(s) and the will of the commander makes conflicts especially difficult and complex. *Uncertainty is always present* and pervades these situations because of a lack of knowledge regarding the suspect, terrain, weather, innocent bystanders, and even other law enforcement personnel. This uncertainty requires commanders to make decisions based upon probabilities for which they are invariably lacking accurate and timely data. This is one of the most pervasive attributes in these situations and is described by a concept called "fog." **Fog**[13] is that condition which prohibits a tactical commander from obtaining accurate information in a timely manner. A complete and reliable view of any tactical situation is thus impossible. To a greater or lesser degree, fog is present in all crises, but especially conflicts. Consequently, the information needed to make reliable decisions will never be entirely satisfactory.

Aggravating the lack of information is the *uncontrollable element of chance*. **Chance** consists of turns of events that cannot reasonably be foreseen and over which we (or an adversary) have no control. Uncontrollable factors, accompanied by the inherent risk in trying to dominate them and compounded with the element of chance, create a condition called "friction." **Friction** is the force that resists all action. It makes the simple difficult and the difficult seemingly impossible. Friction may be psychological, as when a commander becomes overwhelmed by the amount of risk, or when chance favors the suspect. It may also be self-induced, such as when a commander suffers from indecision, fear of failure, or a lack of a clearly defined goal. It can also be physical, as when the suspect succeeds in some endeavor or the commander encounters an obstacle.

Only a commander who has experienced the disappointment and frustration of trying to read in darkness or rain, or in attempting to control a situation with a broken radio, can truly appreciate the impact that physical obstacles have on emotional feelings and mental attitude. Thus, friction will always have a psychological, as well as a physical impact. As with fog, we must attempt to reduce friction wherever possible while at the same time recognizing that it will always be unavoidable to some extent.

Second, because of the countless factors that impinge on tactical situations, a commander must accept some degree of risk. *Risk is inherent in every tactical situation*. Some risk is personal, such as when the decision maker is exposed to physical or emotional harm, or when failure can result in career hardships or setbacks. There will also be risk to others, as when efforts to achieve a successful resolution will increase the peril of subordinates. Nearly always, there is organizational risk. Organizational risk may involve a loss of equipment, assets or prestige. Commanders attempt to reduce risk by seeking better, timelier and more accurate information, but since this is never entirely possible, risk is unavoidable. Notwithstanding, it is an implied duty of command to reduce risk to the greatest practical extent.

Risk, in and of itself, is comprised of two distinct factors. The first factor is the *probability of occurrence* of an adverse event. This is expressed as either a ratio or a percentage. For example, if the chance of a person being injured in a traffic accident at a given intersection is one for every one-hundred vehicles, the risk for any given driver passing through the intersection would be one in a hundred, or 1%. The second factor is the *circumstances of exposure*. Circumstances of exposure refers to the conditions that create a danger. The risk of the car becoming involved in an accident at the intersection in question drops to zero if the driver avoids the area entirely. Risk can thus be reduced by affecting either the probability of an event occurring or the consequences of harm if it does. Nevertheless, risk is inherent in crisis situations and can never be completely eliminated.

Third, each episode in an operation is the result of a unique and temporary combination of circumstances. Unique, because each circumstance is dependent only upon those factors which are present at the particular time and place; and temporary, because an outcome, of any kind, affects the next set of circumstances. In a conflict, the opponent who can most quickly exploit circumstances to his benefit gains an advantage. Moreover, a decision and/or action delayed is often rendered ineffective because the circumstances will have changed. Thus, *all tactical operations are time sensitive*. Further, when an adversary is involved, they are not only time sensitive, but also time competitive. Time or opportunity neglected by one adversary can be exploited by the other. The aggregate resolution of these episodes will eventually determine the outcome of the conflict.

Fourth, there is *always a potential of severe consequences*.

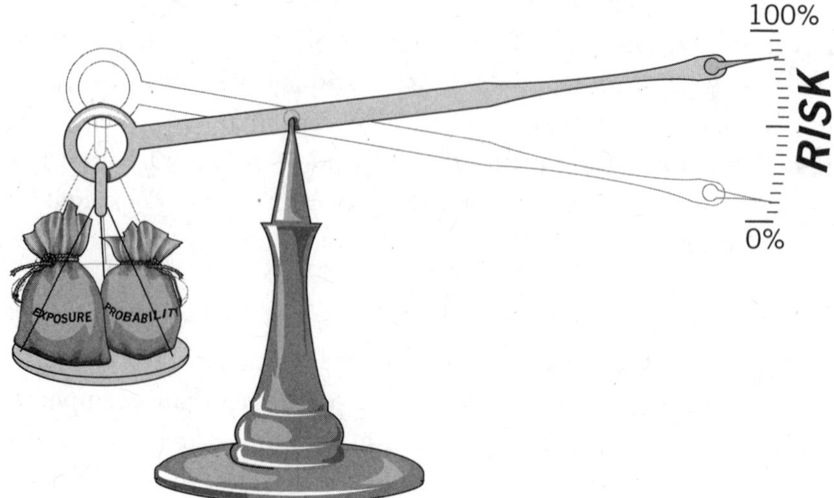

FIGURE 2-2 RISK SCALE: As illustrated with this scale, risk can be decreased by reducing either the probability of occurrence of an adverse event or reducing the exposure to harm if it does.

For example, consider a situation in which a local shopping mall is being plagued by graffiti and vandalism from loitering teens during school lunchtimes. Law enforcement can reduce the likelihood of these acts by maintaining a high visibility, questioning suspicious persons and strictly enforcing truancy and loitering ordinances. They might even ask school officials to close their campuses during these periods. Likewise, they may reduce the damage and incentives by employing abatement actions such as immediately removing the graffiti and encouraging business owners to utilize conspicuous video surveillance and graffiti resistant paints and materials. So it is with tactical operations. While risk can never be completely eliminated, it is the responsibility of tactical commanders to reduce it to the greatest practical extent.

Because all crises are defined by an impending, abrupt and decisive change it is virtually impossible to achieve such definitive results without a potential of calamity. The significance of this single factor cannot be overstated. A timid and lackluster response will not provide the necessary countermeasures to thwart events that will ultimately lead to disaster without an effective intervention. Likewise, an intervention that is uncoordinated, disorganized, or unfocused is highly unlikely to avoid a catastrophe.

Fifth, *a human element is always present*. In fact, without an impact on humans, it is impossible to experience a crisis. Earthquakes off the California coast, hurricanes in the Caribbean Sea or mid-Atlantic Ocean and range fires in open fields and distant forests occur with frightening regularity, but it is only when humans are impacted that those events can become a crisis. Moreover, because interventions are always human activities, human characteristics such as training, experience, maturity, emotion, prejudice and discipline, deeply affect individual and collective efforts. Because the most fundamental factor in conflicts is the irreconcilable disagreement between adversaries, these situations are especially susceptible to, and will be inflamed and shaped by, human emotions and personalities. Consequently, any doctrine or plan that attempts to reduce tactics to ratios of forces, weapons or equipment, or attempts to rigidly impose an algorithm on how to resolve them, neglects the impact of the human will on the conduct of the operation and is therefore inherently flawed.

These five characteristics manifest themselves in countless ways and combinations in every tactical operation. Tactical commanders who recognize that they are intrinsic in each and every crisis are not as likely to be surprised or discouraged when they are experienced. In the ever-changing and confusing environment of uncertainty, frustration, ambiguity and risk, tactical situations inevitably gravitate toward disorder. Each encounter in a tactical situation will tend to grow increasingly more complex and disordered over time. Since the situation is continuously changing, a commander is forced to improvise again and again until the final actions frequently have little resemblance to the original scheme.

PHASES OF EMERGENCY MANAGEMENT

Because the circumstances that define a crisis are always unique and temporary, it stands to reason that each response will also need to be somewhat unique. Nevertheless, the scope and complexity of large tactical operations and major disasters benefits from a methodical and calculated approach. This is especially critical in that while it may be impossible to avoid a calamity like an earthquake or hurricane, it is still possible to attenuate some of the consequences when they do occur.

Generally, the first phase in emergency management is **mitiga-**

tion. Mitigation is often called the "cornerstone" of emergency management and refers to those activities designed to prevent and/or reduce losses from disaster. Mitigation efforts almost always involve long-term actions such as reinforcing structures, installing backup power sources for critical installations, educating the community and sanctioning strict building codes and zoning ordinances. When compared with the activities involved in the other three phases, these actions tend to be the most cost effective and effectual.

The second phase is **preparedness**. This phase is focused on planning and preparing for an effective response. Of necessity, this includes establishing priorities and organizing, equipping and training personnel for their expected roles when they are needed. Likewise, this phase includes conducting practice exercises for testing plans, making improvements and ascertaining the true state of readiness. Other activities related to this phase include designating evacuation routes and refugee centers, identifying critical facilities and personnel, securing contracts for specialized equipment, stockpiling food, clothing and medical supplies, and so forth.

The third phase is the actual **response** to the situation. The response phase involves the mobilization and deployment of personnel and equipment to respond to an anticipated or unfolding situation. Actions in the response phase are, by necessity, tightly focused on preserving life and property and include such actions as evacuations, quarantines, searches and rescues, first-aid, firefighting, arrests, feeding, sheltering, and sanitizing. While this phase may include civil servants and community volunteers, it is predominately staffed by professionals from the safety services, particularly the fire services and law enforcement.

The last phase is **recovery**. To the extent possible, activities in this phase are concentrated on quickly restoring an affected area and people to their former state. This phase often overlaps the response phase and begins as soon as the threat to human life has subsided. Like the mitigation phase, the recovery phase tends to be prolonged and in fact often intermingles with a new mitigation phase in preparing for another episode. Structures that have fallen during an earthquake, for example, can be rebuilt to more stringent building codes and areas that have been inundated in a flood may be rezoned to prohibit any buildings at all!

UNDERSTANDING FORCE

Of the three types of crises most often handled by law enforcement, conflicts will always require the threat or use of force. Accordingly, an understanding of the nature of force becomes critical.

Force is defined as the exercise of strength, energy or power in order to impose one's will.[14] It can be focused on a person or a thing, as in using force to push a car.[15] In resolving a conflict, however, it is always focused on one or more people. Without question, force is the most scrutinized aspect of any conflict and frequently a point of contention. It behooves everyone, but especially planners and decision makers, to thoroughly understand force as a concept, in all its forms and uses.

The most obvious division of force is that between lethal and nonlethal. These are not antithetical concepts however, but rather two levels of the same spectrum. The opposite of force is surrender—zero force—which means nonlethal force[16] is in between lethal force (at one end) and compliance (at the other) on the continuum of force.

The separation between lethal and nonlethal force is deeper than first appears though, because the distinction is the intent of how they are used and not the capabilities of the option itself. This is a critical distinction in that lethal force options provide the capability of killing an adversary and there is no way to employ them as force without that intent. Nonlethal force options, however, may result in a death but that is *never* the intent! In simpler terms, deaths from lethal force are a consequence while deaths from nonlethal force are an accident.

The next division of force is that between appropriate and inappropriate force. While there are many definitions of appropriate force, the most common understanding is simply that which is reasonably necessary to effect an arrest or overcome resistance. It is important to understand that appropriate force does not require the least amount of force but rather only a reasonable amount.

Accordingly, there is also no requirement to begin with lesser force and gravitate to higher levels.

Inappropriate force generally falls into two distinct categories; excessive force and unreasonable force. **Excessive force** is that which is deemed to be more severe than is necessary in either kind or duration. Excessive force by kind is that which inflicts more pain, suffering or injury than is deemed proper to accomplish the tactical objective. This almost always entails choosing the wrong weapon. Excessive force by duration is when force is applied longer than is necessary. Hitting a suspect with a baton may be necessary and reasonable, for example, but when applied longer than is required to achieve the tactical objective would be excessive.

Unreasonable force is the use of any force when it is unjustified. The most common mistake associated with complaints of unnecessary force is lack of urgency. In such cases the situation simply did not merit the use of force at the time it was applied even when it might have been called for eventually. While these distinctions may seem subtle, failure to fully understand their nuances leads to misunderstandings that are translated into inferior planning and poor performance.

Another natural division of force is between physical and psychological force. As its name implies, **physical force** is any force that is perceptible to the senses and subject to the laws of physics. Physical force is tangible and it can be measured. **Psychological force** is that which is focused on the mind or will of a person. The effects of psychological force are imperceptible and unable to be measured. Accordingly psychological force is inherently less predictable than physical force. While physical force can take any number of forms, psychological force is limited to a threat of some sort.[17] There are two types of threats, expressed and implied. An **expressed threat** is the most well-known and occurs when the consequences of defiance are made known. Two familiar expressions from early "cops and robbers" TV programs were "Come out or we'll come in and get you!" or "Stop or I'll shoot!" and serve as good examples of expressed threats. Because adversaries are made aware of the consequences for failure to comply, expressed threats provide them with an ability to make an informed decision. Thus, expressed threats may not provide sufficient intimidation to achieve success as an effective tool for deterrence or compliance.

An **implied threat** is one in which the consequences of defiance are left to the imagination of the adversary. Because even absurd and bizarre options are possible in our imaginations, the implied threat is far more powerful. This is because what an officer is able to do and what she is willing and authorized to do are usually farther apart than most suspects realize. Even without words, for example, pointing a lethal weapon at a person creates an implied threat. Similarly, "sparking a Taser" to intimidate a suspect creates an implied threat. While controversial in some circles, this type of threat has proven an effective method of gaining compliance because at best no force is necessary while at worst no harm is done.

Force is an indispensable tool in resolving conflicts. Like any other tool, it has a purpose and place and should not be over-relied upon to achieve tactical objectives that can be better attained with other means. Neither, however, should it be neglected when called for. In these types of situations the judicious use of force is authorized by law and expected by the community. A commander who fails to recognize and accept this requirement surrenders the advantage to a suspect who will not.

FORCE MULTIPLIERS

When force is required the most self-evident principle is that it needs to be greater than that of the opposition. It is advantageous, then, to increase the amount of force available and this is done through some type of "force multiplier." A **force multiplier** is defined as any capability or advantage that, when appropriately employed, significantly increases the potential of an individual or group, and thus enhances the probability of success. Force multipliers are very diverse and can be as complex as a superior weapon or as simple as a better idea. The only requirement is that the option provides some markedly greater advantage. To be certain, physical force multipliers are the most well-known, but these types really represent just a small fraction of the possibilities. In point of fact, a force multiplier can be anything that forces adversaries to consider the consequence of their actions. This is why a mere threat can be so powerful.

Physical force multipliers nearly always take on some form of superior weapon or equipment. One excellent example was the invention and wide-spread use of the .45 caliber Colt "Peacemaker" in 1873. This invention was so critical that it was dubbed, "the gun that won the West." The physical size and strength of a gunfighter was suddenly irrelevant. An ability to effectively employ this weapon put anyone in parity. Likewise, a force multiplier may make a unit or person more resistant to force. Many a police officer has prevailed in a deadly conflict, for example, because of a ballistic vest or helmet.

Conversely, force multipliers can be intangible. Such intangibles include training, preparedness, ingenuity, and morale. Consider the advantages in having critical equipment staged and ready for use or in fortifying a location before having to defend it. Even more important is personal preparedness such as proficiency gained by training, education and experience. Similarly, the skills and abilities of a highly trained team are closely associated with personal preparedness but are of even greater importance. This is so because the innate human failings of a single individual can be compensated for by teammates. Thus, a team of people collaborating in harmony creates a synergy surpassing numbers alone.

One of the most effective but frequently neglected intangible force multipliers is ingenuity. An imaginative approach to any problem—especially those involving adversaries—provides unexpected methods and options that not only surprise opponents but may even leave them dumbfounded and unable to employ effective countermeasures.

Regardless of the form a force multiplier takes, however, two general characteristics predominate. The first is that greater possibilities lie outside the physical realm. Consequently, some of the most seemingly benign actions can have profound effects. The second is that they tend to be nonlethal. This is because most force multipliers are incapable, in and of themselves, of inflicting death, but rather work either by enhancing the effective employment of lethal force or by creating conditions where it may not be necessary at all.

FORCE CONTINUUM

Fundamental to employing force options is a thorough understanding of a concept called the "force continuum." In the simplest terms, a **force continuum** is simply a tool used to describe a succession of force options from minimal to maximum. It is one of the most common concepts in understanding force for law enforcement applications but it can also be one of the most bewildering, because like many concepts, the interpretation is not as simple as the idea.

The choice of whether a force option is minimal or maximal is largely dependent upon the interpretation of the two philosophical underpinnings on which force continuums are based. The first is that the type and amount of force authorized should be based upon the amount of injury likely to be inflicted on a suspect. Thus, options like pepper spray or TASERs that seldom result in serious injury are logically placed near the entry level in the application of force. The second is not based on the amount of *injury to* a suspect[18] but on the degree of *defiance by* a suspect.[19] Accordingly, these same options can justifiably be placed much higher on the spectrum based upon the belief that the suspect's actions are the determining factor.

A force continuum is a simple concept but becomes particularly troublesome when one law enforcement agency places a force option at one end of the spectrum while another agency places the same option near the other end. This is because a force continuum is descriptive rather than prescriptive; that is it characterizes an array of force options without mandating specifically which ones should be used, how often or in what order. Consequently, many departments avoid using them in court where lay juries are even more easily confused; opting instead for quadrants, matrices or wheels. In point of fact, however, these new configurations are simply reconfigurations of a continuum.

Historically, tactical objectives have been achieved by killing or destroying an enemy. Force was always deadly, hence effectiveness was judged only to the extent and speed at which death or destruction could be introduced. A huge gap existed between presenting a threat and carrying it out. When force is viewed as a continuum, however, an array of options presents themselves. The beginning of this continuum is initiated by a threat, while deadly force takes its proper position at the other end. Nonlethal alternatives allow a commander to increase and decrease the amount of force necessary to accomplish a mission. Movement up and down the force continuum is generally continuous and seamless, yet a careful examination reveals some general categories.

Entry into the force spectrum almost always begins with a threat of some sort, even if only implied. This is because even the mere presence of a law enforcement officer creates a psychological escalation of force because it requires adversaries to contemplate the consequences of their actions. Thus, an implied threat is inherent in virtually every encounter.

The next major category involves physical force of some type but force which is not coercive in nature. Generally, this includes those devices that engage antagonists strictly on their own volition without requiring an intervention by a law enforcement officer. Examples may include concertina, barbed wire and other similar obstacles. They are placed relatively low on the force continuum, not because of the amount of injury likely to be sustained, but because they are benign without the willful defiance of the individual attempting to thwart them.

Higher on the continuum would come munitions that cause physical discomfort but fall short of inflicting serious trauma. Examples of these options include flashbangs, tear gas, pepper spray and the like. Although the discomfort or injury may be substantially less than that from a caltrop or concertina wire, the employment of these options requires a decision to intervene and is thus subject to the idiosyncrasies of the individual employing them. Factors such as training, experience, maturity, discipline, prejudice, emotion and judgment all play a part in their application and require them to be viewed more closely than those options that involve only one will.[20]

Still higher on the continuum are those munitions that inflict trauma and require a decision to employ them. Examples might include batons, saps, stingballs, bean bags, pellet munitions, and so forth. This is generally the point on the force continuum which separates nonlethal from lethal force.

Highest on the spectrum are lethal options. Although the particular conditions that merit deadly force should be identified, lethal options should always be regarded as part of the force continuum and not as separate options altogether. This avoids ambiguity and confusion as to when they are authorized. Many situations rapidly evolve from less dangerous circumstances before requiring deadly force to resolve. A police officer who is free to employ a variety of options is more likely to be proactive, to retain the initiative and to recognize situations requiring deadly force more quickly than would one compelled to examine a situation isolated by "either/or" parameters.

Because of the nature of a continuum no category is easily distinguished from its neighbors. In reality, some natural divisions have emerged that serve as guidance for determining where specific force options are placed in a continuum. The most historical division separates the lethal options from those that are less lethal. Because the level of provocation necessary to justify lethal force is usually very discrete and easily discerned, force options naturally gravitate to one or the other of the two divisions.

Another common division is the natural separation between options used to enforce compliance or defend against defiance. While some force options, such as pepper spray may be used for either purpose, many others naturally fall into one of the two divisions. Stun bags fired from shotguns, for example, would be nearly impossible to justify for simply attaining compliance.

The third division is between passive and active options. Passive options do not require a decision to intervene while active options require a separate and conscious decision to employ them. Passive options are routinely used for area denial;[21] such as those incorporated into the protection of sensitive buildings and to prevent the introduction of contraband or escape of inmates in prisons and jails. Active options are typically selected and employed by an individual or tactical force in response to a specific threat.

The fourth division is that between actual force and the threat of force. While a case can be made for the fact that threats are not force per se, courts have ruled in many circumstances that anything that is coercive in nature is a type of force. For example, a credible threat of lethal force is a nonlethal option since adversaries will necessarily consider the consequences and adjust their behavior accordingly. This issue is especially contentious with warning shots, which may be out of policy, but by definition, are not an application of lethal force.

A force continuum is a useful tool for conceptualizing what type and how much force is reasonable given a specific set of circumstances but ascribing too much precision or exceeding its limitations is a recipe for disaster. While not perfect, this tool has proven to be one of the most reliable methods for understanding, comparing and teaching force options.

---

11. A Latin proverb which implies that the situation can go in more than one direction.
12. As used here, a "will" is simply a desire, purpose or determination held by one or more people. Thus, a single will can represent an opposing position from any number of suspects or terrorists.
13. The military refers to this concept as "the fog of war."
14. In other tactical settings, the term "force" can also be used as a noun to describe a body of troops, such as a military force, police force, or labor force.
15. Force used in this context is inherent in all forms of crises, including natural disasters.
16. The term nonlethal force is an ideal and has not yet been achieved in practice. Other terms, such as less lethal, less than lethal, minimal force, etc., are often substituted to more accurately convey this apparent inconsistency.
17. While a case might be made that a threat is not force, the stronger argument is that without force there can be no threat.
18. Force options based upon this philosophical understanding are also called "effects based."
19. Force options based upon this philosophical understanding are also called "behavior based."
20. As used here, "will" identifies the mental faculty by which an individual deliberately chooses a course of action; or in other words, a conscious choice or decision.
21. Nonlethal options are generally divided into five broad functions, anti-personnel, anti-materiel, anti-mobility, anti-infrastructure and area denial.

EMONs

Generally, management of the many is the same as manage-ment of the few. It is a matter of organization.

—SUN TZU[22]

EMERGENCY RESPONSES HAVE BEEN DESCRIBED AS "COME as you are parties."[23] This is because the nature of the circumstances does not allow detailed planning and prolonged preparation. First responders arrive with whatever is at hand. Likewise, the response organization that forms is comprised of a variety of personnel who have responded when the call for help was sounded. Understandably, these people participate because they are available and not because of their particular knowledge or skills. Accordingly, an early management task is to rearrange these responders to match their knowledge, skills and abilities to maximize their collective efforts. An understanding of organizational development then, especially relating to emergencies, becomes imperative.

All organizations are designed to distribute power, affix responsibility and allocate resources. They are generally divided according to conventions associated with a concept called the division of labor. In the simplest terms, **division of labor** refers to the categorization of specific knowledge and skills in the performance of roles within an organization. For example, police agencies have specialists in patrol, investigations, custody, and so forth. Similarly, the fire services have specialists in firefighting, rescue, hazardous materials, and the like. These categories are grouped within an organization for maximum efficiency and effectiveness.

Even the best of these organizations, however, are ill-suited to function well during periods of intense pressure because the circumstances of a specific emergency do not precisely coincide with the configurations of any agency. Specialty units that are essential for handling missions involving tactical interventions, investigations, searches, or explosive ordnance disposals, have different chains of command. The first common senior[24] who exercises command for all these disparate units may well be the Chief of Police. Needless to say, this is not practical. The problem is compounded when multiple agencies, disciplines and venues are involved, something that is commonplace in emergencies.

RESPONSE ORGANIZATIONAL IMPERATIVES

The solution is to build a temporary organization that is focused solely on resolving the particular problem and incorporates all the necessary specialties into a single chain of command.[25] This requires a **command and control architecture**; that is a design or system to provide for the interaction of the essential components and assure that all efforts are directed toward achieving a common goal. This architecture[26] is necessary to effectively define lines of authority, distribute power and allocate resources. The military describes this framework as a "set of associated command and control elements arranged in a command structure and communication network to enable a commander to plan, direct, coordinate and control the operations of his forces."[27] There are eight characteristics that need to be incorporated into these organizations to enable them to deal with the confusion and complexity of emergency situations.

First, and foremost, the infrastructure must establish a *unified command*. All the specialists, units, agencies and disciplines must report through a single chain of command to a single individual. Many incidents, such as the 1992 riots and 1994 earthquake in Los Angeles, and Hurricane Katrina in New Orleans involve multiple jurisdictions. Fire, police, military, disaster and health service organizations are all called upon to work together. A unified command structure requires that the implementation of the plan be accomplished under the direction of a single individual who has been designated as the incident commander.

Second, there must be a *manageable span of control.* This identifies the maximum number of personnel that can be supervised effectively by a single individual. It is especially important because organizations handling emergencies grow faster than a commander's ability to handle them. A commander can quickly become inundated with decisions that would better be made by subordinates. Such a situation is characterized by the term "**OBE**," which stands for "**O**vercome **B**y **E**vents."[28] OBE occurs when decision makers lose the ability to efficiently prioritize between competing interests when they become overwhelmed with their magnitude and complexity. Understandably, this situation needs to be avoided. One way to avoid OBE is by reducing the span of control. Generally, the span of control for people with emergency management responsibilities should be smaller than for those conducting routine operations. Factors such as the nature of the incident, complexity of the tasks, hazards and safety factors, all exert considerable influence on the number of subordinates an individual can effectively supervise. Generally, this has been determined to be about five subordinates. Another way to relieve command pressure is by insisting that decisions be pushed to the lowest possible level. In fact, this is so important that it is a precept for handling these types of situations.

Third, there must be *common terminology and procedures.* This may sound trivial, but has acute significance when multiple agencies and disciplines are involved. For example, shouting "fire" means something entirely different to a firefighter than to a police officer. The problem is further exacerbated if two components of an organization which must work together employ different procedures. All police and fire agencies depend upon mutual aid for large-scale civil disorders and the like, and many smaller agencies routinely depend on each other during complex tactical operations.

Fourth, the organizational structure needs to develop in a *modular fashion.* In addition to the command and control function, there are at least three areas that must be developed and assigned in every tactical operation. The intelligence section is assigned the duty of providing accurate and timely intelligence to the commander. It is responsible for the gathering, recording, evaluating and disseminating of all information pertinent to the incident. The operations section provides the coordination and implementation of the tactical response and is responsible for the planning, assignment, coordination, execution and evaluation of all tactical missions. The logistics section obtains and provides support, including personnel, as the operation progresses. This component is responsible for the acquisition, identification, tracking, staging and recovery of all personnel and logistical assets used in the operation.

If the organization remains small, a single individual may handle all of these areas but larger operations will require that at least one subordinate is assigned to each area. Each of the modules must be capable of adding additional personnel and equipment as it becomes necessary. Extremely large, complex or prolonged operations may require an entire staff wholly committed to a single function.

Fifth, every incident needs a *plan.* Though this sounds obvious, and though smaller incidents do not require a written plan, some guidance is always necessary. Without a plan, an incident commander is unable to seize the initiative and dooms the effort to one of reaction. Generally, a written plan should be considered necessary whenever resources from more than one agency are used, or when the incident is prolonged and requires changes in shifts of personnel or equipment.

Sixth, *predesignated incident facilities* need to be established. Critical facilities, such as evacuation shelters, command post locations, staging areas, helicopter landing zones and trauma centers need to be identified. Checklists for persons to be notified, as well as procedures for opening buildings, need to be developed. Simple things like "Who has the keys?" or "Who knows where . . .?" can be "showstoppers" without prior arrangements. By making these preparations before they are needed, memoranda of understanding, leases, contracts and insurance matters can be completed without further burdening an incident commander.

Seventh, is the need for *comprehensive resource management.*

Besides identifying potential resources, a plan needs to be developed for efficient distribution and accountability of equipment and personnel. Some resources have a limited service time, and replacements must be considered. For example, batteries may have to be recharged or replaced. Other items consume fuel, coolant and lubricants, or perhaps toner, ribbons and paper. Maintenance may also be necessary. Still others require special operator skills. For instance, large generators, heavy equipment and aircraft, all require specially trained personnel.

In addition to equipment, personnel must be fed and relieved. Sanitation facilities may be required or transportation arranged. Keeping track of all these factors requires assigning a current status condition to every resource to allow for maximum efficiency. Some method of accountability must be in place to avoid losing the equipment or over-fatiguing personnel.

Eighth, is a requirement for an *integrated communications system*. Communications systems need to provide flexibility, reliability, speed and security. Although all these four are critical, reliability is, by far, the most important. In the military environment, communications is called the "voice of command," for when a commander cannot communicate, he[29] can neither command nor control. As a matter of fact, this concept is seen as so intrinsic and essential in the command and control function that it is often abbreviated as "C^3" which stands for "Command," "Control" and "Communications." The communications infrastructure needs to identify the tactical channels[30] necessary to function. This frequently includes a tactical channel, a command channel and a logistics channel. Like the modular organization it serves, each of these channels supports a function, and needs to expand or contract to meet the needs of the organization as a whole.

EMERGING MULTI-ORGANIZATIONAL NETWORKS—EMONs

Sociologists refer to these "self-evolving" organizations as **EMONs**, or **E**merging **M**ulti-**O**rganizational **N**etworks.[31] They are designed specifically for resolving the immediate issue and although they depend on the "parent" organizations for resources, they have a "life" and "personality" of their own. Because EMONs are in response to situations that are always somewhat unique they take on different forms, sizes, and configurations depending on the circumstances presented. A fire, for example, will require a different approach than will a flood. Likewise, they "pulse" with the intensity of the situation and will respond accordingly, often by shrinking or expanding as the circumstances demand. Conversely, regardless of the circumstances, these organizations commonly share six characteristics.

First, they are *crisis driven*. This means that the nature of the situation defines the intensity, tempo and composition of the organization that attempts to control it. Even with organizations that commonly handle emergencies, such as law enforcement, fire services or military units, EMONs change according to each particular emergency. Moreover, they change during the same emergency depending on the circumstances at the time.

Second, they are *task oriented*. Routine duties and normal operations cease for persons assigned to handle an emergency. The entire focus centers on resolving the crisis. Further, there are no "collateral" responsibilities. While an EMON will certainly have supporting roles and functions, as a whole, it is solely concerned with solving the problem at hand.

Third, they are *self-evolving*. EMONs will evolve without conscious effort on the part of the management or executive functions within an organization. Although conscious effort will certainly influence the ultimate configuration of the EMON, their existence cannot be prevented. With, or without the assistance of authorities, people will take actions to preserve life and property. Accordingly, it is in the best interests of everyone to develop and implement protocol and procedures to make these temporary organizations more effective.

Fourth, all EMONs are *time sensitive*. Because all tactical situations are time sensitive, it follows that the organizations that are called upon to deal with them are also time sensitive. Even an ineffective EMON will change over time in its attempts to achieve a successful resolution. As the intensity of the operation ebbs and flows, so too does that of the organization attempting to influence it. Darkness, shift changes, and inclement weather are only a few examples of factors that may require an EMON to be reduced, enlarged or reconfigured. Thus, an EMON at the end of an operation will almost always look considerably different than what it did at the onset.

Fifth, all EMONs are a *composite*. This means that they are comprised of various individuals, units, agencies and disciplines who are required to work together to achieve a successful resolution for a given problem. Even the smallest EMON will be comprised of personnel with varying skills that must be integrated into a unified effort to achieve a satisfactory resolution. Particularly complex or unique situations may require consultants, experts or disciplines not found within the "parent" organization but who have rather been recruited to specifically assist in the endeavor.

Sixth, EMONs are *temporary*. They are ad hoc, and cease to exist as soon as they are no longer needed. Even agencies which are regularly called upon to handle emergencies do not have the ability to have a "standing" organization for these events because each situation will require a different set of skills, personnel, agencies or functions. Although EMONs evolve without conscious effort, they are most often canceled by a decision. "Return to normal operations" or "break it down" are common expressions familiar to law enforcement and military professionals alike, and describes the end of these temporary organizations.

SPLITTING EMONS

All events requiring a tactical intervention tend to evolve from a simpler form to one that is more complex. A warrant service that escalates to an operation with barricaded suspects is one example. Fires that eventually require evacuations, and protests and marches that erupt into riots, are other examples.

As the complexity and scope of a situation increases so too must an EMON. More and different types of resources from any number of agencies, jurisdictions and disciplines are added to enable a suitable response. A problem occurs when at some point the organization exceeds the abilities of the original incident commander's ability to manage everything effectively and subordinates will need to be assigned responsibility for components and/or functions. The question then becomes: how should such an organization be split?

Fortunately, law enforcement has been learned from the business world experiencing the same difficulties, albeit in a more leisurely fashion. This is because the division of labor concept not only results in groupings of workers by skills but along five general categories. These are by time—when they work; by area—where they work, by purpose—what they do; by process—how they do things; and by clientele—who they do it for. These categories create natural "seams" in an organization that allow divisions with a minimal amount of confusion or friction.

Time is the most common method of splitting a response organization and quite naturally sorts itself by the seams of shift changes. During emergencies, EMONs are ordinarily divided into "operational periods," often exceeding the common eight-hour shifts and expanding to "twelve and twelves," meaning twelve hours on and twelve hours off. Regardless of the length of the operational period, each shift is commanded and staffed by different personnel and the organization itself often requires different functional specialties, especially when the shifts overlap periods of daylight and darkness.

A second method is by geographical *area*, especially if the situation is unfolding in noncontiguous areas of operation. Grouping people by where they are physically located and working allows closer coordination and supervision. It also provides a means of creating impromptu expertise by providing a capability for novices to work alongside experts, not only learning from those experts on the job but collaborating in completing essential tasks too urgent to allow a wait for more specialists.

A third method is *purpose*. Purpose refers to the objective or end on which an activity is focused. When EMONs are separated by purpose they are almost always by function. For example, all personnel assigned to a single function like traffic control, containment, communications, evacuations, and so forth, could be grouped into a single command. Component units of an EMON grouped according to purpose are commonly assigned missions that cross jurisdictional and geographical lines, and even across shifts. This occurs when the activity is deemed so critical that the component is granted semi-autonomy and required to operate with only minimal instructions from higher headquarters. One of the best examples is the logistical function. Once an operation is underway and an EMON is established, those personnel assigned to logistics are required to anticipate, procure, and distribute food, tools, ammunition, equipment and all other logistical needs to sustain the operation without separate instructions for every activity or location.

A fourth method is dividing by *process*. Process refers to the methodology or ongoing series of actions to accomplish some activity. Separating an EMON by process is useful when knowledge of a process is a major contributing factor in accomplishing a similar, but not identical activity.[32] Say, for example, that a major evacuation is required and one of the desired factors is the tracking of refugees for early reunification with families and loved-ones. This is especially important when refugees like young school children, invalids, and the like, are incapable of assisting. Besides all the critical requirements like transportation, housing and feeding, knowing where people are physically located and how to contact them can be critically important. The incident commander may split the response organization by grouping persons with the necessary skills to provide this ability. Because tracking inmates is a similar process to that needed to track refugees, custody and correctional personnel will not only have personal knowledge of how best to accomplish the assignment but also possess special equipment for that task, such as wristband identification, computers, software, and so forth.

The last method is by *clientele*. Clientele refers to a grouping of people, regardless of how they are identified or assembled, and for whom some service is required. Although not as common for splitting an EMON as the other four methods, one example of splitting an EMON by clientele might be when there are a large number of refugees, as during a flood, fire or earthquake. An incident commander who is actively involved in life saving operations will not want a competing interest, even one as important as caring for refugees. Consequently, one method of splitting the EMON is to assign all tasks related to refugees to a single command. This component of the larger organization would then be responsible for all duties related to refugees, such as transportation, shelter, food, and security, regardless of where the refugees are physically located.

The advantages of splitting an EMON along these natural divisions should be apparent. It should also be clear that these methods allow close coordination and supervision even when personnel are separated geographically, separated by time, or working alongside of but with a separate mission from other components of the EMON. A commander who understands this natural division of labor is better able to make informed decisions and to exploit the individual and collective expertise inherent in all such organizations.

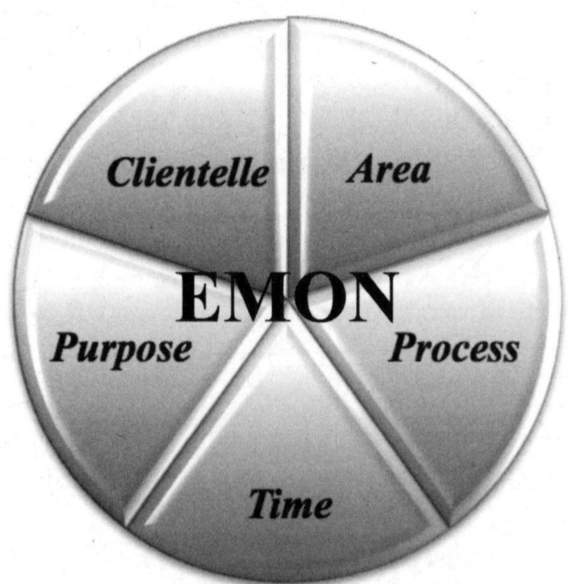

FIGURE 3-1 SPLITTING AN EMON: Even temporary organizations, like those that develop when responding to emergencies, have natural seams within themselves. When they grow in size and complexity beyond the capabilities to be easily managed they must be divided and a supervisor assigned to each division. The most efficient and effective way is along these natural seams.

22. Sun Tzu, *The Art of War*, c. 500 B.C.E
23. Capt. (ret.) Richard "Odie" Odenthal, commander of the Los Angeles Sheriff's Department's Emergency Operations Bureau and later Public Safety Manager for the City of West Hollywood, CA
24. The "first common senior rule" states that conflicts between various personnel and or units within an organization are decided by the first senior (supervisor) that is common to all involved.
25. This single chain of command exemplifies the criticality of the principle "unity of command" discussed in more detail in Chapter 4—Guiding Principles.
26. Also called a "table of organization," "job summary chart," or "organizational chart."
27. *United States Marine Corps Command and Control Master Plan*, published by the United States Marine Corps, August 1987.
28. Often referred to as *Overwhelmed* by Events. The acronym is not pronounced as a single word but rather by each letter, "O-B-E."
29. Throughout this book, officers and commanders (and, for that matter, criminals and suspects) may be referenced as "he." This is neither preference for male leaders nor reflection of today's law enforcement reality, in which commanders are of course both male and female. Rather, it is to avoid the awkward "he/she" concatenation and the distraction of such a reference. "He," therefore, will be used generically and no further inference should be drawn.
30. While many think of a communication channel as a radio frequency, as used here it has a much broader definition and includes all means of communication, to include telephone, fax, computer, messenger, email, web, and any combination.
31. Sometimes called *Evolving* Multi-Organizational Networks.
32. If it were an identical activity the most likely separation would be by purpose since it would constitute a function.

SECTION 2

SECTION 2

UNDERSTANDING AND DEVELOPING STRATEGY

> *Strategy is a system of makeshifts. It is more than a science, it is the application of science to practical affairs; it is carrying through an originally conceived plan under a constantly shifting set of circumstances.*[33]
>
> —HELMUTH VON MOLTKE

ONE ASPECT COMMON TO ALL SCIENCES IS THAT THEY ALL USE principles to provide guidance. Some, like the laws of physics, are inviolable. Most of them, however, provide general guidance for thought and actions toward norms and expectations. This is especially true for the soft sciences like psychology, sociology or history. So it is with tactical science. While there are no algorithms to resolve tactical problems there are a number of reliable principles that reduce ambiguity and provide direction. Like a doctor asking a patient, "Where does it hurt? Is it a sharp pain or a dull pain? Is the pain throbbing or steady? Does it occur often or seldom?" so a knowledgeable tactician can cut through the confusion and begin identifying the factors and influences involved. Because principles are crafted and tested by experts they provide novitiates with an ability to start where the experts left off in dealing with a developing situation.

This section is focused on understanding and developing strategies based upon sound doctrinal principles. It opens with a description of the most well-known grouping called "the principles of war." Notwithstanding the obvious focus, these principles have far broader application and provide guidance in all types of crises. They are frequently cited in business books and professional magazines, for example, and serve the same purposes.

The next chapter provides a means of looking into the future to anticipate outcomes, both satisfactory and unacceptable. Needless to say, those that are satisfactory are sought, while those that are not are avoided. This simple understanding provides a foundation to bring about a desirable future by identifying and encouraging favorable factors while discouraging those that are not. Of all the factors, two are so powerful that an ability to control them is decisive. Because they may not be apparent, the chapter continues by describing how to identify them. It concludes with methods to identify probabilities from limitless possibilities to avoid wasted efforts on unrealistic strategies and plans.

The final chapter in this section is devoted entirely to strategy, tactics and techniques and not only explains the differences but how they interact. It describes the two general categories for all strategies and the type of strategies that terrorists must employ to succeed. The chapter concludes with the tactics that are most often employed by law enforcement agencies when handling conflicts, to include a comparison of each of their advantages and disadvantages.

---

33. Field Marshal Helmuth Graf von Moltke (the elder), *On Strategy*, 1871. Helmuth von Moltke was the Chief of Staff of the Prussian Army for thirty years and is regarded as one of the great military theorists of his time. He was a staunch disciple of another famous theorist, Carl von Clausewitz. Unlike a system of rules advocated by another contemporary, Antoine-Henri Jomini, von Moltke considered the ability of adapting strategy to fit changing circumstances far more critical. He remains influential to this day and "Moltke's dictum, " which (paraphrased) states, "Plans are worthless but planning is essential" encapsulates his thoughts on the importance of not using a plan as a script but rather using the process for understanding how best to adapt it. Because he had two famous nephews with the same name, he is often identified as "the elder" to avoid confusion.

GUIDING PRINCIPLES

Get your principles straight; the rest is a matter of detail.

—NAPOLEON[34]

PRINCIPLES ARE FUNDAMENTAL LAWS OR TRUTHS FROM WHICH others are derived. They work as mental constructs by providing insights into reality. Principles are not rules, per se, but rather basic generalizations which focus attention and provide guidance. As such, principles are especially valuable in discerning the relevant factors and influences involved in chaotic and confusing circumstances. Even when no answer is apparent, a principle provides a glimpse of where to look.

The origin of principles for handling tactical operations can be traced as far back as 500 B.C. in Sun Tzu's *Art of War*, but they were first explicitly listed in Carl von Clausewitz's *Principles of War*[35] in 1812 and later still in Baron Jomini's *The Art of War* in 1838. Through the years, other strategists have also identified principles from their own perspectives that have served to deepen the understanding of the subtleties and undercurrents so easily missed at a quick glance.

PRINCIPLES OF WAR

Among the best known of all tactical principles are nine tenets called the **Principles of War.**[36] There is nothing exceptional about these particular nine except that they have withstood the test of time and trial and remain relevant to this day. The United States Army first published its discussion of these principles in 1921, but they were taken from the works of British Major General J.F.C. Fuller,[37] who published them originally in 1912 and continued to refine them until they reached their present form in 1925. Fuller's work set forth in concise terms, nine interacting and related factors that have stood the test of analysis, experimentation and practice. Each principle is present, to a greater or lesser degree, in every tactical operation. The fact that a commander may neglect or even ignore them makes them no less important—it merely affects the outcome. These nine principles play a key role in the development of tactical plans and have revolutionized the ways in which personnel and equipment are utilized and deployed.

The principle of **maneuver** is well known but not well understood. In fact, persons with no knowledge of tactics sometimes confuse it with the entire body of tactical principles. Indeed, the impact this principle has on any tactical plan can hardly be exaggerated. Maneuver can be defined as the movement of troops and equipment to gain an advantage. It is important to understand that maneuver is more than simply movement. Like two boxers vying for position around one another, maneuver in tactical operations seeks to gain a temporary advantage by position. As such, maneuver must accommodate for factors such as terrain, weather, lighting and other contextual factors.

Maneuver has at least two interrelated dimensions, flexibility and mobility. *Flexibility* describes the need for versatility and pliancy in thought and plans. It provides an ability to react rapidly to unforeseen circumstances. Without flexibility an organization will be unable to adapt to changing conditions. *Mobility* is then necessary to enable prompt actions and reactions. This principle is a key contributor to sustaining the initiative, exploiting success, preserving freedom of action and reducing vulnerability.

The principle of **objective** is called the master or controlling principle. This is because it is the basis from which all planning necessarily must follow. In the simplest terms, objective means purpose. Accordingly, the objective in tactical operations and disaster responses is the end to be attained through the employment of forces. Every operation must be directed toward a clearly defined, decisive and attainable objective. Although it often appears that tactical objectives are readily apparent, they are in fact frequently obscured by emotions, uncertainty and vague commands. No plan, no matter how brilliant, can overcome the confusion created by a vague, ill-conceived or undeclared objective. A commander *must* decide upon an acceptable resolution and direct the efforts of his forces to that end.

Since the most effective and decisive way to pursue and attain an objective is through the seizure, retention and exploitation of the initiative, offensive action is required in all tactical operations. This is because whatever forms offensive action takes, it is the only means by which a commander holds the initiative, maintains freedom of action and imposes his will on the circumstances. Since **offense** is required to reach a conclusion, a commander who neglects this principle surrenders the initiative. While defense is valuable, it cannot, in and of itself, be decisive because the initiative cannot be gained or maintained while in a defensive posture and so the best that can be hoped for is a stalemate. Notwithstanding the importance of this tenet, it is one of the most misunderstood and neglected of the nine principles.

Because crises, by their very nature, are plagued with confusion and chaos, **simplicity** in plans and actions becomes essential. A plan that cannot be understood cannot be implemented. "Direct, simple plans and clear, concise orders are essential to reduce the chances for misunderstanding and confusion."[38] Since friction is inherent in all tactical operations, even the simplest plan can become difficult to execute and the difficult plan becomes all but impossible. Consequently, plans which are readily understood and unencumbered with complications are more likely to succeed. The concept of simplicity is often emphasized by an adage called "*Occam's razor*," which states "the simplest solution is usually the correct one."[39]

Economy of force suggests that, in the absence of unlimited resources, a commander must accept some risks in non-vital areas to enable him to achieve superiority at a decisive place and time. Since no commander has unlimited resources, the principle of economy of force is inherent in every tactical operation. Even when a commander has all the personnel and equipment he can use, time will require a change of shifts and conservation of resources to allow for sustaining the operation. Accordingly, this principle is especially critical in prolonged operations. An astute commander will determine what personnel and assets are available, and when and where they will be needed. He then distributes his forces accordingly.

Mass is the reciprocal of economy of force. This means that the two principles are interrelated and complementary. Economy of force is necessary to create mass and mass requires some economy of force. The principle of mass requires that those limited resources must be used so that sufficient power can be concentrated at a decisive time and place. Without an economy of force it will not be possible to mass. This often happens when a lack of understanding obscures the ultimate objective since prioritization becomes impossible.

It is important to understand that massing effects are not simply a concentration of forces. Proper application of mass more precisely means incorporating and synchronizing sufficient forces and resources of all types to achieve decisive results. Thus, being at the right place and time with the right equipment, even a numerically inferior force can prevail. For example, in a riot situation a law enforcement commander who encounters a large group of rioters may deploy forces in such a manner that the rioters must consider multiple threats from multiple directions. By massing his forces at a time and place of his choosing, the law enforcement commander gains a substantial advantage when the suspects are slow or unable to effectively react. A series of such maneuvers can deplete the adversaries' forces to the point where continued resistance is futile.

In any tactical situation, there is a point at which a final decision must be made. That decision must be made by a *single* authority. This assures that coordination and control are focused toward attaining the objective. The principle of **unity of command** ensures that all efforts are focused on a common goal. Unity of command is achieved by vesting a single commander with the requisite authority to direct, coordinate and control the actions of *all* forces employed in reaching the objective. This principle is so critical that Napoleon once stated that it was better to have one bad general than two good ones![40]

Similar, but fundamentally different, to the principle of unity of command is a concept called **unity of effort**. While unity of command refers to a single commander ultimately responsible for every objective, unity of effort refers to the collaboration of all forces toward a common objective even though they may have different supervisors and report through different chains of command.

Surprise results from striking an adversary at an unexpected time or place, or in an unanticipated manner. It is not necessary that an adversary be taken completely unaware, only that he becomes aware too late to effectively react. Surprise can provide advantages that decisively affect the outcome of tactical operations. In fact, for law enforcement, it is often the key factor in the success of many drug raids and high-risk warrant services. Surprise is one factor that may assist in creating sufficient mass against a numerically superior or more powerful adversary because a commander can trounce an adversary before effective countermeasures can be brought to bear. As a concept, surprise is so powerful that it may allow success to be attained out of all proportion to the effort expended.

The principle of **security** denies an adversary an ability to acquire an unexpected advantage. The principle of security encompasses far more than just secrecy, however, and may be better described as protectiveness. It encompasses everything in which a tactical force engages. Plans must be kept secret; equipment and movements must be guarded; command posts must be defended and communications protected. "Security enhances freedom of action by reducing friendly vulnerability to hostile acts, influence, or surprise."[41] Moreover, security is, to a large degree, related to the principle of surprise because while it is possible to have security without surprise, it is not possible to have surprise without security. Consequently, compromised plans for actions that may not even seem controversial can create friction if exploited by persons with an agenda contrary to the overall objective. One of the most well-

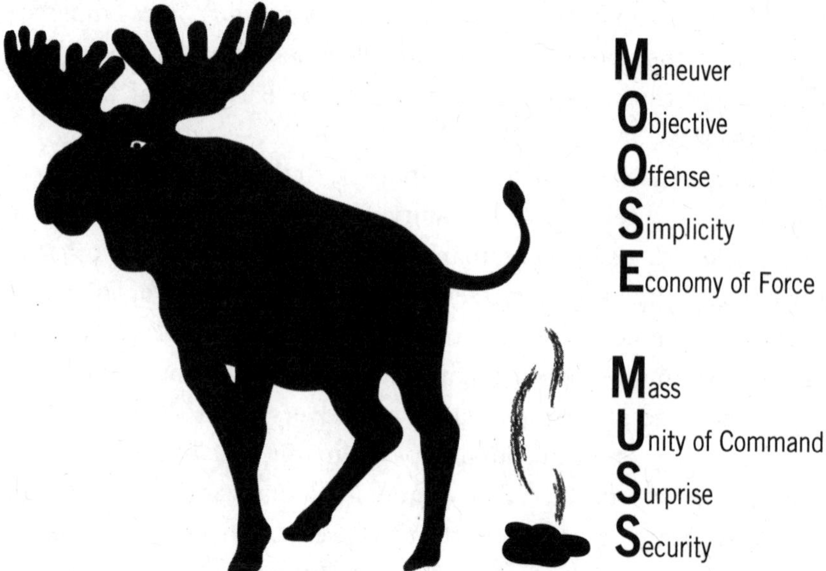

FIGURE 4-1 MOOSEMUSS: "MOUSE MOSS," "SUMO MOSES," and "MOM USE SOS," are a few of the many acronyms used to help remember the principles of war. Probably the most common, however, is "MOOSE MUSS." Each of the letters stands for one of the principles. Maneuver, Objective, Offense, Simplicity, Economy of force, Maneuver, Unity of command, Surprise and Security.

known adages concerning the principle of security is "Plans known are plans defeated."

These nine principles are used so often that they are committed to memory by many tacticians. A useful tool for remembering them is the mnemonic used by the U.S. military: **MOOSEMUSS.** Each of the letters identifies a principle and keeps them mentally available for review. Because these nine principles have withstood the test of time and trial, a commander who appreciates their significance is much better able to understand some of the latent factors inherent in all tactical operations.

THE 10TH PRINCIPLE

While it would be nice to use these nine principles as a checklist or formula, they are by no means sacred. Over the years, strategists have suggested a number of others, at least one of which is worthy of discussion here because it so strongly applies to law enforcement tactical operations. The principle of **legitimacy** is sometimes called the "10th Principle of War." It identifies the absolute necessity of maintaining the confidence of the community of the lawfulness and morality of actions. The U.S. military learned the significance of this principle the hard way when they lost the support of the American people for the Vietnam War and ultimately withdrew. The lesson should not be lost on domestic law enforcement who are constantly scrutinized as a matter of course.

Like the principle of surprise, legitimacy is also related to the principle of security. This is because one of the most indispensable ingredients for legitimacy is an informed public. While this might seem to conflict with the principle of security, it is not necessarily so. How an operation is conducted is not usually as important as to what was done and why. As long as the actions taken were necessary and reasonable the public tends to be forgiving of mistakes. This is not the case when attempts are made to conceal or falsify information that rightfully belongs in the public domain. Accordingly, public access to information should be an essential component in gaining and maintaining their trust. While some information, such as personal information and forthcoming operational plans, will need to be kept private, they also enjoy the protection of law and so support the principle of security. Although some may argue that politics have no role in tactical operations, as public servants the law enforcement community answers directly to the people. Neglecting or ignoring the principle of legitimacy is a recipe for disaster. In fact, win or lose, legitimacy can be the decisive element when actions are examined after the fact.[42]

PRINCIPLES FOR SPECIAL OPERATIONS

Some types of conflicts are, in and of themselves, noticeably distinct and/or somewhat peculiar when compared with others. Lacking a more descriptive term they are lumped together under the umbrella of "special operations." In the military these include operations dealing with counterinsurgencies, hostage recoveries, counterterrorism, dignitary protection, and other unconventional assignments that do not neatly match the roles of the military services in general. Similarly, the law enforcement community has had to respond to critical incidents for which special weapons and tactics were required.[43] Adopting the same concept, the law enforcement community has also formed special teams to deal with complex, difficult and/or unusual assignments like high risk warrants, hostage recovery, counterterrorism, barricaded suspects, snipers, dignitary protection and others that require specially trained and equipped personnel.

The principles and precepts that govern other tactical operations are no less relevant for special operations but some tend to take on increased significance. This is not only because of the uniqueness of the assignments but the fact that small units are incapable of duplicating the capabilities of large ones, especially in sustaining operations. Accordingly, special operations are nearly always of short duration where the objective is to temporarily gain an advantage that can be exploited. This concept is called relative superiority.

Relative superiority can be defined as that temporary advantage gained by a smaller force over a larger one or a well-defended opponent.[44] Relative superiority is derived from and closely related to the principle of mass described earlier but where mass is needed to bring overwhelming power at a specific place and time to achieve decisive results, relative superiority needs only to gain a temporary advantage that provides a decisive advantage if properly exploited. Likewise, the force gained by mass almost always requires superior numbers of personnel and equipment, even if only temporary, while relative superiority achieves the same advantage by the use of a smaller, but highly trained force tightly focused on an objective.

Relative superiority has three fundamental conditions. First, it is only effective at the pivotal point of an engagement. Too early or too late and it cannot provide the necessary advantages to be decisive. Second, it must be appropriately exploited. This is because smaller forces are unable to indefinitely sustain the advantage. Strategically then, relative superiority is always in a supporting role as part of a larger operation. Finally, if it is lost it is difficult to recover. Because overwhelming force is not available to a small unit, other factors, especially speed and surprise, are used to gain relative superiority. Understandably, once these advantages are lost they are nearly impossible to recover and so relative superiority is likewise affected.

The value of the concept of relative superiority is in its ability to reveal positive factors and influences in achieving success without relying on overwhelming numbers. One factor is that the earlier in the engagement relative superiority is attained the better the chances that the mission will be a success. This is because it reduces vulnerability to unforeseen circumstances and opposing actions. Because relative superiority serves to provide a focal point on a pivotal stage of an operation, critical factors and influences that might be obscured during planning and preparation tend to become apparent.

As with any operation, not every factor or influence can be controlled. Notwithstanding, those that can be should arouse special attention and more effort. While the nine principles of war will serve in the role of "general purpose;" six principles specific to special operations have proven to predominate these types of operations. These are *simplicity*, *security*, *repetition*, *surprise*, *speed* and *purpose*.[45] Not only are these six principles important individually, but interact with one another and so neglecting one can also adversely impact others.

Of the six principles, simplicity is the most crucial in special operations. By its very nature, relative superiority is tightly focused on a pivotal stage of an operation which is intended to be crucial to overall success. Accordingly, plans and execution for this assignment require simplification to the maximum possible extent. Generally, there are three ways of achieving simplicity. First, is by limiting the tactical objectives to only those that are vital to attain relative superiority. Second, by reducing the number of unknown factors and variables to the maximum practical extent. This requires good intelligence. Third, by using imagination and innovation to avoid or overcome obstacles that would otherwise complicate the mission.

Security for special operations is particularly important but is nearly never complete. For example, criminals always take precautions to prevent police from locating and confiscating contraband and other evidence. These range from simply hiding the contraband to elaborate fortifications that provide time to destroy evidence before it can be confiscated. Moreover, the precautions are always based upon a preconceived idea of how police will attempt to overcome them. The information most needed to be protected then, is when and how an operation will unfold. A lack of security, however, allows even the most inept criminal an ability to develop effective countermeasures.

The **principle of repetition** can be defined as any series of drills, exercises or practices intended to increase proficiency in preparation for an actual event. Repetition reduces unfamiliarity, increases confidence, and enhances the speed necessary for surprise. Repetition, then, indirectly contributes to gaining and maintaining the initiative. Because it improves the skills of both individuals and units it tends to refine procedures and enhance simplicity. It is not unusual for special operations units to conduct comprehensive dress rehearsals, especially when success may hinge on critical procedures and/or sequences. Dress rehearsals have the added advantage of revealing weak points in a plan so that corrections and/or reinforcements can be incorporated prior to the execution.

Because relative superiority does not require overwhelming force, surprise is often the best alternative. In special operations, surprise is most often attained through deception, timing and/or exploiting vulnerabilities. Deception is used to create a vulnerability by distracting an adversary long enough to take advantage of a weakness. Deceptions are usually difficult to achieve, however, and so should not be a critical juncture in a plan without a reliable contingency. Timing provides an advantage of surprise because the choice of "when" lies with the special operations unit. Since no force can indefinitely maintain a constant state of utmost readiness there are periods when vigilance is reduced or made more difficult (i.e. darkness, inclement weather, etc.) that can provide opportunities for exploitation. The last method involves identifying and exploiting vulnerabilities. Even the most formidable adversaries are unable to develop an absolutely fool-proof defense. An opponent's apparent lack of weakness is almost always attributable to a superficial search.

Regardless of how surprise is achieved, it is important to understand that, in and of itself, it is not decisive in nature. Of all the factors that affect sustainment, surprise is the most transient. It merely contributes to gaining relative superiority and should never be viewed as a standalone option.

The **principle of speed** refers to the rapidity and quickness of actions. It includes all functions and operations involved in a tactical operation, but is especially critical in a conflict. Because overwhelming power is not practical for special operations units, speed of execution can provide some compensation by rapidly overcoming an adversary's ability to effectively resist. Moreover, speed is one of the most effective methods for gaining surprise and seizing the initiative. Speed is also required when reacting to unexpected setbacks and adapting to new circumstances. Like repetition, speed is not one of the principles of war but is such a potent influence to the outcome of special operations it deserves examination on its own merits.

The last principle is purpose. Purpose is derived from the principle of objective but provides two important aspects. First, it describes the precise goal of the special operations mission, and second, it instills a sense of personal commitment and dedication. Special operations, by their very nature, are ambiguous and gravitate toward perplexity. Without a clear understanding of what is needed and the personal dedication to accomplish it, it is easy to become disillusioned and distracted by setbacks. A clear purpose provides an ability to adapt to changing circumstances accompanied by the determination and perseverance to accomplish it regardless of interference and obstructions.

While each of these principles is important in its own right, none exist in isolation from the others. For example, repetition enables faster actions and speed directly contributes to surprise, which in turn is dependent upon security. Likewise, simplicity greatly facilitates purpose, and so forth. Ignoring or neglecting the impact of any one principle severely degrades the likelihood of success when missions are exceptionally unusual and/or dangerous.

OTHER PRINCIPLES

The principles described previously are by no means an exhaustive list. Other schools of thought have held that the principles for maritime operations are different than for those on land and both of these are different than for air operations. Still others point out that other critical factors are ignored completely. For example, it has been suggested that because of the dynamic nature of tactical operations and disaster responses, flexibility is absolutely essential. Other perspectives insist that factors like sustainability, morale, and collaboration are as equally important. Opposing views point out that each and every one of these is inherent in all the other principles and as such should be considered as a given without having to examine their influences separately.

In point of fact, the principles described in this chapter represent those which have proven of value over time and have withstood the test of scrutiny and challenge. That is not to say, however, that other principles don't have equal value in specific circumstances. The value of any principle is attributed directly to how well it provides insight and guidance in situations that are inherently confusing, chaotic and ever-changing.

---

34. Napoleon Bonaparte, 1769-1821, Emperor of France and considered one of the greatest military minds in history.
35. Carl von Clausewitz is better known for his seminal work, *On War*, but this essay entitled *Principles of War*, was written around 1812 and served the purpose of today's monographs. It was written to instruct the young Prussian Crown Prince Friedrich Wilhelm, who Clausewitz was tutoring at the time.
36. In attempts to assuage the feelings of those who object to the term "war," these principles have sometimes been identified as the "Nine Governing Principles of Tactical Operations" and similar politically correct terms. For clarity and simplicity, the original, and/or most common terms, will be used throughout this book.
37. British Gen. John Frederick Charles (J.F.C.) Fuller published a military journal article in 1916 called "The Principles of War, With Reference

to the Campaigns of 1914–1915." This article is credited as being the first description of the modern principles of war.

38. *Operations*, FM 100-5, Headquarters, Department of the Army, Washington D.C., May 1986, p. 177.
39. Over the years, Occam's razor has been used to emphasize the importance of simplicity in many sciences. It is attributed to a 14th-century English logician by the name of William of Ockham. It is also commonly referred to with the Latin phrase "lex parsimoniae" which translates to English as the "law of parsimony" or the "law of economy." For no discernible reason, the term is commonly spelled both "Occam" and "Ockham.
40. This concept was well-known and applied by the time of the American Civil War. President Abraham Lincoln paraphrased it during his First State of the Union Address on December 3, 1861 when he said, "It has been said that one bad general is better than two good ones, and the saying is true if taken to mean no more than that an army is better directed by a single mind, though inferior, than by two superior ones at variance and cross-purposes with each other."
41. *Operations*, FM 100-5, Headquarters, Department of the Army, Washington D.C., May 1986, p. 176.
42. Other suggestions as principles of war include perseverance, speed, flexibility, cooperation, sustainability, morale, readiness, initiative, and many others. The nine presented here are simply those that have withstood the test of time and trial and are the most often cited in American operations.
43. The generic term for these teams is "SWAT" which was coined by the Los Angeles Police Department at the inception of the law enforcement special operations concept in the mid-1960s and has been nearly universally adopted throughout the United States. While agencies have chosen other names, such as Special Emergency Response Team (SERT), Special Weapons Team (SWT), or Crisis Reaction Team (CRT), and many others, they are all based on the same concept. One definition, adopted by the State of California's Commission on Peace Officer Standards and Training, describes the nature of these teams and their assignments as: "A Special Weapons and Tactics (SWAT) team is any designated group of law enforcement officers who are selected, trained, and equipped to work as a coordinated team to resolve critical incidents that are so hazardous, complex, or unusual that they may exceed the capabilities of first responders or investigative units."
44. This definition is paraphrased from that provided by William H. McRaven in his book, *Spec Ops: Case Studies in Special Operations*

Warfare Theory and Practice. Presidio Press, Ballentine Books, New York, New York, 1995. McRaven, a SEAL in the U.S. Navy, is both a practitioner and a student of special operations. After analyzing historical special operations he identified six principles that so heavily influenced the outcomes of these types of operations that they merited special attention for planning, preparing and executing missions that required innovative thinking and extraordinary measures. McRaven wrote the book while a Commander in the U.S. Navy and has commanded at every level of the military special operations community, to include commander of the Joint Special Operations Command (JSOC). The book has become an outstanding text in the special operations community for both military and law enforcement special operations teams. The principles and concepts described in this section are derived entirely from it.

45. Of note is that four of the six principles for special operations are either the same or derived directly from the nine principles of war. These are simplicity, surprise, security and purpose (objective). While the other principles of war are still important, these four are particularly relevant for successful special operations.

END STATE

As for the future, your task is not to foresee it; but to enable it.

—ANTOINE DE SAINT-EXUPÉRY[46]

MANKIND'S EARLIEST EFFORTS TO INFLUENCE THE FUTURE almost certainly began with the hunt for food and shelter. Factors like experience with prey, knowledge of the terrain, availability of weapons and the skills of other hunters all played a part in the venture. The first debriefings probably existed as tales around a campfire. As humans continued to gain knowledge, however, the significance of critical factors became more and more apparent. Successful clans exploited lessons the group had learned and held skilled hunters in high esteem. As these groups began competing for the same limited resources they fought with each other and discovered that the knowledge and skills they gained in seeking food and shelter were also applicable in defending themselves and in exploiting weaker tribes.

This ability to work together and maximize the group's lessons learned served to encourage the formation of armies and government. Armies gained fame for their innovations in warfare and conquered vast areas of the world. Over time, the effort to reduce uncertainty and to apply scientific principles to achieve tactical success has grown into a large body of doctrine. From this knowledge, sound plans can evolve. One crucial concept is the end state.

THE END STATE

Most people probably do not think of law enforcement officers as futurists. Contemplating a future satisfactory resolution, however, constitutes a critical aspect in operational planning, particularly in responding to major disasters with their harsh time constraints, rapidly unfolding and ambiguous circumstances and far-reaching consequences. This resolution is most often referred to as an **end state** and is defined as those required conditions that define achievement of the commander's objectives.

In the simplest terms, the end state describes the desired result, or final outcome, of a tactical operation. It is never a return to the way it was before because any situation that requires an intervention to achieve a resolution has already indelibly altered the future. Thus, it is impossible to return to an identical previous state. Consequently, commanders must develop a clear picture of a satisfactory end state to provide a focal point for directing efforts to attain it.

Without this vision, the operation will run on its own inertia, lacking both guidance and impetus. In short, the operation becomes an end in itself, neither efficient nor effective. Inasmuch as the end state may occur hours, days, weeks, or even months into the future, commanders cannot obtain a totally clear vision of the final resolution. Although a certain amount of vagueness and ambiguity will always exist, commanders can reduce it by limiting the possibilities to a range of likely outcomes. The more precisely that this range can be defined the easier it is to focus efforts on achieving a favorable outcome. This has momentous implications for strategic planning.

To illustrate the importance of this concept consider the following scenario. Two young men hiking in the woods encounter a hungry bear and begin running to escape. The bear begins chasing them, and as time passes, it becomes clear that it will eventually catch them. Nearly out of breath, one of the boys stops and retrieves a pair of running shoes from his backpack. As he sheds his heavy hiking boots and dons his running shoes his friend watches in astonishment. Anxious to be on their way he questions, "What are you doing? You're still not going to be able to outrun the bear." His friend instantly replies, "I don't have to outrun the bear!"

The first young man had defined his end state as outrunning the bear. Because of this understanding he continued on a course of action even though he knew it would eventually fail because he could think of no better alternatives. The second young man had defined his end state as not being eaten by the bear. This subtle difference provided options that were not obvious to his friend. The point of the joke is that he could out run his friend who would then be caught by the bear, but other options, not as funny but just as viable, were also available. He could climb a tree or jump into a river, for instance.[47] The point this illustrates is that the better the vision of the end state, the greater the ability to achieve it. So it is with tactical operations and disaster responses.

THE MANAGEABLE FUTURE

For some tacticians, the future is intimidating because it is fraught with uncertainty. For others, this very uncertainty is used as an excuse for failure in the belief that since the future cannot be foreseen their response is as good as anyone else's, a lack of understanding or knowledge notwithstanding. A closer examination, however, reveals that uncertainty is not equally distributed. For example, there is less uncertainty in the near future than the far future. Likewise, there is less uncertainty in situations that are deemed more likely to occur than those that are bizarre and exceptional. An understanding of what is likely and what is not enables planners and decision makers to focus on those actions that will encourage positive influences for a favorable resolution. Conversely, it may be just as effective to inhibit negative influences to avoid their consequences. Without a clear vision of the desired end state, commanders' directions become aimless and devoid of a cohesive strategy. Two concepts that help understand how uncertainty is unequally distributed in the future are the event horizon and scenario reviews.

The **event horizon** describes that portion of the future in which decision makers can reasonably anticipate the consequences of their actions. It is the far threshold of a range in time called the foreseeable future. Beyond this range uncertainty is so prevalent that reliable decisions are impossible. Within the range, however, commanders can make plans and decisions with a degree of assurance. Plans and decisions focused near the present are more reliable than those focused farther into the future but tend to have minimal effect on an outcome. Conversely, those focused farther into the future are bolder and have more effect but beyond the event horizon there is so much uncertainty that they become rash. Understandably, better plans and decisions are those that are bold enough to have the desired effect but are neither timid nor reckless.

Of necessity, commanders must anticipate some actions relatively close to the present, while others may have far-reaching effects. Generally, the higher up an organization the decision maker the farther into the future the event horizon will be oriented. For example, in a tactical operation, a sergeant most likely would be concerned with the detailed deployment of subordinate officers and their immediate well-being, while a lieutenant may be considering rest periods or shift changes that would occur twelve or more hours into the future. In the same fashion, a captain would be interested in actions that will ensure the eventual success of the operation several days into the future, whereas the chief of police may be looking at ways to enhance the abilities of the department for similar operations in the months and years to come. Each of these sets of decisions has their own criteria and a differing event horizon. Understanding an event horizon provides a means of identifying that portion of the future that commanders can realistically influence and so becomes a foundation for planning.

Commanders never remain completely ignorant nor become all knowing; rather, their level of confidence gradually increases the closer it approaches the present. In fact, commanders never will be surer of a decision than at the moment they make it; thus, the level of confidence is always highest at the present. After commanders make a decision, their level of confidence begins to drop sharply because they, like everyone else, cannot determine precisely what the future holds. Eventually, commanders reach a point where they

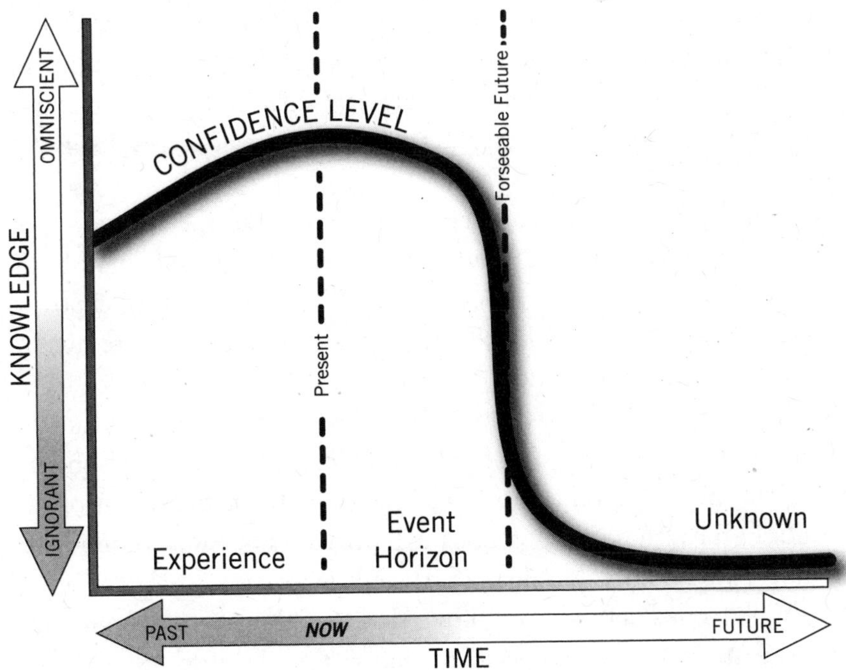

FIGURE 5-1 EVENT HORIZON: The graph illustrates the quest for certainty and visually depicts the event horizon. The Y-axis (vertical arrow) represents knowledge and runs the gamut from complete ignorance to omniscience. The X-axis (horizontal arrow) delineates time and extends into both the past and the future. The curved line depicts the confidence level, which represents the degree of assurance that decision makers can anticipate the consequences of their actions. It always increases until the time of decision since it is not possible to be surer of a decision that at the time it is made. The two remaining lines on the graph represent two extremes—the close (timid) versus the distant (rash) limit that defines the event horizon. A plan oriented too close to the timid line has minimal effect on the outcome. Conversely, a plan oriented so far into the future as to make the consequences unpredictable proves reckless because such proposals rely more on guesswork than reliable factors and sound reasoning. Therefore, an indifferent disregard for the consequences can result in catastrophic repercussions.

can no longer reasonably anticipate the impact of their decisions, and their level of confidence drops dramatically. This defines the farther limit of the event horizon.

However, the closer commanders orient their decisions to the present, the less efficiently they generally can achieve their ultimate objective. Lackluster actions often result from overcautious and anxious commanders and usually are not bold enough to alter the future sufficiently to achieve a successful resolution. Commanders who fail to implement actions to achieve their end state surrender the initiative and remain in a reactionary posture. This results in the situation being driven by events.[48]

While the event horizon defines the range into the future where reliable decisions can be made and plans formulated, it fails to identify the scope of the possibilities. While the number of possibilities is limitless, those that merit serious consideration are not. A **scenario review** is a method that identifies likely probabilities from boundless possibilities. A scenario is simply an outline, or model, of a set of expected, or supposed, sequence of events. Commanders take the premises that support a scenario from the situation at hand. In turn, these suppositions will provide some idea of the best, worst, and most likely things that can happen.

When considering everything that could happen, commanders use the *best-case scenario* to define the absolute upper limit, if everything proceeds well. This scenario takes all factors into account and assumes effective actions and favorable influences. It provides the upper limit of the potentialities, but stops short of the miraculous. On the other hand, the *worst-case scenario* represents the absolute lower limit and describes the worst possible outcome. Like the other, this scenario takes all factors into account, but assumes that actions will prove minimally effective and unfavorable influences will exist. It provides the lower limit of the potentialities, but stops short of unreasonable, catastrophic consequences. The third type of scenario is called the *most-likely scenario*, and describes the outcome that, based upon all known factors, is most likely to occur. This scenario always lies somewhere between the best and worst-case scenarios. Not surprisingly, the farther away from the most likely scenario a plan is oriented, the more unpredictable its outcome. Commanders use the most likely scenario primarily to provide direction and focus to their efforts while not ignoring the worst-case possibilities.

When planners use the scenario review process in conjunction with the event horizon, they can readily discern that the **manageable future** lies between the present and the event horizon and the

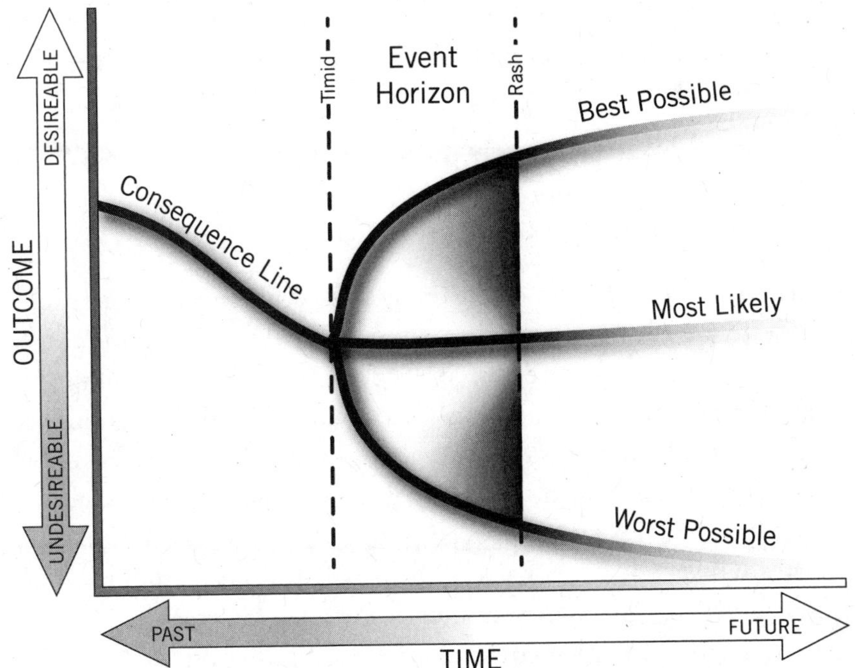

FIGURE 5-2 SCENARIO REVIEW: The graph illustrates the manageable future and identifies the limits of the scope of possibilities. The consequence line depicts the chain of events pertaining to their effects (and anticipated effects) on the desired end state. The lower the line moves the more undesirable the consequences. Conversely, the higher it goes the more desirable they become. In contrast with the confidence level used in depicting an event horizon, the consequence line almost always descends from the past to the present. If it ascends (the situation is improving), the need for intervention may not be necessary. Also, as the line continues moving past the present, it reflects not on what has happened but what could happen. Thus, when the line moves from the past into the future it becomes a forecast; that is, what commanders think is going to happen based upon their assessments. Accordingly, it forks into a forecast of the three scenarios with the best and worst-case scenarios defining the scope of possibilities that merit attention.

best and worst-case scenarios. The most likely course of events lies closest to the present and along the most likely scenario line.[49]

By understanding that the indefinable future is not quite so uncertain, planners and decision makers can begin to collect the information that will enable them to reliably forecast an acceptable outcome to a situation. Then, by looking at a variety of possibilities, from best to worst-case scenarios, managers can plan their courses of action with greater certainty of success. In turn, they will create a manageable, and more desirable, future for themselves and the citizens they serve.

CENTERS OF GRAVITY AND CRITICAL VULNERABILITIES

Assisting commanders in determining an acceptable and achievable end state are two concepts that help to identify a focus for those factors that have the greatest influence. These are determining a center of gravity and identifying critical vulnerabilities. In conflicts, a **center of gravity** refers to something a suspect is dependent upon for success, and which, if eliminated, damaged, diminished or destroyed, will severely impact his opportunities for success. To illustrate this concept, consider a barricaded suspect situation. The suspect's center of gravity is most often the structure itself. The structure provides a sanctuary that prevents the authorities from observing his actions and may even shield him from bullets. In order to defeat him, the advantages provided by the structure must be eliminated in some manner. This is often done with an entry but may be done in a variety of other ways. For instance, insertion of chemical agents may not allow him to remain inside, his movements may be observed with infrared night vision scopes or a garage may have the vehicle door pulled open to facilitate entry. In the same manner, this concept can be applied to disasters in that factors that diminish the effects on a community can tremendously attenuate the adverse consequences. For example, early identification and support for critical roads and bridges will greatly reduce the disruption to community services and facilitate support during storms. In fact, the more resilient the infrastructure in general, the less impact a storm, flood, fire or earthquake will have on a community when it does occur.

A **critical vulnerability** identifies a weakness which, if exploited, will create failure. Common examples of critical vulnerabilities for suspects include lack of mobility, lack of relief (will tire over time) or lack of logistical sustainment (food, water, power, ammunition and so forth). Because none of these are normally a problem with authorities, it may be possible to defeat a suspect by simply waiting him out. It hardly merits comment, but to avoid unfavorable outcomes we must also examine our own organization for its critical vulnerabilities.

While easy to describe in concept, both centers of gravity and critical vulnerabilities may be difficult to identify in actual situations. To make them more conspicuous, two additional concepts are useful. The first is critical capabilities. **Critical capabilities** are defined as those inherent abilities that enable a center of gravity to function. Critical capabilities answer the question: What are the ways of attaining the desired end state?

Because all critical capabilities have necessary conditions and resources to enable them to operate, they in turn have critical requirements. **Critical requirements** are those conditions, means and resources that enable a critical capability. More simply put, critical requirements are inherent preconditions for critical capabilities and answer a different question: What is necessary to enable the identified critical capabilities?

Each critical capability may need a number of critical requirements to be fully operative. For example, helicopters need both pilots and fuel and the lack of either renders the helicopter useless. It follows that interfering, inhibiting or degrading a critical requirement then impairs the capability it supports.[50] Thus, a critical vulnerability is simply a critical requirement that is vulnerable.

To illustrate how these concepts work together, consider the following actual incident. In protest of a hotly contested political reform a militant group had been demonstrating regularly at a federal courthouse but had not been getting much attention because the counter-demonstrators usually outnumbered them. After weeks of frustration a radical element within the group decided to incite a riot with either the counter-demonstrators or the law enforcement officers who routinely policed the protests. The plan was discovered by law enforcement, however, and a tactical response was developed to prevent the riot.

During the situation assessment it was noted that the area where the confrontation was expected to take place was a large, treeless lawn surrounded by paved parking lots, streets and sidewalks. Consequently, any weapons to be used or missiles to be thrown would have to be brought to the site and dispersed amongst the provocateurs.

To better grasp how these concepts apply to this scenario think of ends, ways and means. The goal (end state)[51] for the radical element was to create a violent confrontation that would attract the necessary attention to emphasize their fierce opposition, especially from the ever present news media. The ways to accomplish it (critical capabilities) were to attack either the counter-demonstrators and/or the police. The means to attack (critical requirements) would be with clubs, or more likely, some type of thrown object. Because neither the weapons nor the missiles could be picked up at the scene they would have to be transported and dispersed among the agitators prior to their assault. Consequently, if the weapons could be seized before distribution the entire plan would collapse. Because there would be large numbers of law-abiding protestors who would be present but not rioting there would be no way to distinguish those with evil intent from those simply intending to protest. Thus, this critical requirement was also a critical vulnerability. Undercover police officers soon confiscated buckets of golf balls, wheel weights and old spark plugs that were intended to be thrown and arrested those responsible. The riot never materialized.

As can be seen, these four concepts identify the critical nodes involved in defeating an adversary and allow commanders to craft plans focused precisely on them. Early identification of centers of gravity and critical vulnerabilities provide direction and substance for sound tactical planning. They can easily become the cornerstones in developing and implementing effective intervention strategies. The success of many tactical operations have hinged on far less.

TRENDS, POTENTIALS, CAPABILITIES AND INTENTIONS

When scrutinizing an agglomeration of data, four factors provide insight for assessing the impact. These are trends, potentials, capabilities and intentions.

Trends are a combination of measurement and prediction used to identify a general tendency, inclination, predisposition or frequency. Trends are discerned by identifying and measuring events and provide value for both measurement and prediction. An **event** is a single, discrete one-time occurrence that has an impact on a given issue. When two or more events can be identified as being related to an issue, a prediction can be made as to another. The more events and the greater precision with which they can be measured, the more accurate and reliable becomes the prediction. When time permits, as in strategic and operational intelligence, this might be done statistically and presented with graphs. Because of the harsh time constraints inherent in tactical operations, however, trends for tactical intelligence are more often based on appraisals and estimates. In this case, events may be specifically related to the issue at hand or drawn from similar situations which have occurred in the past.

Potentials describe the ability or capacity of something. Because the second, and most important, part of a trend is a prediction, they are always an approximation. Potentials set limits on the possibilities. These are often defined using a best-case scenario, worst-case scenario and most-likely scenario described previously. Since potentials delineate possibilities, they are used to assess the impact of trends. Thus, trends and potentials are inseparable and interrelated.

Capabilities describe the ability of a specific opposing agent to successfully accomplish an action. When the agent is an adversary, capabilities provide a measure of ability in terms of logistical support or operational sophistication. When the agent is a natural or mechanical disaster, capabilities provide a calculation of the degree of impact on a region, function or organization. It is important to understand that capabilities identify not only what an agent can do, but what it cannot do, because both are essential for planning and conduct of operations. In many respects, capabilities are related to trends, however, where trends are used to identify a pattern or class of antagonist, capabilities are specifically applied to a discrete, identifiable opposing force.

Intentions refer to the actual or potential activities of an opposing force. Intentions answer the question, "What is likely to happen?" When applied to an adversary, they generally identify their aims and likely courses of action and when applied to natural or technological disasters, intentions identify probable behaviors and consequences. For example, disasters such as fires and hurricanes have typical behaviors, while earthquakes and hail storms have predictable consequences. Once an opposing force can be identified, capabilities provide the possibilities and intentions identify the probabilities. Consequently, capabilities and intentions are also inseparable and interrelated.

---

46. Antoine de Saint-Exupéry, *The Wisdom of the Sands*, trans. Stuart Gilbert (New York, NY: Harcourt, Brace and Company, 1948), 50.
47. It is reported that legendary bodybuilder, Arnold Schwarzenegger, in advising young bodybuilders hoping to emulate him illustrates this endstate idea when he asks them, "Why are you in the weight room? To lift weights or get strong?" Clearly he understands that the means can easily be (and often are) mistaken for the ends.
48. "Driven by events" is a term that describes a condition in which the organization is responding or reacting to events, rather than managing them.
49. It is important to understand that both the event horizon and scenario review techniques are conceptual tools to help understand the distribution of uncertainty in the future and not planning tools per se.
50. These definitions are taken from the excellent monographs by Dr. Joe Strange, Marine Corps War College, entitled Perspectives on Warfighting, Number Four, 2nd Ed, *Centers of Gravity & Critical Vulnerabilities* and Number Six, *Capital "W" War: A case for Strategic Principles of War*, Marine Corps University, Quantico, VA, 1996 and 1998, respectively. Likewise, one of the most clear and cogent explanations is Eikmeier, Col. Dale (USA (ret.), "Centers of Gravity," *Marine Corps Gazette*, November 2010, pp. 97-105
51. Adversarial situations, by definition, involve an opposing will. It goes without saying that the suspect will have a different and opposing end state.

STRATEGY AND TACTICS

Strategy without tactics is the slowest route to victory. Tactics without strategy is the noise before defeat.

—AUTHOR UNKNOWN[52]

STRATEGY, TACTICS AND TECHNIQUES

The most critical element of any plan is the scheme that it describes. To a greater or lesser extent, every plan attempts to maximize the likelihood for success by focusing effort, affixing responsibility, distributing authority and allocating resources. Depending on the scope of the plan, it may be broad and far reaching or tightly focused and detailed. Plans that are wide-ranging in application and/or far-reaching in the future are said to be "strategic." Conversely, those that are more narrowly focused on specific near-term objectives are "tactical." It has been said that "tactics win battles but strategies win wars." Accordingly, successful operations will require both.

The differentiation of strategy and tactics is a relatively recent understanding and is usually attributed to the Swiss-born[53] military theorist, Antoine-Henri Jomini who wrote during the Napoleonic era. Since that time the concepts have been refined and are now taught at every military academy in the world. Notwithstanding, much confusion remains, especially because the differences are largely in degree and not kind.

Strategy may be defined as the planning and development of large-scale and/or long-range operations to ensure a satisfactory end state. Strategies link the ends and means and provide a "game plan" that tells us how personnel will be employed and resources will be distributed to achieve objectives. By nature, strategies employ a broad perspective and look at the problem as a whole. They treat problems in a holistic manner rather than simply as a collection of the component parts. It goes without saying that a flawed strategy will have momentous consequences.

Similarly, **tactics** may be defined as the methods and concepts used to accomplish particular missions. Thus, they are in a supporting role to, and drivers of, strategy. In fact, it has been said that "tactics are the handmaiden of strategy." Even if successful, tactics without strategy will not progressively promote the accomplishment of the overall objectives. Conversely, strategy without tactics cannot adapt or adjust to circumstances and so becomes easily stymied by relatively minor obstacles.

While the differences between strategy and tactics may seem confusing, one tactics instructor explained it this way. After becoming lost in a desert a hiker climbs a small hill and discovers the tracks of a bicycle leading off into the distance toward a mountain pass. Having no better alternative the hiker realizes that the tracks provide the most promising route to safety and so studies them carefully and begins to follow them. As the hours pass he notices that the path is not really as straight at it first appeared but rather zigs and zags around rocks and bushes. In fact, the tracks from the front wheel are continually making minor corrections to avoid these, and many other obstacles that would otherwise stop the bicyclist. It is only when looking at the tracks from a distance that they look straight. The bicyclist is clearly focused on the mountain pass and makes corrections quickly after surmounting the many minor diversions. The point of the story is that the bicycle track leading to the mountain pass is the long-range direction that provides the essential focus. Without it, every small detour around the rocks and bushes could easily lead the bicyclist astray. On the other hand, without the ability to navigate around obstacles the bicyclist would be stopped by the first serious obstruction. So it is with strategy and tactics.

A third related concept is called a technique. A **technique** is simply a procedure or process for performing a specific task or function. Techniques almost always involve the employment or utilization of a weapon or piece of equipment. Using the same analogy of the hiker lost in the desert, techniques would be those procedures the bicyclist uses to stay on course, maintain balance and traverse obstacles. So it is in tactical operations which utilize techniques for everything from sighting a weapon while wearing a gas mask or speedily clearing a malfunction to pulling the pin on a diversionary device without losing grip on a weapon or building a field expedient litter. Techniques provide the specific "know how" for complex assignments and are the major component of hands-on expertise; consequently they provide the critical individual skills lacking in tactics.

In the law enforcement community an example of a strategy is the "default" surround and negotiate strategy used for hostage situations. Common examples of the supporting tactics include establishing a containment, conducting a crisis or stealth entry, using a coordinated sniper initiated assault, and so forth. Techniques would include everything from how weapons and equipment are carried to how they are used.

While strategy and tactics tend to be more closely associated with operations that involve adversaries,[54] they are also critical for other types of operations. Consider a large brush or forest fire that threatens homes. A strategy is needed for whether to encourage early evacuation, last minute evacuation, or shelter in place. Tactics are needed for conducting evacuations, protecting life and property and avoiding interfering with the firefighters' actions. Techniques are needed to alert the homeowners, avoid traffic congestion, and so forth.

Much of the confusion about strategy, tactics and techniques occurs because there is no sharp line between them. They are more similar to each other than they are different with the only clear distinction being their particular focus. Notwithstanding, each play a critical role in providing the essential capabilities for successful tactical operations.

SYMMETRIC AND ASYMMETRIC STRATEGIES

Generally, strategy can be divided into two types. The one that people are most familiar with is a **symmetric strategy** in which one force attempts to match—or rather, to overmatch—an adversary's strengths. In other words; beating him on his own terms. A good example is defeating the fortifications on a "rock house." Dope dealers place bars over the windows and tactical teams pull them off. If the dope dealers get stronger bars, tactical teams get bigger ropes and trucks.

Symmetrical strategies have been successful in law enforcement largely because we can nearly always wield greater force, both in amount and duration. Nevertheless, symmetrical strategies are encumbered by two shortcomings. First, lacking overwhelming strength, symmetrical strategies can easily lead to "wars of attrition."[55] Poignant newsworthy examples include the 51 day "siege" of the Branch Davidian compound in Waco, Texas, the 81 day wait to arrest a militant group in Jordan, Montana and the 38 day standoff in Illinois to arrest a single 51 year-old female suspected of being mentally unstable. Second, without overwhelming strength, symmetrical strategies leave little or no room for error. This is especially true in attempting to arrest armed criminals. Taking guns away from criminals at gunpoint is a "pass/fail" exercise. Success and survival become synonymous. Adherents to symmetrical strategies are understandably zealous in demanding increased firepower for law enforcement officers in order to exceed that of criminals.

The other type of strategy is called an asymmetrical strategy. An **asymmetric strategy** is one that attempts to apply strength against weakness. More simply put, this is using some means to which an adversary cannot effectively respond in kind. This may mean using dissimilar techniques, technologies or other capabilities to maximize our strength while exploiting weaknesses in an adversary. Take for example a wealthy drug dealer who has equipped his house with the latest anti-intrusion appliances such as video cameras, seismic intrusion devices, infrared and ultrasound alarms, and so forth. Serving a warrant on such a location is a most formidable undertaking and defeating or avoiding all these alarms and cameras is nearly impossible. An asymmetric strategy might be to use the alarms against the suspect by intentionally and simultaneously setting them all off at once to overwhelm his ability to effectively respond. He might even attribute such a catastrophic failure of his elaborate alarm system to a malfunction and ignore the danger completely.

Another way of fighting asymmetrically is by using surprise. One of the "nine principles of war," surprise is achieved by striking an adversary at an unexpected time or place, or in any unanticipated manner. Since all humans are handicapped by an inability to instantly process and react to a new stimulus, surprise deprives a suspect of his ability to effectively react. Using the previous example, a tactical team encountering an elaborate alarm system might ignore the alarms altogether and serve the warrant at a time when the suspect is sluggish from sleep, in a swimming pool, away from his house or simply by moving to their objective so fast that he is incapable of mounting an effective response.

Asymmetrical strategies provide an additional advantage of offsetting technological or firepower advantages. One of the most cost-effective examples is terrorism because a terrorist attack can be as accurate and effective as any multi-million dollar laser-guided bomb or missile, but infinitely cheaper. As a matter of fact, even a credible threat can achieve everything[56] but the actual destruction.

More common manifestations of asymmetrical strategies employed against law enforcement agencies can take the form of "sit down strikes" or blockades of streets, sidewalks and buildings. The nonviolent nature of these activities precludes virtually every type of force lest an agency be accused of overreacting. An asymmetrical counter might be to simply reroute traffic and close the buildings and contain the protestors where they sit, because the attention they seek is largely gained through their ability to disrupt. The key factor in all asymmetric approaches is that they focus on a weakness. Thus, ingenuity, adaptability and innovation play especially critical roles in developing and employing asymmetric strategies.

In reality, effective plans usually attempt to combine the best of both symmetric and asymmetric approaches. Thus, whether a strategy is considered to be symmetric or asymmetric is almost always one of degree rather than kind. A proficient strategist should not be biased in favor of one or the other. The most effective strategy for any situation must be adapted to those unique circumstances present at the time. Frederick the Great once said, "War is not an affair of chance. A great deal of knowledge, study and meditation is necessary to conduct it well."[57] The same holds true for all tactical operations because the objective is to win—not to fight.

BOND RELATIONSHIP TARGETING

One of the most difficult aspects in implementing an asymmetric strategy is identifying a weakness that can be exploited. A prepared adversary presents few weaknesses and a cunning one guards even those. One of the most overlooked weaknesses is the relationship bonds that link people or organizations together. Like all tactics, bond relationship targeting is equally useful to both sides of a conflict, but is particularly vulnerable within the criminal element because of the self-serving nature that makes those people untrustworthy to begin with.

In its most simple terms, **bond relationship targeting** may be defined as focusing an attack on the association, connection or cohesion that binds two or more people or organizations. This is often a particularly desirable target because once the relationship is broken; other vulnerabilities are ripe for exploitation. When attacking a bond relationship, trust is especially susceptible to gaining an advantage and depending on the circumstances, can be exploited by increasing or decreasing the amount of trust that binds the relationship.

To better understand how this tactic works let's use an example. Suppose that you are involved in defeating a violent, international drug cartel and you've just arrested one of the couriers with 100 kilos of cocaine. The amount of drugs and conditions of arrest will most assuredly result in an extremely long prison sentence but intelligence indicates that this individual possesses information that would bring the ultimate downfall of the entire organization. Consequently the U.S. Attorney offers a deal to the arrestee for the information. If the courier cooperates, he will be set completely free. If not, he will receive a lengthy prison sentence that will keep him incarcerated for many years. No one is surprised, however, when the courier rejects the deal out of hand. His decision is understandable given that the worst that is going to happen at the hands of the authorities is a long prison term. If he betrays the drug cartel, however, he can expect death. The bond to the cartel is stronger than the incentive to defect.

This scenario is manifested in real-life in any number of ways, but let's add one permutation. When the news of the arrest is released, only 50 kilos of cocaine is reported to have been seized. Still a sizeable amount, and one that will guarantee the same prison term, but what must the cartel think about the other missing 50 kilos? The relationship bond between the courier and the cartel is now strained, if not shattered completely, and since it will be nearly impossible for the courier to adequately explain away the missing drugs, he can realistically envision both the long prison term and death upon his release! Thus, the bond has been targeted and the likelihood of cooperation is increased.

While bond relationship targeting is most often used to weaken the relationship bonds between two or more individuals or organizations, it may also be advantageous to strengthen them. The most common situation where this method may be useful in domestic law enforcement is when hostages are involved. The well-documented **Stockholm Syndrome** is an emotional attachment between hostages and hostage-takers that develops when a hostage is threatened with death and unable to escape. In coping with the experience, a hostage often comes to see the situation from the perspective of the criminal and loses touch with their original perspective, which now seems unimportant or even counter-productive to their survival. But an important aspect of this relationship is that it is bidirectional. That is, the hostage-taker frequently forms a similar, albeit less intense, bond with the hostage, thus making it harder to harm them. With this understanding comes the logical conclusion that strengthening the relationship bonds between the hostage-takers and the hostages works to the advantage of the eventual safe release of the hostages.

Besides the tactical opportunities provided by bond relationship targeting, it also has strategic implications. This is particularly so when dealing with terrorists because terrorism, is by nature, an asymmetrical strategy. It relies on weaknesses that can be exploited and avoids open confrontation with stronger forces. Terrorists cannot win pitched battles. Accordingly, bond relationships are not only appealing; they usually offer the only possible chance for success at a strategic level.

The bond relationship that terrorists most often target is that between the people and their government. Since the most fundamental responsibility of any government is the protection of its people, a government that appears ineffectual or inadequate in this regard loses both their respect and their support. Thus, even though terrorists are relatively weak when compared to the government they attack, they are able to exert an inordinate amount of pressure with a smaller force. It is for this reason that seemingly insignificant physical targets, such as the safety of passengers on mass transportation or the inconvenience of losing electrical power, are especially attractive to terrorists since they are often weakly defended, if at all. Such acts drive an emotional wedge between a government responsible for providing these services and the people who rightly expect to be protected.

Clearly, the importance of bond relationships cannot be discounted. While the short durations of most domestic law enforcement tactical interventions make it difficult to attack bond relationships, tacticians and strategists should miss no opportunity to weaken an adversary or exploit a set of fortuitous circumstances. By taking a holistic approach to the problem, bond relationship targeting provides targets that are difficult to defend and often taken for granted. Only the most naïve tactician will downplay the significance of relations as a force multiplier. For this reason a unit with high esprit de corps is far more formidable. As Napoleon once said, “In war, moral power is to physical as three parts out of four.”[58]

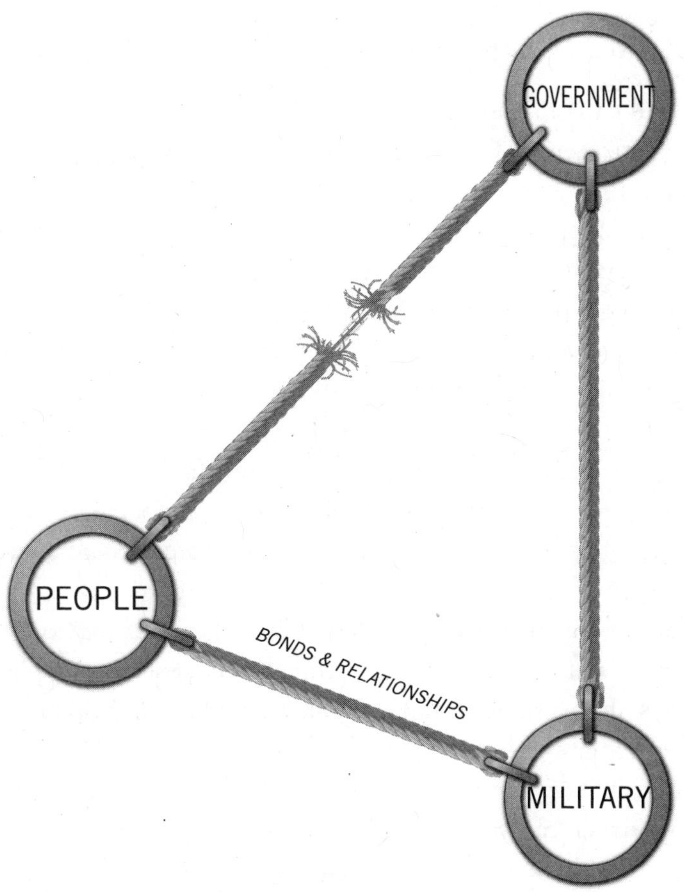

FIGURE 6-1 BOND RELATIONSHIP TARGETING: Relationships are inherent in every human enterprise. Depending on the nature of the interaction, bonds may take the form of familial, trust, love, fiscal, respect, or even fear. Some are so common as to be legally formalized with written contracts, such as business partnerships, mortgages, retainers, marriage and adoption. Regardless of what form they take, bond relationship targeting provides a means of defeating an adversary by indirect attack. For example, drug users need dealers who in turn need suppliers who in turn use smugglers who in turn need growers and/or manufacturers. Severing any of the essential bonds can be even easier and more devastating to the enterprise than attacking the nodes.

The illustration above is sometimes referred to as the "Trinity of War," "Clausewitzian Trinity," or the "Social Trinity" and represents the three most critical relationships thought necessary for a viable nation. Strategists point out that the U.S. military had never lost a major battle in Vietnam and that the end of the involvement in the Vietnam War was a result of the degradation of the bonds connecting the people and their military. Likewise, terrorists are also unable to defeat the military and so attack the bonds that connect a people with their government by forcing dilemmas between individual rights and intrusive protective measures.

DEPLOYMENT STRATEGIES

Nearly all calls for service in domestic safety services involve some type of emergency. Consequently, the responses require the individuals and organizational units to stop what they were doing and handle the emergency. In most instances, the response strategy used is called a ramp-up strategy. A **ramp-up strategy** is one in which the size and type of units needed to adequately handle a situation are estimated and dispatched. Upon arrival, the handling unit or on-scene commander is free to call for more assistance if needed. Since only the units necessary to handle a situation are actually engaged, the ramp-up strategy is the default for nearly all emergencies because it is the most cost effective. It becomes problematic; however, when a rapidly evolving situation threatens to exceed the intervention efforts before reinforcements could arrive.

When a threat is recognized that has the potential to be catastrophic if not immediately controlled the preferred deployment method is often a surge strategy. A **surge strategy** is one that intentionally overestimates the immediate need and attempts to quickly provide a decisive intervention to avoid potentially devastating consequences. While guidance can be provided by policy, the choice to use a surge strategy is ultimately the responsibility of the senior commander involved. This is because while surge strategies are very effective they also tend to be very costly. Overuse not only results in depletion of funds but excessive wear on equipment and fatigue of personnel.

When comparing the two strategies the distinguishing feature is the response. While a ramp-up strategy attempts to provide just enough personnel and resources to adequately handle a situation with reinforcements available as needed, a surge strategy attempts to provide overwhelming resources to quickly achieve decisive results with excessive personnel and equipment relieved when they are deemed unnecessary. In the fire services, a surge strategy might be chosen to handle a small brush fire when weather conditions, fire load, or proximity of structures present extraordinary threats if allowed to get out of control. A similar example in the law enforcement community might require a surge when a drunken fight breaks out after a championship game or during a protest. The ability to

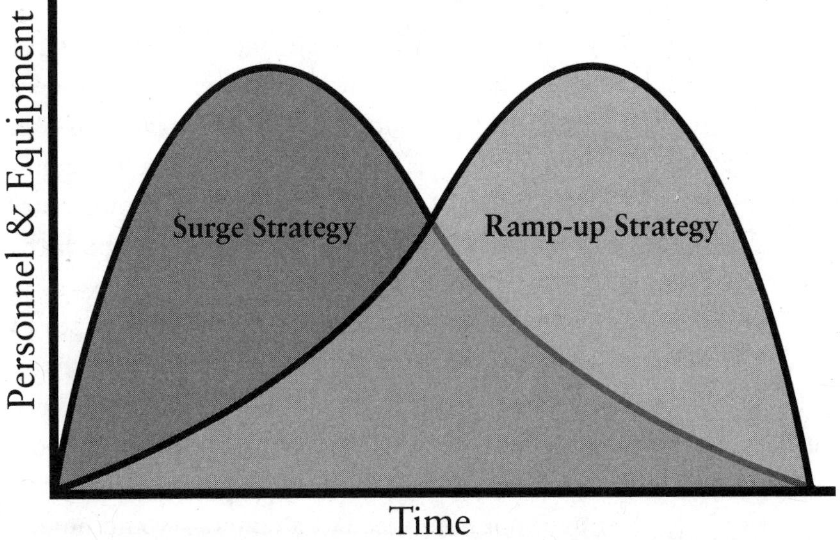

FIGURE 6-2 DEPLOYMENT STRATEGIES: Ramp-up strategies are the default mode for both the fire services and law enforcement because they are more efficient. An assessment of what and how much is needed is estimated by a dispatcher and then verified or amended by supervisors at the scene. They gradually build to a point where the situation can be resolved with the minimum amount of personnel and resources. Conversely, surge strategies are not as efficient but more effective because they attempt to overwhelm a situation with personnel and resources which are then returned to routine duties as the situation warrants. Surge strategies are normally reserved for those situations deemed too critical to allow to escalate.

quickly employ overwhelming force is often enough to avoid an escalation of the disturbance into a full-fledged riot.

THE TACTICAL TRIO

All tactical maneuvers unfold in both space and time. The tactical objective in space is to gain and maintain control of key terrain while the tactical objective in time is to create and exploit opportunities. Likewise, all successful tactical maneuvers have two fundamental underpinnings; flexibility in thought and mind and mobility to create and exploit opportunities. A rigid application of either principles or tactics is a recipe for disaster and even the most insightful tactician is rendered powerless without the mobility to follow through. A shrewd commander is thoroughly familiar with the underlying concepts of the various tactics as well as the situational awareness of the present situation to enable confident decisions for the best course of action. As one general noted, "In tactics, the most important thing is not whether you go left or right, but why you go left or right."[59] Accordingly, even a rudimentary understanding of how tactics work provides insight into both the selection and adaptation of tactics to specific situations.

Typically, law enforcement responds to one of three types of situations; natural disasters, such as floods and storms; mechanical disasters, such as car accidents and train wrecks; and conflicts, such as barricaded suspects and riots. Of the three, conflicts are the most complex because they involve an adversary who is in active opposition. Each situation is comprised of a temporary and unique set of circumstances that require somewhat unique tactics but when the situation is a conflict three time-tested tactics are predominant. These are the "hammer and anvil," the "envelopment" and the "pincer." When properly applied these tactics work by overwhelming a suspect's ability to effectively resist.

The **hammer and anvil** is one of the oldest tactical maneuvers and was used effectively by Philip of Macedon and his son, Alexander the Great, during the Peloponnesian Wars more than 2,400 years ago. The hammer and anvil tactic works by using two forces, one stationary and one mobile. The stationary force "fixes" the adversary and prevents escape while the mobile force moves toward it with the adversary caught between. This creates a dilemma since the adversary can't flee because of the stationary force (anvil) and can't stay because of the moving force (hammer).

In law enforcement operations the hammer and anvil is commonly used against barricaded suspects where a containment team functions as the anvil and an entry team functions as the hammer. The more astute will quickly recognize the importance of terrain on this maneuver since a barrier[60] can be used in place of the anvil. The hammer and anvil tactic is simple to implement, but because overwhelming force is the primary factor it has a disadvantage in that it usually requires substantial personnel and/or firepower to ensure success. Because these are normally not limitations for domestic law enforcement, hammer and anvil operations are both popular and common.

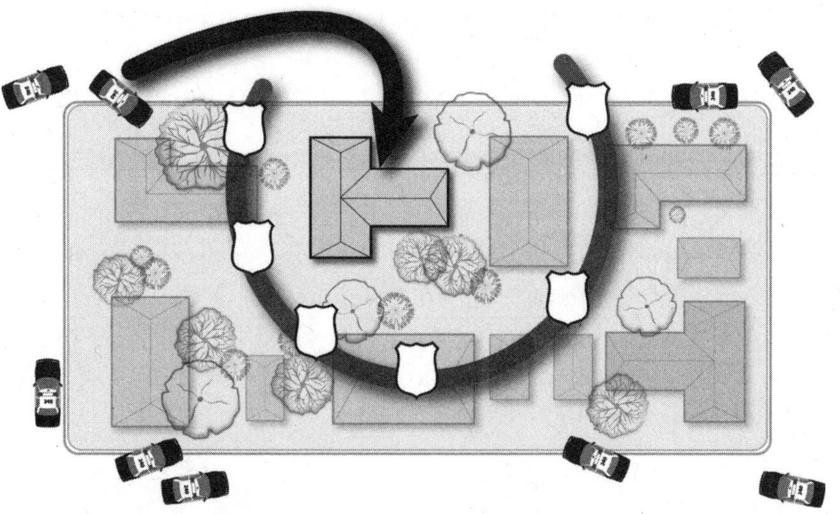

FIGURE 6-3 HAMMER AND ANVIL: While there is no way of saying for sure, the hammer and anvil tactic was almost certainly derived from the hunts of early man. Using terrain features, like cliffs, swamps, rivers and lakes, as an anvil, a group of hunters could kill even gigantic animals. As tactics and weapons improved, the terrain used for the anvil was augmented and even replaced by other hunters.

The hammer and anvil tactic works by using a stationary element to fix an adversary in place and prevent escape while a mobile element maneuvers to force the adversary from hiding or a protected position. This creates a dilemma since the adversary can't flee because of the stationary element and can't stay because of the moving element. As depicted in the graphic, this tactic is commonly used in law enforcement applications for a barricaded suspect. The containment serves as the "anvil" (depicted by the white badges) while the entry team works as the "hammer."

The second tactic is an **envelopment**. Like the hammer and anvil, it has been around for at least two millennia and was used successfully as far back as the Battle of Cannae in 216 B.C. when Hannibal used it to nearly destroy the Roman Army. Unlike hammer and anvil tactics, envelopments do not rely on overwhelming force but rather seek to apply strength against weakness. It works by attempting to fix an adversary's attention on one area while the main force exploits a weakness in another. It avoids the "front," which is usually more heavily guarded, and strikes from one of the flanks. Thus, envelopments are more easily understood as flanking maneuvers. Law enforcement frequently uses this method when serving search and arrest warrants and resistance is expected. One of the most common adaptations is to give a "knock and notice" at the main entrance and when a suspect refuses to comply the entry team (main force) forces entry at a rear door or window while the suspect's attention is focused on the front. Another common method is to use a diversionary device to distract a suspect's attention while an entry team exploits the temporary confusion by flanking the suspect from a different direction. The advantage of an envelopment is that it requires fewer personnel than the hammer and anvil but because of the high degree of necessary coordination it requires more extensive and detailed planning.

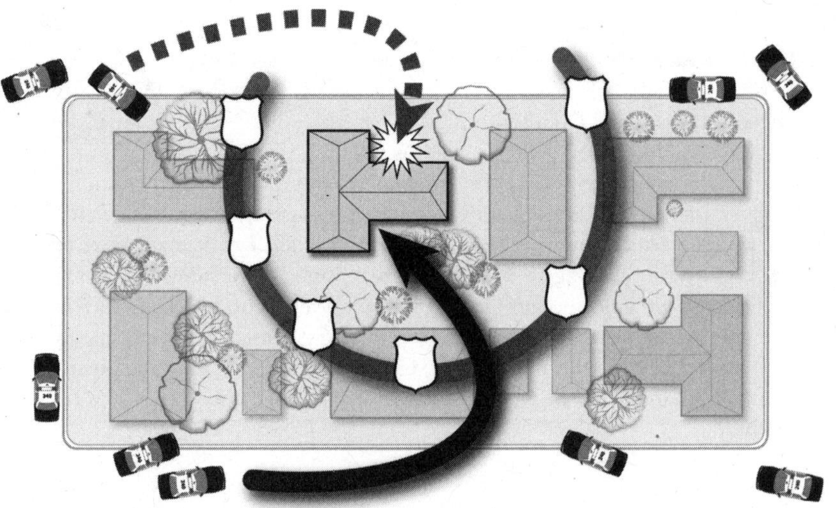

FIGURE 6-4 ENVELOPMENT: An envelopment is a tactic that works by creating and/or exploiting a weakness. Because it avoids areas where adversaries are prepared and waiting it is often referred to as a "flanking attack." As depicted in the graphic above, envelopments are commonly used in law enforcement applications to serve search and arrest warrants when suspects will not comply with a "knock and notice." One element seeks to draw a suspect's attention while another attacks from an unanticipated direction.

The third tactic is called a **pincer**. Fundamentally, a pincer movement is a variation of an envelopment but instead of a single maneuver element it has two.[61] It works by employing two moving forces closing toward each other with the adversary caught between them; hence it is sometimes referred to as a "double envelopment." Like the other two tactics, pincers have been used since antiquity and are described in Sun Tzu's *The Art of War* dating back to 500 B.C. Law enforcement frequently uses this tactic during foot pursuits when the rapid and unpredictable movements of a suspect make establishing a blocking force impractical, and so diminishes the value of using a hammer and anvil or envelopment. The advantage of a pincer movement is that it is quick to set up and so provides an effective response but pincers have several disadvantages. First, they are difficult to coordinate because keeping track of everyone is nearly impossible. Second, broken terrain makes it difficult to ensure that all avenues of escape are covered because there is no containment. Third, shifting gun-target lines create potential friendly fire problems.

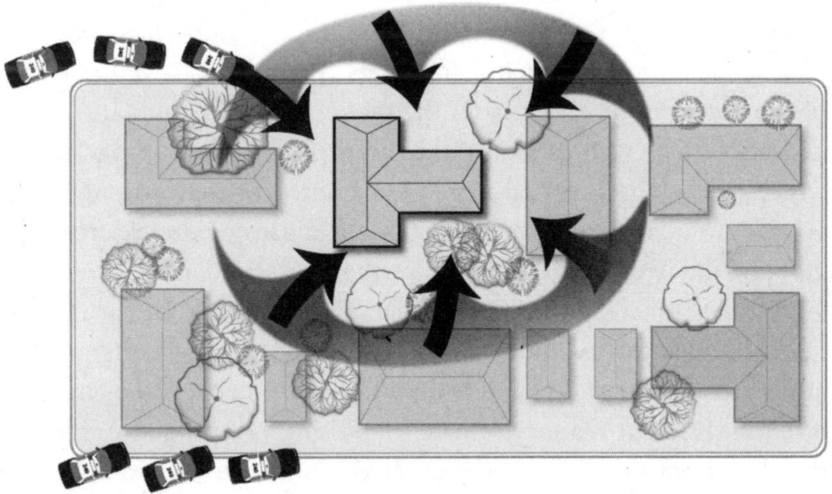

FIGURE 6-5 PINCER: A pincer tactic is fundamentally a variation of an envelopment but instead of a single maneuver element it has two. It takes its name by the way it works when the maneuver elements move toward one another with the adversary caught in between. Because of the two maneuver elements it is sometimes referred to as a "double envelopment." Pincers are both more complex than either the hammer and anvil or the envelopment tactics and more dangerous because of the shifting gun target lines. Nevertheless, they are an effective tactic and are commonly used in law enforcement applications for capturing fleeing suspects during foot pursuits (as depicted above).

SWARMING TACTICS

Some types of conflicts are exceptionally difficult and dangerous; none more so than an active shooter situation. History has shown that the vast majority of casualties resulting from these types of incidents occur within the first few minutes of the incident. Moreover, most of these shooters have no intention of surviving the confrontation; they will die, either by committing suicide or being killed by police. The suddenness and extreme violence of such attacks, coupled with the deadly nature of the suspect(s), requires a response tightly focused on quickly preventing further injuries to potential victims.

Because urgency is the critical factor in these situations, conventional tactics that involve containments, negotiations, and massed assaults are far too sluggish to prevent further casualties. One tactic that provides such a rapid response is called "swarming." Simply put, a **swarming tactic** is one in which the scheme of maneuver involves multiple semi-autonomous units that converge on a single target from many directions. The name, as well as many of the concepts, is taken from the tactics of insects like ants, bees and hornets as well as from other animals that hunt in packs like wolves and sharks. An adversary confronted by a swarming tactic is put in a quandary in that a defense against one attack creates a vulnerability from another and is further frustrated as more maneuver elements[62] create multiple threats. Ignoring any threat creates opportunities for exploitation. In prolonged engagements attacks at different times and places from different maneuver elements and often in different manners create a "pulsing" effect that continues the deterioration. Effective countermeasures are exceedingly difficult in that it is nearly impossible to determine from where, how and when the next attack will come.

Generally, swarming tactics take one of two forms. The first is called a "**massed swarm.**"[63] This type of attack forms after the maneuver elements have massed at a staging area or from another formation and then disperse to attack simultaneously from multiple directions. The second is a "**dispersed swarm**"[64] which involves maneuver elements that are already dispersed and converge on a

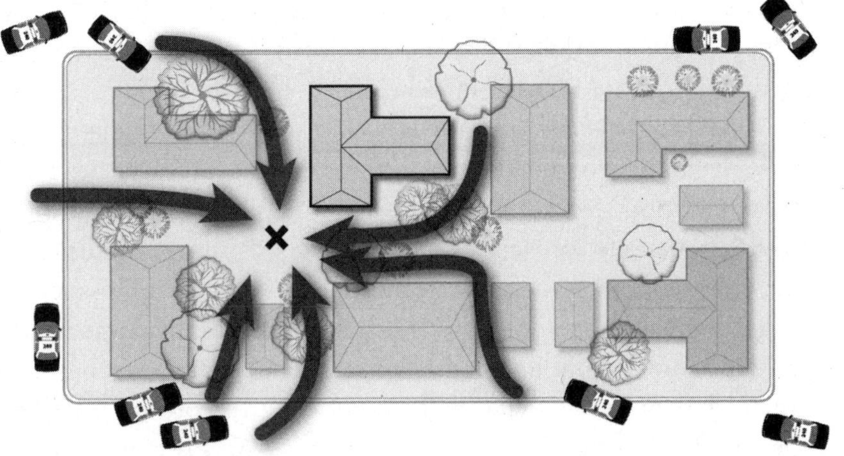

FIGURE 6-6 SWARMING: Like other tactics, the originations of the swarming tactic were taken from watching the animal kingdom. Insects, like bees and hornets, and animals, like wolves and sharks, defeated much larger and stronger animals by converging from many directions. Attempts to thwart an attack from one direction creates vulnerabilities from others. Swarming tactics have long been used by law enforcement in handling "officer needs help" calls and are a favored tactic in dealing with active shooters. As depicted above, a swarming tactic is characterized by numerous maneuver elements all converging on a location or suspect from many directions. In law enforcement applications they enjoy an advantage over other tactics by the rapidity with which they can bring overwhelming force to a situation. Notwithstanding, they are among the most complex and dangerous of all law enforcement tactics because of the difficulties in coordination and increased chances of fratricide.

target from many directions. Of the two, the second is most appealing for law enforcement applications since patrol units are typically already dispersed throughout an area and collecting them into a staging area before dispersing them is almost always counterproductive.

Because of the difficulties in controlling the larger number of maneuver elements involved in swarming operations coupled with the rapidity of their movement and necessity for immediate action, collaboration is more critical than command and control. Thus, each of the maneuver elements must be vested with decision making authority traditionally reserved for a higher headquarters. This renders them semi-autonomous and enables them to seek, create and exploit opportunities based upon their individual situational awareness. Understandably, the objective must be clearly understood lest divergent perspectives create confusion. The necessity for high-levels of training, discipline, maturity, communication and coordination should be self-evident.

Critical to the success of any law enforcement swarming operation is the ability to quickly respond and engage an adversary with little or no input from higher authority. Initial reports are always somewhat sketchy and confusing. Even good information grows stale very quickly and so the situational awareness necessary to make effective tactical decisions is largely gained at the crime scene. In order to create cohesion and facilitate collaboration amongst the maneuver elements it is vital that situational awareness is shared in order to create a common operational picture. Accordingly, reliable and efficient communications are a critical requirement for any successful swarming operation.

Like any other tactic, swarming is not without its drawbacks, not the least of which are the formidable challenges to conventional—even cherished—methods for command and control. The absolute necessity to relinquish control normally reserved for higher headquarters to the maneuver units is nearly incomprehensible to some of the more staid. Nevertheless, without the authority to make decisions based upon the local conditions and unfolding situation the entire effort becomes mired in antiquated protocols and loses momentum. Nearly as daunting is the need for close coordination among the maneuver elements to maximize the swarming effects without friendly casualties. This requires constant communication, usually by radio, which in turn requires strict radio discipline to avoid squelching other communicators.

While swarming tactics represent a significant departure from conventional tactics for military operations, they are simply an extension of "business as usual" for the law enforcement community. In fact, swarming tactics have been the preferred method when responding to "officer needs help" calls long before they were considered for active shooter situations. Regardless of the specific circumstances for which a swarming tactic is used as a remedy, the primary objectives are to find, fix and defeat the adversary.

Because of the relatively large number of maneuver elements that comprise a swarming tactic, finding an adversary is greatly facilitated when compared with more conventional approaches since a larger number of maneuver elements can cover a larger area faster. This nearly always occurs in at least two phases. The first is "movement to objective" in which the notification serves as an execute order and the command and control remains unchanged. The second is the "actions on the objective" in which case the maneuver elements are authorized more control as they move with relative autonomy and coordinate with each other to locate and

TACTIC	MAJOR ADVANTAGES	MAJOR DIS-ADVANTAGES	PRIMARY FACTOR	COMMONLY USED FOR:
Hammer & Anvil	• Simple to employ	• Abundance of personnel and equipment	• Overwhelming force	• Barricaded suspects
Envelopment	• Economy of force	• Higher degree of planning and coordination	• Exploits a weakness	• Warrant services
Pincer	• Quick response	• Coordination difficulties • Difficult containments • Potential friendly fire	• Exploits a weakness	• Foot pursuits
Swarm	• Speed of execution • Does not rely on containment	• Command & control challenges • Requires highly robust communications • Potential friendly fire	• Contemporaneous collaboration	• Officer needs help • Active shooters

FIGURE 6-7 TACTICS COMPARED: While there is no "size small, fits all" tactic suitable for every encounter, these four are the most commonly used in law enforcement situations. Each has its own advantages and disadvantages and is adaptable to circumstances. A tactician who understands how they work and why gains a considerable advantage over one who does not.

fix the suspect(s) before attempts are made to "defeat in place."[65] Once a suspect is located and fixed conventional methods can be effectively employed to neutralize the threat.

In spite of the difficulties in employing such complex tactics, swarming provides advantages that cannot be achieved by other means, especially speed of execution. Since the immediate objective in responding to an active shooter is to prevent further casualties, any interference or disruption of the suspect's plans works in the favor of innocent victims and the authorities alike. The value of preparation and training cannot be overestimated.

---

52. This quote is most commonly attributed to Sun Tzu, the author of *The Art of War*, circa 500 B.C. and while it is certainly compatible with his published writings it does not appear in any known translation and the authenticity remains doubtful.
53. While Jomini was born in Switzerland, it was as a French officer under Napoleon and later as an officer with the Russian army that he gained his greatest fame.
54. More simply known as "conflicts."
55. Rather than some decisive action, a "war of attrition" is one which is resolved through the gradual diminution of forces and/or resistance by constant stress, exhaustion or casualties.
56. Because terrorism seeks an audience, the evacuations, lengthy searches for bombs, chemicals, etc. coupled with the disruption to businesses, merchants and the general public can gain nearly as much attention without actually employing a device of any kind.
57. Frederick the Great, *Instructions to His Generals*, 1747
58. Although unverified, this quote is attributed to Napoleon Bonaparte (1769-1821), and is sometimes stated as "the moral is to the physical as three is to one." It was first noted by Maturin M. Ballou, *Treasury of Thought*, p. 407 (1899). Regardless of the precise verbiage, it would certainly not be out of character as Napoleon has been quoted in other references that corroborate his strong belief in the importance of morale. In another quote he states, "A man does not have himself killed for a half-pence a day or for a petty distinction. You must speak to the soul in order to electrify him."
59. General A.M. Gray, 29th Commandant of the U.S. Marine Corps
60. A barrier is any terrain feature that prevents movement across or through it. Typical terrain features that can be used as barriers are riv-

ers, lakes and even some large walls or fences. For more information on terrain see, Chapter 15—Terrain.

61. While there is nothing to prevent more than two maneuver elements they are exceptionally rare because of the increased complexity and need for coordination.
62. A maneuver element is a simply a component of a tactical formation capable of changing position in order to gain a position of advantage. For simplicity and clarity, the term is used throughout this chapter as a generic substitute for all typical law enforcement maneuver elements, such as radio cars, patrol cars, squads, platoons, or mobile field forces.
63. Also called a "cloud swarm" in that even though the "swarm" is loosely collected it arrives and remains comparatively together.
64. Also called a "vapor swarm" in that the formation never coalesces into a definable group.
65. While the terms, "movement to objective," "actions on the objective" and "defeat in place" are sometimes novel to law enforcement officers they are well-known to the military community and are used here for clarity and accuracy.

SECTION 3

SECTION 3

COMMAND STAFF

No commander can know everything. He must rely on deputies, competent in the narrow areas assigned to them.[66]

—LT. GEN. ALEKSANDER LEBED

CONTEMPORARY TACTICAL OPERATIONS AND DISASTER responses are some of the most complex undertakings imaginable. It is not possible for a single individual to exert the requisite amount of control over such a multi-faceted operation. This is not a new phenomenon and has been recognized since the late 1700's during the land wars in Europe. At about that time it became apparent that it was not humanly possible to oversee so many units scattered over so large of an area. Napoleon is usually credited with developing the first modern staff function as a permanent part of an army when he established his *Corps d'état Major* (staff corps) in 1795. His chief of staff, Louis Alexandre Berthier, was known for his quick comprehension and complete mastery of detail. Although not a particularly strong field commander, Berthier was a seasoned veteran and fought in the American Revolution with the Generals Rochambeau and Lafayette before returning to France with the rank of Colonel. Berthier is credited for supervising the details necessary for Napoleon's campaigns and was considered Napoleon's most valuable assistant. The so-called "Napoleonic Staff" has evolved into three major functions; operations, logistics and intelligence. The more astute will quickly recognize the presence of all three of these functions in the modern Incident Command System and the National Incident Management System.

This section is focused on the major supporting roles necessary to handle the largest and most complicated tactical organizations. It begins with the role of command and explains the differences between command and control as well as some of the ways that this function provides the direction for ensuring a unity of effort. Of particular importance are the command relationships that are formed when more than one agency and discipline find themselves working together.

The second chapter explains the role of the operations function in managing the activities of all the maneuver elements in fulfilling the overall guidance from command. It explains how to incorporate reinforcements and the types of orders used to direct actions. Despite the best of intentions, friction is inherent in tactical operations and the chapter concludes with measures to reduce conflict without having to personally intercede in every dispute

The intelligence function is the focus of the next chapter and begins by explaining the difference between intelligence and information. It then explains the various types of information and how they can be organized before becoming more focused on the three ingredients that form intelligence to support planning and decision making. After explaining how the intelligence process works it continues by describing the logic supporting the strategies of how intelligence is gathered and disseminated. The chapter closes by explaining the characteristics necessary for good intelligence and a six-step format for submitting field intelligence reports.

The logistics function is the most scientific of all the staff functions but, arguably, one of the least understood. Logistics sets the limits of operational capabilities and the chapter addresses the logistical process from the onset. It proceeds from there with a brief description of each of the tasks associated with the logistical function. The subject is concluded by explaining some of the science behind logistical strategies.

The section concludes with a discussion on communications. Although not part of the original Napoleonic staff, or even part of the modern National Incident Management System, communications is a critical part of all military staffs and has been included here. After a brief explanation of the critical contribution of communications in controlling tactical organizations, the major requirements for effective communications are identified. The discussion is continued by describing the forms communications can take and the various types of communications systems.

---

66. Lieutenant-General Aleksander Ivanovich Lebed, quoted in *Time*, February 27, 1995. Lt. Gen. Lebed was a popular Russian soldier and politician who was known to be extremely blunt in voicing his opinions. Among other things, he was highly critical of the Russian Defense Minister, Pavel Grachev, and his poor handling of the Chechen War. He was known to back up his words and defended Boris Yeltsin's headquarters during an attempted coup in 1991. He served as Secretary of the Security Council and was the National Security Advisor to the President of Russia. This quote was taken from an interview with two *Time* reporters in Moscow in answer to a question on how he would react if he were criticized.

COMMAND

An army of deer led by a lion is more to be feared than an army of lions led by a deer.

—PHILIP OF MACEDON[67]

OF THE FOUR PREDOMINANT FUNCTIONS NECESSARY FOR managing disasters and handling tactical operations, none is more critical than the role of command. The primary duty of the command and control function is to identify and state the ultimate objectives to be accomplished as well as providing essential planning guidance to achieve the necessary cooperation and coordination among the other functions. All other functions are subordinate to this one. Command provides the essential focus to assure that all efforts are concentrated on completing essential tasks necessary for a satisfactory resolution

An implied responsibility for this component requires the monitoring of all activities within the tactical organization, especially concerning the other three functions of intelligence, operations and logistics. Ultimately, everything that happens, or should happen, is the responsibility of command, for while authority can be delegated, responsibility cannot!

ROLE OF COMMAND

The role of command, in and of itself, is not inextricably linked to rank or title. It is better understood as an assignment. Of all the decisions that are made during crisis situations, none has more impact on a successful resolution than the selection of the commander. For better or worse, it is the commander who will determine the direction and set the tone and tempo for the action which are to follow.

In law enforcement, commanders of tactical operations have not traditionally been selected for demonstrated skill or knowledge. Instead, they have been chosen because of either their rank or assignment. When considering rank, it has been generally accepted that a person with greater rank will be more able than one of lesser rank. Since experience is the deciding factor in this argument, it only has merit when comparing two people who have similar backgrounds. It fails when the experience of one individual has provided them with greater tactical skill or knowledge than the other. This becomes particularly bothersome when the person with the greater expertise is of lesser rank.

The argument for assignment also uses experience as the determining factor. In point of fact, experience must be distinguished from tenure. Experience implies a personal involvement or observation of some relevant topic. It is experiential knowledge; that is knowledge personally derived from achievement or conversely, adversity and misadventure. Knowledge gained by this method tends to be the most useful, since it is retained longer and is more easily adaptable to present circumstances. Tenure, on the other hand, simply refers to the length of time a person has held an assignment. A person may hold an assignment without gaining experience. The knowledge possessed by this person is derived knowledge. Derived knowledge is better than none, but not as useful as experiential knowledge. An old English proverb says it well when it advises, "Only the wearer knows where the shoe pinches." Thus, a strong argument can be made for seeking tactical commanders with experience.

Another attribute, which should be considered when selecting a commander, is simply whether that person is capable of performing the task at hand. Not everyone is suitable to be a commander. Although this statement may not be controversial in some circles, it strikes at the very soul of police officers. Some people have little or no aptitude to acquire the necessary skills to function in the dynamic, stressful and confusing environment that is inherent in every tactical operation. A commander who does not work well under stress, or is indecisive or disorganized, is more out of place than a claustrophobic coal miner. Regardless of their technical skills, it is not fair to the individual, and dangerous for subordinates, to force upon this person duties for which they are not suited.

Although this inability does not prohibit a person from advancing in the ranks of a law enforcement organization, it should preclude him or her from becoming a commander in a tactical operation. But in fact, as an individual rises in rank the chances of being called upon to handle the largest and most complex tactical and disaster operations increase as well. Just as absurd (but much less dangerous) is the common practice of choosing these people to examine and critique tactical failures. There is a bitter irony in listening to a person who has gained respect and acclaim as an administrator, but who has minimal experience, and little skill or knowledge, in the tactical arena, criticizing an operation for which they have only a modicum of understanding. Indeed, a flawless plan is as mythical as the unicorn, and like the unicorn, anyone can tell you what one looks like without ever actually having seen one.

COMMAND VS. CONTROL

One of the most confusing aspects of tactical operations has been one which deals with the concepts of command and control. Although each describes distinct aspects of directing human endeavor, they are closely related and often mistaken for one another. The military considers them inseparable and identifies their relationship with the abbreviation "C^2." However, each describes a different characteristic. Where **command** is the power one holds because of their position in an organization, **control** is the influence exerted by personal expertise, persuasion or charisma. Command involves *delegated authority*; that is authority that a person possesses by virtue of their position within an organization. Control however, involves *perceived authority*, which is authority bestowed upon a person by those they seek to direct.

The responsibilities and duties of a commander differ significantly from those of a manager, supervisor or director. Yet words like "commanding," "managing" and "leading" are often used interchangeably as if no difference existed. A "leader" attempts to guide or direct a person, often by persuasion or influence, to a course of action or thought. Similarly, a "manager" attempts to get a person to do his or her wishes by skill, tact, flattery, and so forth. "Command" however, implies the formal exercise of absolute authority, as by a sovereign or military leader. The functions of leading and managing are of considerably longer duration than commanding and tend to be more of a process than an event. Granted, there are common elements in all types of direction concerning human endeavor. However, none even approach the absolute power exerted by a commander. Further, they are seldom performed under the crisis conditions which require a commander. In fact, command has been defined as "the ruthless application of power." The critical need for obedience overrides concern for personal feelings.

Regardless of the knowledge and skills of even the most adept commander, no individual is capable of controlling every facet of even the smallest tactical operation. Secondary missions must necessarily be supervised by persons who work for the commander. Experts are frequently called upon to perform missions such as explosive ordnance disposal, mountain or urban rescues, canine searches and firefighting. A commander would dictate the missions for these units but should not attempt to control the personal efforts of the individuals involved. For example, a person may command the pilot of a helicopter, but he certainly wouldn't be in control of the aircraft. It is just as absurd to expect one person to control the actions of other specialized personnel as they attempt to disarm an explosive device, conduct a canine search or make an entry. In fact, it is not unusual for a person to be in command but not in control, and conversely, be in control and not in command. A litmus test for determining whether one has command or control is the ability to inflict punishment. If the person has the ability to compel action under penalty of punishment, they are in command. If penalties for disobedience are not present they may still be in control but they are definitely not in command.

PROVIDING DIRECTION

Like the supporting functions of logistics, intelligence and operations, the command and control element is responsible for a multitude of things but the most critical is defining and achieving a satisfactory end state. Accordingly, some method is necessary to ensure that subordinates comprehend what is required without over-supervising them and limiting their initiative. This is accomplished through a declaration called the "commander's intent." The **commander's intent** is simply a statement that describes the desired end state and how it is expected to be accomplished. While it is often written, it is just as likely to be verbal, especially in the early stages of a rapidly unfolding situation. Nevertheless, complex operations are those which most benefit from a written plan and in like manner, a written statement of commander's intent is even more important when a written plan is also required. It provides the focus for all subordinate elements. Even when changing circumstances result in a plan or concept of operations becoming unsuitable, the commander's intent provides the direction of what needs to be done to achieve a satisfactory end state and subordinates can improvise, adapt and overcome obstacles without becoming stalled while waiting for further direction.

The commander's intent is formed and provided during the earliest stages of planning[68] and is based upon a commander's estimate of the situation. In law enforcement operations it is more often than not issued verbally. A written commander's intent is done in "free form" (without a standard format), and describes both the commander's vision of an acceptable end state and a concept of operations to achieve it. Additionally, it may also include "follow-on actions." **Follow-on actions** are those intended procedures and activities that follow others. It is important to note that follow on actions are often contributory to a desirable end state but are not necessarily prerequisites. They are typically preparatory in nature in that they anticipate and prepare for additional requirements. An example of an order for a follow-on action might be, "Upon completion of your mission, move to location A and prepare to support unit B."

To illustrate how a commander's intent is used for planning, consider the following scenario. A law enforcement agency is called upon to handle the security for a large political rally concerning a highly controversial election issue. The rally will undoubtedly draw activists on both sides of the issue and in past incidents violence has erupted between the two groups. Typical control measures for mobs and riots have included dispersing the mob, isolating and containing the rioters or early intervention by identifying and arresting the provocateurs. Each of these strategies requires different tools and methodologies and the choice of one will affect everything from the selection of personnel and how they are equipped to the logistical support and reinforcements required.

Furthermore, they are often in competition with one another. In this scenario for example, a strategy that advocates mass arrests and one that promotes dispersing a mob cannot both be simultaneously implemented and preparations for one may actually hinder the other. The decision for the preferred course of action rightfully lies with the senior commander and failing to provide the necessary guidance not only unduly complicates planning but cedes the essential decision to subordinates. To avoid this untenable situation, the senior commander issues guidance on the preferred course of action. This allows planners to develop strategies, identify enabling objectives, gather logistical support, select and stage equipment, and so forth.

Once a grasp of the situation is achieved, a "concept of operations" can be developed. A **concept of operations** refers to a series of actions designed to progressively promote the accomplishment of strategic objectives. It may be understood as a scheme for orienting activity without precisely prescribing what must be done. It always involves a number of missions, which necessarily includes a multitude of tasks. Some missions can be accomplished rather quickly, with only one or two persons, while others may take hours or days and require the combined efforts of a large number of people. Some require special skills while others can be fulfilled by almost anyone. Many of these missions are performed simultaneously, and are in competition with each other for personnel and resources. This results in a competing interest. A **competing interest** is anything that engages the attention and results in a division of attention or resources. In this case, more than one action can be accomplished but not at the same time or with the same personnel and resources. Other missions are incompatible, in that choosing one means forsaking the others. These are caused by conflicting interests. A **conflicting interest** is one where two or more actions are mutually exclusive. Understandably, some method of deconfliction is necessary to allow subordinates to use their initiative to exploit opportunities and maximize resources without necessitating formal authorization for every action. This is achieved by identifying the "focus of effort" and the "main effort."

A **focus of effort** describes a concentration of interest or activity. In tactical operations, the focus of effort is what a commander identifies as the predominant activity or assignment that must be accomplished to achieve a successful resolution. All other assignments and missions are subordinate. Thus, anyone is able to resolve a conflict without burdening a commander with minutia.

Similar in concept but distinct in application is the **main effort.** The main effort identifies the agency, unit or component which has been assigned as the primary means to accomplish the interest or activity defined by the focus of effort. More simply stated, where the focus of effort identifies what needs to be done, the main effort identifies who is to do it. All other units and components are intended to support the main effort.

COMMAND RELATIONSHIPS

Every tactical operation is overseen by an organization specifically designed to assign and direct critical personnel and equipment to resolve an unfolding crisis. Sociologists refer to these organizations as Emerging Multi-Organizational Networks (EMONs). One of the most critical functions of an EMON is identifying who is responsible for whom and what. This function is most commonly referred to as a "command relationship." A **command relationship** may be defined as any formal association between two or more people that establishes a connection through which command is exercised. Of necessity, both superior and subordinate roles will be designated. Each of these superior and subordinate roles separate a layer of command called an echelon. An **echelon of command** is the term used to describe a layer of an organization of which all members have equal decision making authority. Generally, the higher the echelon the greater the responsibility, and understand-

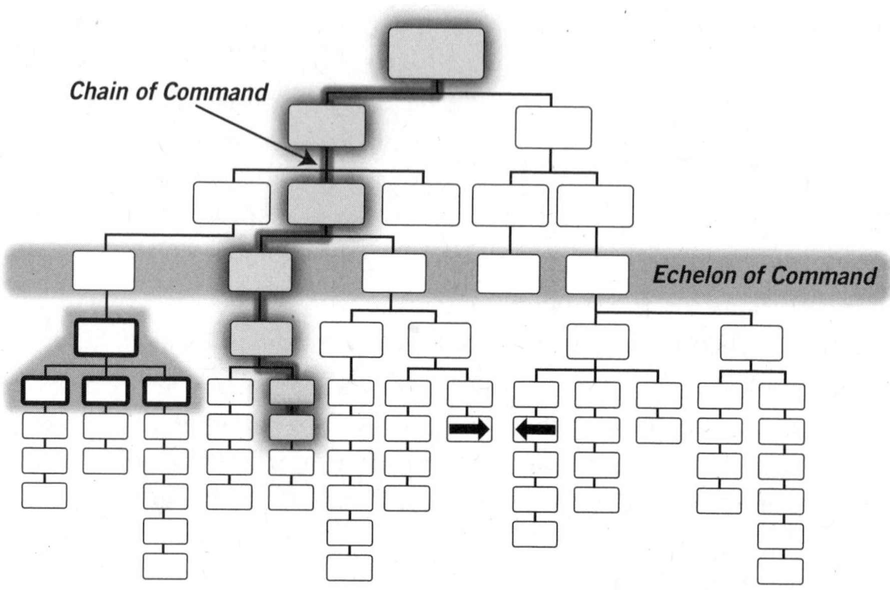

FIGURE 7-1 COMMAND RELATIONSHIPS: While they may vary in size, purpose and configuration, all organizations are designed to distribute power, affix responsibility and allocate resources. A table of organization, sometimes called an "organizational chart," is a chart-like "picture" of an organization that reveals the formal relationships within it. As can be seen in the chart above, each of the positions that comprise the organization is depicted as a box. The higher in the organization the more authority that is bestowed. The lines that connect them identify who reports to whom and are referred to as the "chain of command." Each layer of the organization identifies positions with the same decision making authority and is referred to as an "echelon of command."

It can also be seen that each position answers to a single supervisor. This "unity of command" is essential to avoid confusion with competing and conflicting instructions from more than one supervisor. The number of subordinates under a single supervisor is referred to as the "span of control" and is displayed above with the shading and darker boxes on the left side of the graphic.

Regardless of the care to avoid them, disputes are inevitable. For example, the boxes with the arrows identify a dispute that needs to be resolved. The default method is through the "first common senior rule" which vests the authority to decide with the first supervisor in charge of both disputants. It can be seen, however, that in this case it is the head of the entire organization. This is why temporary organizations are used to meld the necessary skills and knowledge from different parts of the organization, and even other organizations, into a new one under the command of an "incident commander" are so important.

ably, the greater authority. While an echelon is usually composed of equal ranks, the definitive criterion is not rank but authority. For example, it is not unusual to have a subject matter expert in charge of a specialized unit vested with decision making authority otherwise reserved for a higher rank.

Each of these command relationships forms a "chain of command." In the simplest terms, a **chain of command**[69] is the line of authority along which information and instructions are passed between superiors and subordinates. It is important to note that this channel is bidirectional in that instructions are commonly passed from superior to subordinate while information is frequently passed from subordinate to superior. Moreover, higher rank does not entitle a superior with the authority to compel actions if they are "outside" the chain of command.

Command relationships are how an organization affixes responsibility, resolves conflicts and focuses efforts. When disagreements arise between individuals or components within an organization they are resolved using the "first common senior rule." Simply put, the **first common senior rule** establishes the authority to decide

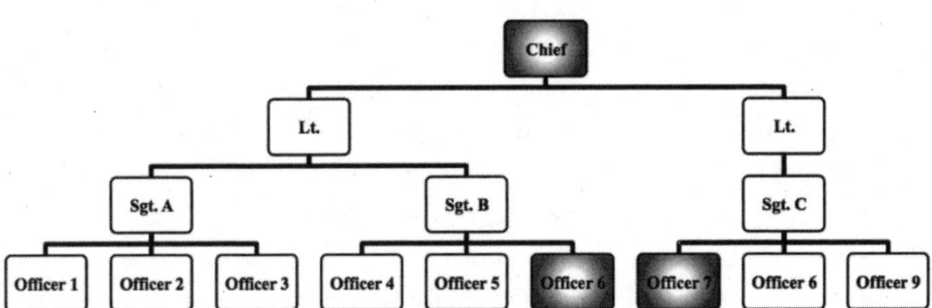

FIGURE 7-2 FIRST COMMON SENIOR: Ensuring maximum coordination and cooperation is a critical aspect in all organizations but is never more important than when handling emergencies. Notwithstanding, conflicts will develop and must be efficiently dealt with less the entire effort become stymied. The first common senior rule establishes decision making authority with the first superior in charge of all disputants and is the "default" mode. In the example above, a dispute has arisen between officers in different divisions but the first common senior is the chief of police. During routine operations this is a nuisance, but during emergency situations it can be ruinous. This is often the case during emergencies when a variety of skills and knowledge are pulled from different divisions, and even different agencies and disciplines. The solution is to assign decision making authority to the incident commander over all aspects and personnel relating to the temporary organization at the scene.

with the first superior in charge of all disputants. This ensures that the concept of "unity of command" is firmly supported.[70]

As tactical organizations increase in size and complexity a point will eventually be reached where it is humanly impossible for a single person to exercise the essential command functions. How many subordinates should be under the direct supervision of a single superior is called the **span of control**. In disaster management and tactical operations a commander can normally supervise about five subordinates. If subordinates are working on extremely complex assignments or are geographically separated the span of control should be reduced. Conversely, if they are working together and performing similar tasks the span of control can be increased.[71]

COMMAND RELATIONSHIPS

When tactical organizations require reinforcements command relationships become especially critical. Generally, the supporting (reinforcing) unit or agency reports to the incident commander of the supported (reinforced) unit and is attached to the existing tactical organization as a separate component. All internal command channels remain the same with the senior commander of the supporting unit subordinate to the original incident commander. Missions and orders are given to the senior commander of the supporting unit and follow the existing chains of command within the attached unit. This command relationship is called **joint command.** Joint command is the "default mode" for quickly incorporating reinforcements and mutual aid. Joint command works just fine in most instances but falls short when the supporting unit is larger than the one supported or when the supporting unit is of another discipline. When either of these conditions exists a **unified command** relationship is most often employed. Unlike a joint command, a unified command incorporates the senior commanders from supporting units into a single command module where command is shared. Collaboration allows agencies to work effectively together without affecting the authority, accountability or responsibilities of the individual agencies.

How a unit is assigned to support also affects command relationships. For example, an agency of another discipline, such as fire services or water and power, are usually in "general support." General support describes the command relationship for a unit whose actions support the organization as a whole rather than any particular component. Units and agencies in general support are responsible for all their own logistics, administrative and operational needs. In comparison, units and agencies whose actions support a specific component of the overall operation are in direct

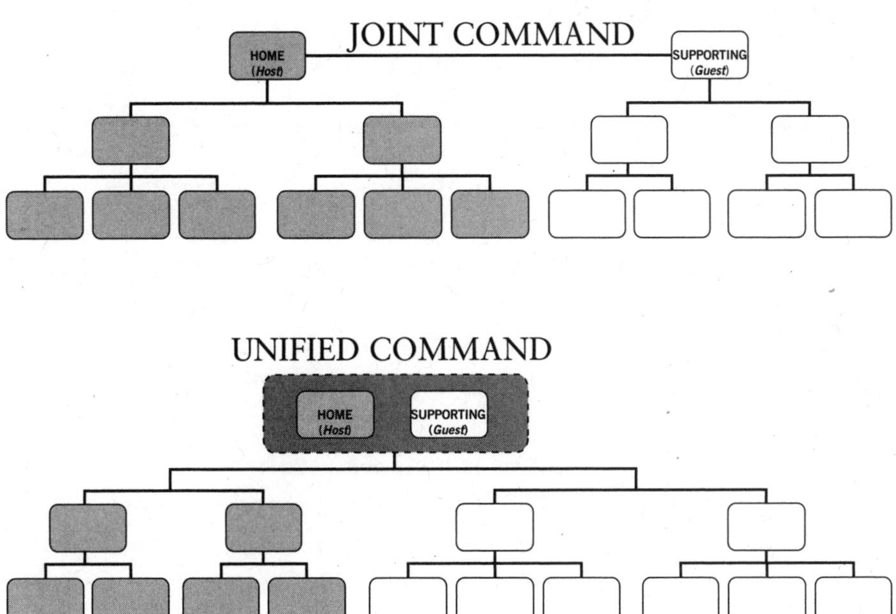

FIGURE 7-3 JOINT AND UNIFIED COMMAND: Protocols for integrating disparate agencies and disciplines assigned to handle the same emergency are essential. With nearly no exceptions, the agency responsible for the jurisdiction is called the "home agency" and is in charge. When reinforcements arrive they report directly to the incident commander from the home agency and use a joint command structure. Sometimes, however, the reinforcements outnumber the home unit and/or have specialized skills and knowledge. In these cases a unified command structure works best by fusing the decision making authority into a single command module.

One easy and informal way of understanding the relationships between supported and supporting units is as "host and guest." The host agency enjoys all the rights and privileges of their home while the guests retain all their own rights but hold only those privileges afforded them by the host.

support. Units and agencies in direct support are under the command of the supported unit commander rather than the incident commander. Moreover, the supported unit commander assumes responsibility for the logistics, administrative and operational needs of the unit or agency in direct support.

Although it is more common in the military than law enforcement operations, command relationships can be further adapted to circumstances by specifying whether a unit is under operational control, tactical control or administrative control. **Operational control**, sometimes referred to as "OPCON," gives a commander authority to assign tasks, organize and employ the supporting unit's assets and give direction throughout the accomplishment of the mission. This relationship is quite rare in the law enforcement community. **Tactical control**, sometimes called "TACON," gives a commander authority for assignments limited to objectives necessary to accomplish specific missions. For example, a commander conducting evacuations might be in charge of reinforcements assisting in the effort who would be under his direction while participating in that particular mission. **Administrative control**, sometimes referred to as "ADCON," gives authority to a commander for controlling all things of an administrative nature. Compared to OPCON and TADCON, ADCON is more common in law enforcement and is sometimes used when operations are exceptionally large and complex. For example, it is valuable when a supporting unit assists by accepting responsibility for prisoners, tracking overtime, feeding and sheltering refugees, ordering supplies and so forth. Because such things as the authority for payment lie with the supported unit, they often specify everything from accounting procedures to how information is tracked and recorded, and even the acceptable forms and invoices.

Command relationships are one of the most common points of friction in any organization but because of the tensions and emotions inherent in crises they are particularly troublesome during tactical operations and emergency responses. One of the most common occurrences is when a change of command becomes necessary. With rare exceptions, the first person on a scene is in command until properly relieved. A change of command is never assumed but must be explicitly delegated and promulgated to ensure everyone involved is aware of who is in charge. While this might seem somewhat rigid and formal it ensures that there is never doubt at any time of who is in charge.[72]

Another occasion is when a commander fails to delegate and assumes more duties than can be easily handled by a single person. This condition highlights the importance of another concept which states that decisions should be pushed to the lowest possible level. To put it another way, it means that the first person with the requisite authority to make any decision should do so. While higher headquarters may be advised, decisions should not routinely be passed up the chain of command.

So important are command relationships to the success of an operation that they are often used as a measure of excellence of the organization itself. An organization with solid and reliable command relationships is quick to react to changing conditions, withstand setbacks and suffer less friction. Accordingly, it is well worth the effort to fully understand their critical importance and refine them before they are strained and tested during times of adversity.

COUP D'OEIL CONCEPT

One of the most valuable attributes of a tactical commander is an ability to quickly and accurately comprehend the factors and influences involved in a particular situation and how they will ultimately affect the outcome. This ability has distinguished some of the greatest leaders and is seen as both a skill and a talent.[73] **Coup d'oeil** (pronounced koo dwee) is the name used to describe this concept. It is a French expression which loosely translated means the "strike of the eye" or the "vision behind the eye." The closest English concept would be that of intuition. Intuition is defined as "perceptive insight" or "the power to discern the true nature of a situation." It explains a commander's ability to visualize what the terrain looks like on the other side of a hill or the floor plan of the inside of a building coupled with an understanding of the impact they will have on an operation.[74] When time is the primary factor, it might involve mentally projecting the impact of flood waters on low-lying terrain or envisioning situations that cause a suspect to react in some predictable manner which can then be exploited.

While a commander who possesses coup d'oeil might be considered gifted, it is more likely that their abilities have been developed. Coup d'oeil involves judgment and judgment can be enhanced with knowledge and practice. An understanding of supporting scientific principles has long been known to increase the effectiveness of a commander's judgment and includes everything from informal debriefings to formal courses of study. Only by a thorough understanding of these principles can they be used to recognize and accurately appraise the impact of subtle influences. Commanders who understand them tend to be more flexible and innovative in thought and actions.

Likewise, coup d'oeil improves with practice. The importance of practice, coupled with a thorough understanding of sound doctrinal principles cannot be overestimated. Anything that broadens experience and exercises judgment increases a person's intuitive skills. Training exercises, debriefings and tactical decision games are especially relevant. To the degree they are conducted in the same operational context,[75] they become even more valuable. In the words of T.E. Lawrence (Lawrence of Arabia), "It [coup d'oeil] can only be ensured by instinct, sharpened by thought, practicing the strokes so often that at the crisis it is as natural as a reflex."[76]

---

67. Philip II of Macedon (circa 359-336 B.C.) was the father of Alexander the Great and was a great military leader in his own right. He is credited with perfecting the phalanx formation, which became a mainstay in ancient armies and remains a generic term used to day to describe a military formation.
68. This stage is normally referred to as "mission analysis" and is focused on identifying what is required for an acceptable resolution, the factors and influences involved and conceiving a general concept of how to succeed.
69. Sometimes referred to as a "command channel."
70. Unity of command is a concept which ensures that every individual participating in an operation reports to one, and only one, supervisor.

It is one of the nine principles of war and is essential to avoid confusion with conflicting or competing instructions or priorities.

71. Generally, the ratio should not be less than 1:3 or more than 1:7 but when organized into platoons and squads, especially during crowd control situations, law enforcement agencies typically deploy with a span of control of 1:10 or even 1:12.
72. This concept is so critical that it is frequently formalized in written policy. This also helps to remove much of the friction since assumption of command is a matter of policy not personality.
73. Napoleon Bonaparte once said, "My great talent, the one that distinguished me the most, is to see the entire picture distinctly." As quoted in Baron Gaspard Gourgand's *Journal inédit de 1815 à 1818.* Likewise, the coup d'oeil concept has been valued by the likes of Col. T.E. Lawrence (Lawrence of Arabia), Captain Sir Basil Liddell Hart, Major General Carl von Clausewitz and Frederick the Great.
74. A gifted commander is not only able to comprehend what is happening but can often predict what will happen next. The Germans call this gift, "fingerspitzengefuhl:" a feel for the battlespace that cannot be taught or fully explained. It comes from experience.
75. Operational context refers to the same circumstances that would ordinarily occur in real situations. For example, requiring a decision maker to define the problem, evaluate and incorporate information which is incomplete, confusing or conflicting and under severe time constraints are all factors that would be expected in actual situations.
76. Colonel T.E. Lawrence, "The Science of Guerrilla Warfare," *Encyclopedia Britannica*, 1929

OPERATIONS

An important difference between a military operation and a surgical operation is that the patient is not tied down.

—CAPTAIN SIR BASIL LIDDELL HART[77]

OF ALL THE COMPONENTS IN A TACTICAL ORGANIZATION THE operations component tends to be the most visible. This is where the proverbial "rubber meets the road." Problems in obtaining timely and reliable intelligence or failing to provide logistical support may be nearly unnoticeable until the operations component attempts to implement some action. Consequently, failures and shortcomings from the other functions are often unjustly attributed to operations. This is one place where the "art of war" becomes the application of the science. The operations component, like its fraternal twins, intelligence and logistics, is part of the triad of specialties involved in every tactical response and while it may be the most conspicuous, it is not the most important. Each of the components relies on and interacts with one another so that a synergy occurs where the combined effect is greater than the sum of the individual efforts. As the old saying goes, "No one can whistle a symphony. It takes an orchestra to play it."

The operations component of a tactical organization is charged with actions focused on reducing the immediate hazard and safeguarding life and property. Accordingly, this is where actions are organized, staffed, coordinated and directed toward a common objective. In the simplest terms, this function is responsible for ensuring that the end state, as defined by the command element, is efficiently and effectively accomplished. It allows the command element to focus on determining an acceptable end state, identifying enabling objectives, and developing strategy, without the necessity of personally supervising each of the subordinate tasks. It is not uncommon for the operations component to be a composite of more than one agency and discipline, especially when the situation is multi-jurisdictional and/or multi-disciplinary. Consequently, the operations component tends to be the largest of all the elements involved in handling emergencies. A large fire, as just one example, will often require the coordinated efforts from both the fire services and law enforcement, and sometimes public works, public health, and even nongovernmental agencies.

SITUATIONAL AWARENESS AND A COMMON OPERATIONAL PICTURE

The greatest contribution of commanders to the success of a tactical operation or disaster response is the decisions they render. While factors such as training, education and experience are critical, a commander's understanding of what is going on has the most impact. This understanding is most often referred to as "situational awareness."[78] **Situational awareness** is a concept that describes a person's knowledge and understanding of the circumstances, surroundings, and influences with regard to an unfolding situation. It also includes everything that is known about the situation leading up to the current episode, as well as the impact it might have on other incidents. It stands to reason that the more complex the operation, the more difficult this is to achieve.

Situational awareness is present to a greater or lesser degree for everyone involved in an operation. Naturally, a person's perspective will have a strong effect on their personal knowledge and understanding. Furthermore, it is never exhaustive, since as more knowledge and understanding is attained, a person's situational awareness is increased. It is easy to see that situational awareness is somewhat unique to each individual at any given time. This disparity is particularly troublesome in large operations when different agencies are involved and different echelons of command are required. Field command posts, located near an incident, have a different perspective and understanding of what is taking place than distant and superior command posts responsible for the operation as a whole. This is frequently a source of confusion and disorder, which highlights the importance of another tactical concept called a "common operational picture."

In its most simple terms, a **common operational picture** is simply the shared knowledge and understanding between individuals, teams or groups. It is particularly critical whenever a number of agencies or echelons of command are involved, such as when handling major disasters or large tactical operations, because of the need for close coordination and cooperation. Even so, because the information used to form a common operational picture is always somewhat incomplete, inaccurate, ambiguous, or even conflicting, a completely reliable and comprehensive common operational picture is elusive.

While similar in nature, situational awareness and a common operational picture are fundamentally different in at least three respects. For example, situational awareness belongs to an individual, while a common operational picture, by definition, belongs to a group. This has two implications. First, each serves a different purpose. Situational awareness is intended to provide an individual with insight and discretion while a common operational picture creates shared understanding to enhance collaboration and create synergy. Second, each will require different methods to obtain. Gaining greater situational awareness relies heavily upon personal effort and the needed information is nearly always in some form of personal observation. Acquiring a common operational picture, however, is heavily reliant upon information provided by others. This always means that it has been "processed" because of the natural "filter effect." The filter effect is a well-known, natural occurrence that results when one person briefs another. The person who is doing the briefing (sender) is forced to condense the information into either what they think the receiver of the information needs to know, wants to know or should know. Understandably, this is never as much as the sender knows and so the information passed is always incomplete and somewhat biased. Third, situational awareness describes a person's understanding of a situation, and not the state of affairs. Observations, in and of themselves, are important only if they contribute to gaining a clearer mental picture. Accordingly, a person's training, education and experience play important roles by putting things into perspective. This is because of the increased understanding that results when current events are compared with those of the past. A common operational picture, on the other hand, provides a frame of reference that an organization needs to achieve effective and efficient coordination and collaboration. Goals and objectives are more easily perceived and easier to agree upon, while priorities are less likely to be contentious when everyone involved has the same general perspective. Opportunities and threats are more easily discerned because the common understanding creates a shared vigilance through all organizational components and echelons of command. The entire decision making process in fact, becomes synergistic because each component or echelon is able to comprehend and contribute according to the common understanding.

It stands to reason that the greater the situational awareness, and the more prevalent the common operational picture, the more likely that decisions will be effective and the organization will run smoothly and efficiently. While always important, the application of these concepts is especially critical in rapidly unfolding events when attempting to restore order amidst chaos and confusion.

REINFORCEMENTS

Support for tactical operations can take on many forms ranging from assistance from other units within a department to other agencies and disciplines responding to a mutual aid request. Regardless of how welcome reinforcements are, they complicate command relationships and logistical support.

In the simplest terms, **reinforcement** is the augmentation of a tactical organization with additional troops or equipment. Reinforcements are commonly required to counter unforeseen threats, or to prolong or renew some action and are provided in either general support or direct support. **General support** describes

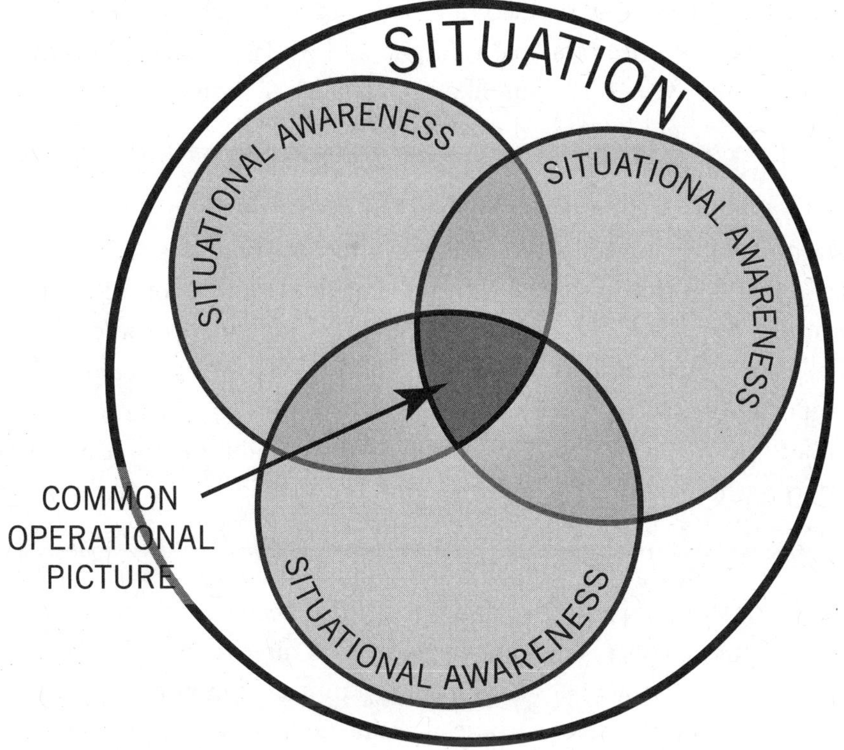

FIGURE 8-1 SITUATIONAL AWARENESS AND A COMMON OPERATIONAL PICTURE: What a decision maker actually understands about an unfolding situation and what is actually happening can be substantial. In this Venn diagram, the large circle represents the situation as a whole and each of the smaller ones represent the situational awareness of a deployed individual or unit. In this manner it can be see that only where they converge and are shared is there a true common operational picture. Accordingly, one of the implied tasks in every tactical operation is to expand this shared situational awareness to the maximum practical extent.

the command relationship for a unit whose actions support the organization as a whole rather than any particular component. When in general support, lines of command and control are essentially the same, with the exception that the portion of the unit actually deployed is under the authority of the incident commander. Additionally, the supporting unit is responsible for all their own administrative and operational needs. This means that personnel replacements and replenishments remain the responsibility of the supporting unit. General support is the "default mode," in that barring instructions to the contrary, specialized units augmenting a tactical response remain "at large" and provide overarching support. Units with functions like air support or bomb disposal are commonly held in general support.

Direct support describes the command relationship for a unit whose actions support a specific component of the overall operation. Reinforcing units are assigned direct support missions by the command authority of the entire operation. Usually, for all but the largest responses, the incident commander personally makes these decisions. Also, unlike in general support, a unit in direct support reports directly to the supported unit commander. This command relationship facilitates integration of the capabilities of the supporting unit with the supported unit and provides a more tailored response for local conditions without requiring approval from higher authority. Additionally, the supported unit becomes responsible for the administrative and operational needs of the supporting unit. Consequently, units assigned a role in direct support are often identified as "attached." Examples of a unit, or component thereof, in direct support might include a canine team attached to a searching team, or a SWAT team attached to a detective unit serving a warrant.

Reinforcements most often come from within the agency responsible for handling the response. When the response exceeds the ability of the agency, however, as is often the case with major disasters, other agencies lend support. Consequently, issues arise because of different procedures, authorized weapons, equipment compatibility (especially communications) rules of engagement, and even who is in charge. This last question becomes especially important when a supporting unit is considerably larger than the supported unit. In law enforcement especially, there are residual issues that can outlast the actual response by months or years, such as which agency is responsible for investigating citizen complaints, allegations of excessive force, or court costs. This last issue can be particularly sensitive when civil suits arise and not only require defense expenses but can result in settlements against a supporting agency.

One of the best methods for resolving these issues is establish-

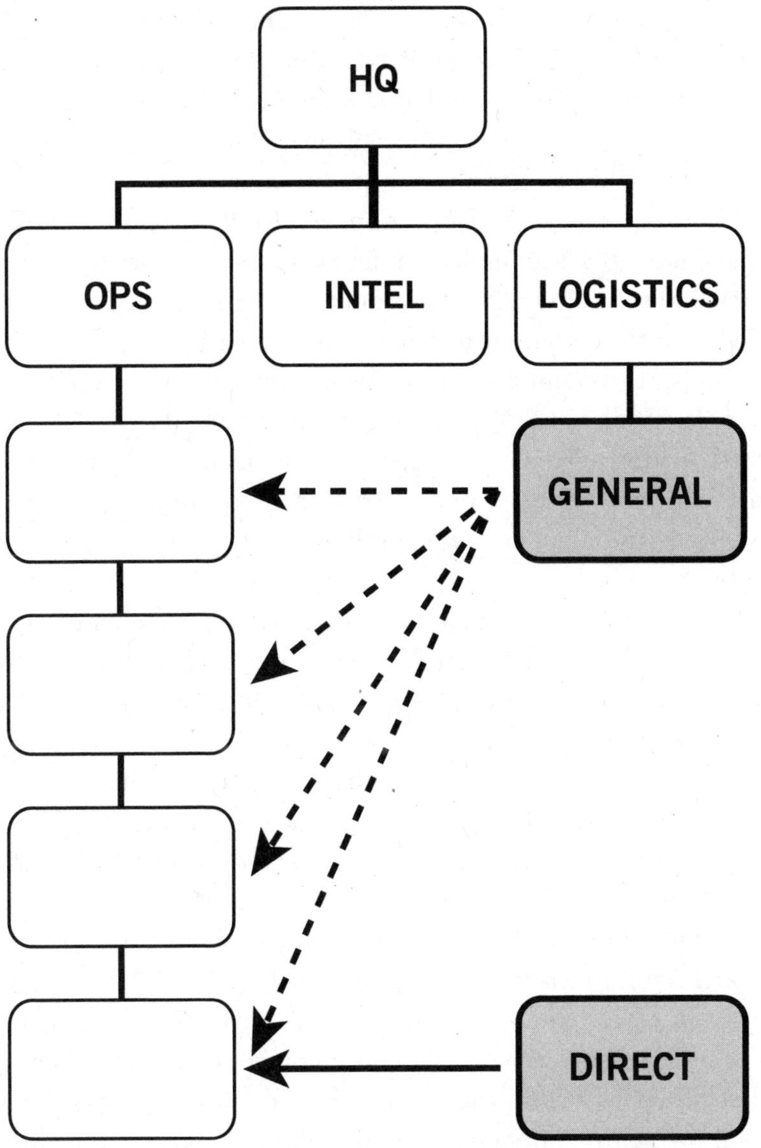

FIGURE 8-2 REINFORCEMENTS: Reinforcements complicate command relationships, especially if they come from other agencies and disciplines. When a unit is in general support it works for the response organization as a whole and the supporting unit remains responsible for their own administrative and operational needs. This is the default mode. Some reinforcements are assigned directly to the supported unit and report through the subordinate unit commander. This is common when reinforcements are highly specialized, such as explosive ordnance disposal, SWAT, search and rescue, and so forth. With some exceptions, the supported unit assumes responsibility for the administrative and operational needs.

ing written agreements between agencies and disciplines in the form of SOPs and MOUs. An **SOP (Standing Operating Procedure**[79]) is a formal policy that standardizes methods and routines within an agency according to established procedures. This provides an ability to quickly and easily incorporate units with complex functions without extensive elaboration. An **MOU (Memorandum Of Understanding**[80]) is an understanding between agencies that assigns responsibility and/or allocates resources according to an agreement. MOUs identify potential resources not ordinarily or readily available and greatly simplify and expedite the means to make them available. While an SOP may be unwritten, an MOU is always a formal written agreement. Together, these documents facilitate the entire planning process, reduce friction in coordinating complex procedures and eliminate role conflicts.

Reinforcements generally come from two places, reserves and mutual aid. A **reserve** is defined as designated personnel or equipment retained or set aside for future use or a special purpose, while **mutual aid** is the reciprocal support that different agencies, disciplines and jurisdictions provide each other in times of need. Even though a reserve is usually from the same agency, the only thing necessary to constitute a reserve is that the support be pre-identified and incorporated into a plan. Thus, outside agencies providing mutual aid can be part of a reserve.

Despite the best plans and intentions, situations will still arise in which reinforcements are required and which no formal agreement is in place. As a result, four useful conventions have evolved that can attenuate some of the more contentious issues. The first is that the agency with original jurisdiction (almost always the one calling for help), is designated as the "host" agency. Accordingly, all responding agencies are "guests." Even without a formal agreement, these designations establish a relationship that closely mimics those that would have been codified had there been more time. For example, it would be exceptionally rude for a guest to order a host to do anything. So it is with command and control in a tactical situation. The host agency remains in command regardless of the size of the response. Guests, however, remain in control of their individual units.

The second convention is that mission tasking is the norm. In the simplest terms, mission tasking requires a commander to tell a subordinate what to do, but not how to do it. This allows a subordinate command the freedom to use their own equipment and procedures without interfering with other organizations, even those assigned identical missions.

Of necessity, mission tasking will be exceedingly difficult if members of responding units do not remain together; that is they deploy together and under their own chain of command. As such they are free to employ their own procedures, policies, weapons and equipment. Consequently, the third convention is that responding units maintain their unit integrity and are not dispersed or intermingled with other units.

The last convention attempts to resolve some of the most contentious issues of all, in that many of the problems resulting from mutual aid responses, especially those requiring law enforcement functions, are residual rather than contemporaneous. Bluntly put, this convention requires all units to "clean up their own mess." This means that investigations of damaged property, allegations of excessive force or other citizen complaints are the responsibility of the accused agency not the host agency. To be sure, this does not remove the host agency from civil liability or any other effects from the aftermath, but it allows the accused agency to assess their actions based upon their own policies and practices.

ORDERS

Orders are so rudimentary to the conduct of tactical operations that they are usually taken for granted. Yet, it is only by timely and unambiguous orders that meaningful and effective collaboration can occur. Hence, an understanding of what orders are (and are not), as well as the roles they play, can assist in avoiding confusion and disruption.

An **order** is a command given by a superior requiring the immediate and full obedience in the execution of some task. Orders differ from similar terms, such as "instructions" or "directives," because they require immediate and strict compliance. While orders can be written, they are most often issued verbally. All orders fall into one of two general categories. These are direct orders and indirect orders. A **direct order** is one that is precisely and clearly expressed directly from a superior to a subordinate. Direct orders may be verbal or written and are the norm when supervisors and subordinates are collocated or connected directly through some type of communications device. An **indirect order** is one that is issued through an intermediary. While it is not uncommon for an indirect order to be issued verbally, they are most commonly written, especially in the form of a policy or instruction. Indirect orders are the norm when a commander issues an order to an entire unit. Notwithstanding, a direct order carries no greater weight than an indirect order and both carry the same obligations of obedience.

Generally, there are four types of orders related to tactical operations and disaster management. An **alert order** is used to initiate a heightened state of vigilance or preparation for some action. It signals individuals or units that they may be assigned a mission concerning a developing situation. Alert orders are sent as soon as it becomes likely that a situation may require the efforts of the notified individuals or units, and provides as much information about the situation as is known, as well as any concept of operation being considered.

A **warning order** is used when it appears certain that an individual or unit will be required, but is not immediately needed. It can also be used to advise that some type of action may be required. This is particularly valuable if the action requires unusual resources or extraordinary preparation. When used in this manner, it is sometimes issued with the admonition to carry out the action "on order." This identifies the need to be ready to immediately perform the assignment upon receipt of the order to execute it. Warning orders provide notice to begin preparations for deployment and furnish as much information about a developing situation as available together with any anticipated problems and the probable mission. Warning orders will usually, but not always, follow an alert order.

Neither alert, nor warning orders should ever be considered definitive since they are always based upon incomplete information. Consequently, more thorough and precise information is required before any detailed planning can occur or committing to a particular course of action. Nevertheless, they perform a valuable role in tactical operations by providing for timely preparation and planning while the situation continues to develop.

An **execute order** is used to implement or carry out some action in accordance with a plan. Execute orders can be initiated in any of three ways. The most common is immediately upon receipt. This happens when a commander gives the order and it is implemented without delay. The second method is according to a preset time. The order may be given minutes or hours before it is actually implemented, but requires no further order to implement. In fact, to stop or delay the action, an additional order must be given. The last way is according to a predetermined event. In this manner, an event which can be anticipated is used as a "tripwire" to automatically initiate action without further orders.

The last type of order is called a **fragmentary or "frag" order**. A frag order is used to modify or rescind any existing order by providing additional details to a situation or by adding to, changing or countermanding a previous order. Because it is only used for changing an existing order, nothing except essential information

TYPES OF ORDERS	
Alert	Used to initiate a heightened state of vigilance or preparation for some action
Warning	Used when it appears certain that an individual or unit will be required but is not immediately needed
Execute	Used to implement or carry out some action in accordance with a plan
Fragmentary (Frag)	Used to modify or rescind any existing order by providing additional details to a situation

FIGURE 8-3 ORDERS: Orders in emergency situations are essential for coordination and direction. As such, they naturally fall into types depending on their particular role.

is provided. Thus, it is incomplete, or "fragmentary," without the preexisting order. Frag orders are very common in developing situations and are used to update personnel and units of new developments or changes to plans.

DECONFLICTION MEASURES

The size, scope and complexity of large tactical operations and disaster responses make detailed oversight difficult. At times, an operation may proceed according to a plan but then reaches a point where further direction is necessary to ensure success. Because these junctures can often be identified with a high degree of certainty, two techniques assist decision makers in providing the necessary guidance without becoming overwhelmed with details. These are "decision points" and "tripwires."

A **decision point** is a technique that is incorporated into a tactical plan to call attention to the need to make a decision. It identifies an event, time or sequence at which further guidance is necessary to proceed. When a decision point is reached, the decision is automatically defaulted to the commander (or a designated person) for further guidance.

A closely related but distinct concept is a "tripwire." Like its namesake used to automatically set-off booby traps, a **tripwire** is used to automatically implement a plan, procedure or series of actions. Tripwires afford instant action within predetermined guidelines without burdening a busy commander with needless concern over decisions which are so apparent that they can be "defaulted." They provide a mechanism to allow complex plans to be developed and briefed yet instantly implemented in the "heat of battle."

Decision points and tripwires are excellent tools to relieve a commander of anxiety by allowing him to concentrate on the tasks at hand without neglecting future operations. This keeps the operation from running ahead of him. Each of these tools can usually be identified on a map or diagram where (or when) a commander must make a decision or invoke some action in order to seize or retain the initiative. The key element regarding the placement of these tools is time.[81] When a decision point or tripwire is reached there must remain sufficient time to implement the commander's decision.

To illustrate how these tools work, imagine an incident involving a barricaded suspect with hostages. The commander is advised that oncoming darkness will have a dreadful impact on a successful resolution. The commander is willing to accept any alternative as long as it leads to the safe release of the hostages, but prefers to arrest the suspect as well. Not wishing to kill the suspect outright, the commander agrees to accept some risk to the hostages to achieve this goal. But if the operation continues into the hours of darkness, the hostages remain vulnerable, while the tactical team's ability to intervene becomes greatly diminished. The risk becomes unacceptable. Therefore, the commander places a decision point at a given time and preparations are made to achieve a satisfactory solution while it remains viable.

A tripwire could be added if the commander decided to use a tactical intervention if a suspect kills a hostage. For example, a tactical team could be predeployed and all other aspects of the operation would continue until a suspect killed a hostage. Without further instructions, the intervention would be executed according to the commander's earlier decision.

Decision points and tripwires are among the most valuable tools available to a commander to avoid becoming overwhelmed by events. These techniques allow detailed planning and preparation without necessitating implementation. This has a profound impact on economy of force by allowing personnel to rest, refugee centers to be set up, food stuffs and equipment to be staged as well as the myriad of other tasks which would be exacerbated, or even prevented, if one attempted to condense them solely into the execution phase of an operation.

---

77. Captain Sir Basil Liddell Hart, *Thoughts on War*, 1944. Hart is a renowned military historian even though he was actually in combat less than two months. After suffering health problems from being gassed in World War I he was retired at the rank of Captain and became a jour-

nalist. He is best known for publishing his debriefings of high-ranking German generals. The remainder of the quote states, "But it is a common fault of generalship to assume that he is."

78. Sometimes called, "situation awareness."
79. While the term "Stand*ard* Operating Procedures" is often used as a substitute, the original, and more accurate, term "Stand*ing* Operating Procedures" is used to identify their changing nature. Regardless, the terms have so long been used interchangeably that for all intents and purposes they can be considered synonyms.
80. Sometimes called a "Memorandum of Agreement." While there may be subtle differences between MOUs and MOAs from a legal standpoint, for nearly all other intents and purposes they serve the same purpose.
81. The time concept is also applicable to tripwires. For example, events such as darkness, daylight, shifting winds, rain and other factors are all events which can be used as tripwires but are impossible to plot on a map or diagram. Moreover, an event itself can be a tripwire. An example might be the intervention plan for a hostage rescue which is automatically implemented if the suspect kills a hostage..

INTELLIGENCE

The great thing is to get the true picture, whatever it is.
—WINSTON CHURCHILL[82]

THE IMPORTANCE OF RELIABLE AND TIMELY INTELLIGENCE IS nearly impossible to overestimate. It not only provides the underpinnings for understanding and insight but establishes a basis to formulate plans and make effective decisions. While scientific principles are critical, this function more than any other also relies heavily on the intuition, ingenuity and experience of the staff to avoid ineffectual searches and other unproductive efforts, as well as discerning relevance and importance from a hodgepodge of random data. It requires a methodical and logical approach, not only to ensure that the product is reliable but that it is available in time to be incorporated into planning and decision making. In this context, late is the same as absent.

The intelligence component is responsible for the gathering, recording, evaluating and disseminating of all pertinent information relating to an incident. An implied responsibility with this component requires the continual assessment of all information to determine its relevance, accuracy and timeliness in forecasting the impact on the overall operation. Of all the components of a tactical organization, the intelligence function is most concerned with the future since virtually all planning and refinements to an existing plan will be dependent upon the availability and usefulness of the intelligence provided.

INFORMATION VS. INTELLIGENCE

Two terms, often used interchangeably, but with distinct meanings in tactical situations are "information" and "intelligence." **Information** is described as the knowledge or news of an event or situation gained through collection of facts or data. **Intelligence**, on the other hand, is specific information related to the situation at hand. Intelligence usually occurs with the "fusion" of information. This means taking bits and pieces of different details and facts and combining them to obtain a more complete picture of the situation at hand. Therefore, information may be better understood as "raw data" while intelligence is "processed data." A good illustration to which we can all relate occurs in a school setting. Copying some fact from a lecture into our notes is "information." Finding out it's on the test is "intelligence."

The term "intelligence" refers not only to the product, but the process. A complete intelligence picture is never possible. It only reflects everything that is known up to the time it is presented. Consequently, efforts at obtaining reliable, relevant and timely information continue throughout the tactical portion of the operation—and even after it is concluded. The lessons learned from one operation lay the groundwork for the next.

INFORMATION AS A CONCEPT

Generally speaking, there are four types of information. **Archival information** is that which seldom, if ever, changes. All historical data is archival in nature, but other examples include things such as the names of terrain features, flood inundation tables, the locations of hospitals and schools, climate conditions, and so forth. The second type is encyclopedic information. **Encyclopedic information** is durable, but not everlasting. Examples include such things as home telephone numbers, work assignments, or special skills. The third type is current information. **Current information** is that which is time sensitive and pertains to details, events or actions occurring in the present or very near past. Weather and lighting conditions would be examples. Current information also has a subset called "dynamic information." *Dynamic information* is simply current information that is in a near constant state of change. Examples include the precise locations of responders, the length of time they have worked, or the amount of fuel in a moving vehicle. The last type is also the most often neglected. This type is called future information. **Future information** is that information that can be confidently derived by forecast or projection. Future information is critical for planning, estimating impact, and assigning personnel and resources. All plans are a type of future information because all planning attempts to alter a future. Other examples include weather forecasts, fuel consumption, fatigue, estimated times of arrival, and scheduled events.

While all four types of information are critical in planning and preparing for tactical operations and emergency responses, it is important to note that archival and encyclopedic information can be collected and stored for later use, but current and future information are "high maintenance" and require continual acquisition and interpretation. This has momentous implications in that a commander who has the foresight to gather and store useful archival and encyclopedic information gains time and resources to concentrate on the other types when needed.

Regardless of what type of information is used, there are only five ways to arrange it. These are by category, time, location, alphabetically and continuum. Arranging information by **category** means to group it by type or variety; fruits and vegetables or apples and oranges, for example. Grouping ammunition by caliber would be a tactical example. Arranging information by **time** is just the sequential order in which events occurred. An operational log is probably the best tactical example of information arranged by time. **Location** refers to a physical place. Personnel assigned to a command post, staging area or traffic control intersection would all be examples. Arranging information **alphabetically** is self-explanatory, but it also includes numerical progression. Personnel rosters are a common example, but so are weapons and equipment inventories by serial number. The last method is by **continuum**. Continuums are used when there is a continuous succession of which no part is readily distinguishable from another except by arbitrary division; smallest to largest, darkest to lightest, weakest to strongest, slow-

TYPE	CHARACTER-ISTIC	EXAMPLES	EFFORT	
			GATHER	MAINTAIN
Archival	Seldom, if ever, changes	Historical events, climate, language skills, names and building addresses	High	Very Low
Encyclopedic	Durable, but not everlasting	Telephone numbers, work assignments and special skills	High	Low
Current	Contemporaneous and time sensitive	Weather and lighting conditions, physical locations and biological needs	High	High
Future	Prospective but worthy of reliance	Weather forecasts, fuel consumption, estimated times of arrival and scheduled events	High	High

FIGURE 9-1 INFORMATION: As important as the gathering and staging of food stuffs, clothing and equipment, preparing for emergencies should always include collecting information and storing it for future use. While the gathering of information can be a time-consuming and tedious process, some types of information can be stored for long periods, even indefinitely, with little or no effort and then tapped when needed and time is short. This not only facilitates planning and decision making but makes them faster and more reliable.

est to fastest, most to least, and so forth. In a tactical application, this method is sometimes used for making personnel assignments or reliefs when factors such as fatigue or strength are critical. Without exception, every folder, filing cabinet, database and software application uses one or more of these five methods for quickly sorting, storing and retrieving information.

EEIs AND OIRs

In its purest form, intelligence is comprised of three ingredient; EEIs, OIRs and Assumptions.[83] The most important bits of information are called **Essential Elements of Information (EEI)**. EEIs are those critical facts that a decision maker must have to reach a conclusion. Some, like the location of a burglary or robbery alarm or the direction of a pursuit, are readily apparent. In fact, this information is frequently so apparent we don't often recognize it as intelligence. Nevertheless, lack of this information is a "showstopper" since no effective tactical plan can proceed until it is obtained. Other EEIs, such as the size of a mob or whether they are armed, are not so apparent and efforts must be made to find out. Identifying these EEIs form the core of a sound intelligence plan.

Other Intelligence Requirements (OIR) is that information which is "nice to have." OIRs complement the more critical EEIs by "filling in the blanks" and providing a more complete picture of the situation. Examples often include weather reports, hours of daylight, suspect motivation and so forth. Although not as important as EEIs, OIRs play an important role by providing the intelligence necessary to develop more comprehensive plans.

The third type of information is an assumption. **Assumptions** are defined as anything that is taken for granted or accepted as true without proof. To be useful, an assumption must be valid; that is a logical inference or deduction based upon all the facts available, (even though incomplete). An assumption is used when an EEI or OIR cannot be obtained in time to be incorporated into the decision-making process. Thus, an assumption performs the role of a "substitute" for either an EEI or an OIR. In fact, a litmus test for determining whether needed information is one or the other is to ask, "If I don't have this information, will I be *forced* to make an assumption?" If the answer is "Yes" than the information should be sought as an EEI.

THE INTELLIGENCE PROCESS

The intelligence component, like all others, benefits from an efficient and methodical process. The intelligence process can be

FIGURE 9-2 INTELLIGENCE PICTURE: While it is true that a complete intelligence picture is not possible, it is also true that it is often not even needed. It is only necessary to reliably determine what the picture would look like if all the pieces were available. What is nearly always missing in the law enforcement community, however, is a focused and methodical approach on how to attain it. Despite the portions of the puzzle that are missing in this picture it is clear that it depicts the rescue efforts after the attack on the World Trade Center in New York on September 11th, 2001.

The intelligence picture is often compared with a puzzle where the pieces are joined to form a more complete scene. Even assembling a puzzle is not without a system, however. For example, a person usually starts by finding the corner pieces and then the pieces with the straight edges to form the perimeter. After that, pieces are sorted by color and texture until eventually a scene begins to be discerned. Even the largest and most complex puzzles can be assembled using the same basic methodology. So it is when attempting to form an intelligence picture to support decision making.

broken down into four sequential but interrelated steps.[84] The first step is **direction** and stems straight from the operational mission. It identifies both the nature of the intelligence sought and the means to attain it. The commander participates in this portion of the plan by determining the critical information needed to make effective decisions, which will then become the EEIs. Next, personnel assigned to the intelligence function prepare a collection plan to ensure maximum efforts are focused on obtaining the essential information in the shortest amount of time.

The next step is **collection**. Collection refers to those efforts made at obtaining the information and making it available. The value of using a collection plan cannot be overstated. It provides both the guidance and focus of effort to efficiently obtain the information to support a commander's direction. Each mission needs a separate plan, and will change with the tactical situation. Information obtained from collection efforts is generally "loose" data,[85] which may take any variety of forms from oral reports, sketches, and diagrams, to computer data, maps or photographs.

The next step involves two activities, **processing and production.** Processing is where the loose data is analyzed and organized into a usable form. Charts and graphs may be constructed and/or maps may be annotated. Data may be put into computer databases and spreadsheets. In short, this step allows the significance of the data to become conspicuous so that it can be further examined and analyzed. Closely related is production. This is where the raw data first becomes intelligence as it is analyzed for relevance, reliability and accuracy. This is the point where "*information fusion*" takes loose data and combines the bits and pieces into new facts and indications through evaluation (determining value), integration (compiling related pieces of data) and interpretation (analyzing related data).

The final step is **dissemination.** This step ensures that the varying organizational components get the needed intelligence in an appropriate form and in a timely manner. There are two criteria that must be met. The first is timeliness. Intelligence that arrives too late to be incorporated into the decision making process places a commander in pretty much the same position as a bystander. The second is to provide it in a usable form. Sending a computer disk to a field command post without a computer may seem absurd, but serves as an excellent example. No matter how valuable the data on the disk, it is not usable. More common incompatibilities may include extremely small-scale maps sent to local units, or color sensitive information photocopied in black and white or sent through fax machines.

GATHERING AND DISSEMINATING INTELLIGENCE

There are two schools of thought in how best to go about gaining intelligence. Traditionally, law enforcement has used a passive strategy. Sometimes referred to as **passive intelligence**, this strategy advocates methods that rely on deployed personnel in the belief that, because they are already in the field, and in many cases personally involved with the incident, they are the most able to provide the necessary information. One of the most common manifestations of this school of thought is the "windshield survey." When a major incident, such as an earthquake, flood, fire or storm occurs, a windshield survey is implemented using field units to report what they observe to a central location, usually a command post, where a more complete picture is assembled and decisions are made. While this philosophy seems very practical, it falls short because intelligence gathering is a collateral duty and duties directly relating to the situation predominate. Field units quickly become involved in fighting fires, rescues, traffic control and other tasks based upon the local situation as it is presented to them. Thus, this method places command personnel in the position of accepting intelligence passively rather than actively seeking it.

The second method advocates a proactive approach and avoids competing priorities. This strategy, called **active intelligence**, assigns intelligence missions to personnel and units whose primary responsibility is to obtain the information and relay it to a command post. Gathering intelligence is no longer a subordinate task, but the primary mission. Even this strategy is not without its drawbacks, however, because it utilizes resources in a supporting role that cannot otherwise be used to resolve the problem at hand. Thus, a dilemma is revealed. A commander who relies solely on a windshield survey is forced to make decisions based upon incomplete information, while one who relies entirely on an active strategy is required to forego early assessments and divert units from the problem at hand. Because both passive and active intelligence gathering methods have drawbacks, a combination of the two is often the most effective. In major disasters, the first information to arrive at a command post is almost always field reports, but they never complete the intelligence picture. Thus, when time and resources permit, the intelligence function is augmented by designated units with specific assignments who "fill in the blanks."

Once the information has reached a command post, it is processed into intelligence for incorporation into the decision making process throughout the tactical organization. Historically, the most common method of disseminating intelligence has been a **push strategy**. This strategy uses higher headquarters to decide who needs to know what, and then to "push" it to subordinate units in the form of intelligence updates and summaries. This is an extremely labor-intensive activity and requires knowledgeable and experienced people devoted to the task of determining what information should be pushed and to whom. In large operations, and those with widely separated geographical locations, relevant information for one component may be completely useless to another.[86] Thus, the intelligence product must not only be prioritized, but separated and routed in different directions.

Another method employs a **pull strategy**. The pull method places information in a central repository where it is available for subordinate units to access as desired. Information can then be pushed as needed, and pulled as desired. In this manner, local commanders are provided an ability to build their own intelligence picture by augmenting what they have been given with whatever else they want to know. Items such as weather, maps and photographs are just some of the more common types of intelligence that are able to be readily stored and "pulled."

While some common methods of storing this information for easy access have included status boards, folders and filing cabinets, their physical location required someone to be present to glean the necessary information. Nowadays, one of the easiest and most accessible locations is in a secure area of the Internet. Any authorized person with access to the Internet can then search and draw from a variety of sources, such as intelligence reports and summaries, graphics, maps, photographs, and the like.

Each of the strategies has its own strengths and weaknesses and there is no "right answer." The most effective solutions have used the advantages of one strategy to off-set the disadvantages of another. For example, a passive strategy can be used to gain whatever information is available in the shortest amount of time, but recognizing that the intelligence picture is still not complete, will assign designated personnel or units specific intelligence missions to augment the initial reports. Likewise, organizations will always find it necessary to push information that must be incorporated into decision making to ensure a common operational picture, while installing information in some common location where it can be accessed at will by subordinate and/or remote units provides a pull capability.

INTELLIGENCE PARADOX AND INTELLIGENCE AXIOM

Two little known characteristics of the intelligence function are the "intelligence paradox" and the "intelligence axiom." A paradox is an assertion that exhibits seemingly inexplicable or contradictory aspects. In tactical situations it occurs when a commander acts on good intelligence to avoid an undesirable event, and if effective, prevents it from happening. Thus, it appears as though the intelligence predicting it was in error. For example, let's say that reliable intelligence is received that a gang fight will occur after a school sporting event. In order to prevent it, a commander saturates the area with extra patrol coverage, stops and interrogates known gang members, or even cancels the sporting event. As a result, the fight is prevented and it appears as if the intelligence was wrong. This is an example of the **intelligence paradox**. It is a paradox in that the better the intelligence predicting an undesirable event, the less likely it is to occur if properly acted upon.

The other characteristic is the intelligence axiom. An axiom is a self-evident or universally recognized truth. The **intelligence axiom** manifests itself in tactical environments because the value of the information necessary for effective tactical decisions is often proportionate to the difficulty in obtaining and evaluating it. This happens because tactical environments are not only dynamic but satisfactory resolutions are inherently encumbered with harsh time constraints. Gaining good, thorough intelligence is often an intensive and time-consuming process. Yet, waiting for the intelligence requires decisions to be delayed, which may then be rendered ineffective because the situation will have changed. This is a fundamental predicament that confronts every commander at one time or another. It stands to reason then, that the faster and easier relevant

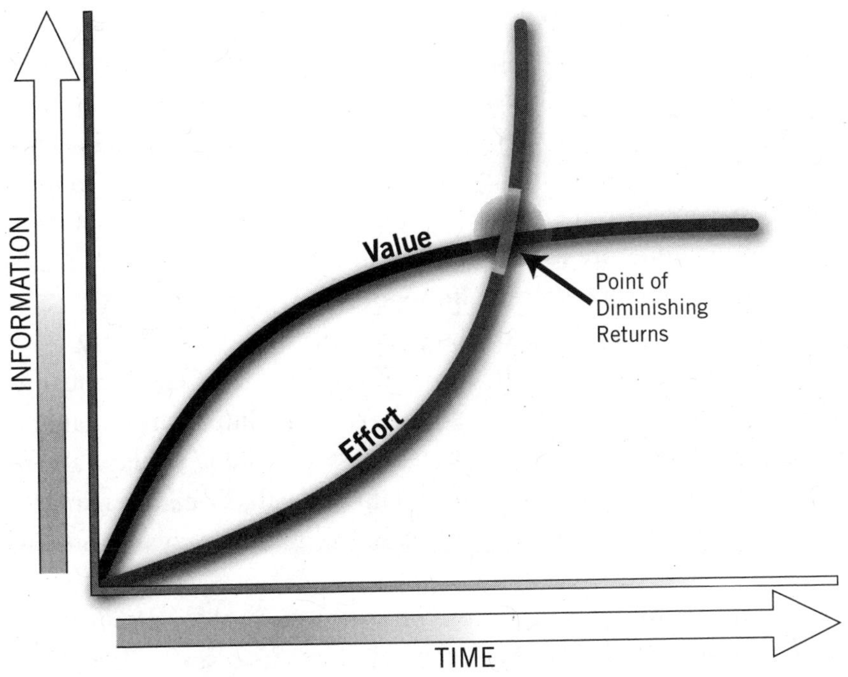

FIGURE 9-3 INTEL AXIOM: Information is essential for planning and decision making but with crises the time necessary to achieve certainty is never available. Initially, any information is useful because it enables decision making while the effort to obtain it is minimal. Later, as a decision maker becomes more aware of the factors and influences in play, additional information provides less and less insight and understanding while the effort to obtain it becomes increasingly difficult. At some point the effort to gain more useful information exceeds its value. Further attempts then are not only unproductive, but even counterproductive, in that effort that can better be used elsewhere is wasted. Thus, it can be seen that anything that reduces the effort automatically increases the value because even information of marginal value can be quickly identified and discarded.

The effort to quickly obtain useful information can be greatly reduced by capturing and storing it for later use, using a trained staff with specialized skills and expertise to seek and evaluate it, using technology to analyze, display and compare data and utilizing tools of analysis to gain insight and understanding.

information can be incorporated into the decision making process, the more value, and the greater impact it will have on the ultimate resolution. Thus an axiom is revealed which states that anything that decreases the effort in obtaining information automatically increases its value.

There are four predominant methods used to decrease the effort. The first, and most popular, is by *expediting access*. This is most often accomplished by arranging information that has been predetermined to have value for easier and faster access. This can be as simple as compiling a phone list with all relevant phone numbers provided in some easily understood arrangement. Other methods include pre-identifying points of contact, subject matter experts, or indexing after-action reports for reference.

Technology is now providing an even more powerful tool for expediting access via the Internet. With the use of email and the World Wide Web, vast amounts of relevant information can be "book-marked" for almost instant access, providing the latest traffic and weather reports, statistical data and subject matter experts. The amount and variety of information obtained in this manner is virtually unlimited.

The second method is by *incorporating specialized skills and expertise*. This always requires a trained staff. Personnel who understand the critical need for certain types of information are more adept and resourceful in obtaining it. They avoid ineffectual searches, duplication of effort and other unproductive efforts. They also tend to be more intuitive in seeking and discerning relevance from a hodgepodge of random data.

The third method is with *technology*. The use of computers to gather, store, analyze and display data is the most well-known. Of particular benefit for prolonged operations or situations with precedents, is the use of databases and spreadsheets to track, analyze, compare and display information in a variety of ways. Other technological advances provide abilities to see in the dark, hear through walls, avoid detection, or silently communicate. In fact, the use of technology to increase the ability to gather and analyze information is limited only by imagination.

The fourth method is by *using analysis tools*. These provide an enhanced ability to quickly discern and display relevant information from a jumble of loose data. They do not have to be complicated or sophisticated. For instance, the use of a standard format is one of the most efficient methods for reducing effort, because it automatically arranges information into categories. This is especially important with field reports from untrained observers because it provides a mental checklist to ensure that nothing significant is overlooked. It also provides an easy reporting arrangement to allow analysts to quickly review a large number of reports for a specific piece of information, without having to read entire documents. Matrices, checklists, spreadsheets, databases, maps, diagrams, charts and graphs, are other examples of analysis tools for determining relevancy and integrating information into usable forms.

SEVEN CHARACTERISTICS OF GOOD INTELLIGENCE[87]

While there are many factors for vetting information, seven predominate. The first characteristic is that intelligence must be *objective*. Objective intelligence is as free as possible from personal prejudices, distortions, feelings or interpretations. Because information can almost always be interpreted more than one way it is difficult to factor out human predilections with absolute certainty. Even the choice of words in a report can skew the understanding. For example, consider the subtle but meaningful differences between words like anger, rage, fury, or wrath. It is critical that information intended to brief a decision maker precisely convey meaning without bias.

The second characteristic is that intelligence must be *thorough*. Being thorough does not mean exhaustive, only that the information is sufficient to allow a decision maker to draw reliable conclusions. Indeed, it is impossible to completely remove uncertainty in tactical situations. Consequently, while attempts must always be made to reduce it, insistence on "all the facts" dooms the response to one of reaction because the situation will change faster than it can be exhaustively evaluated.

The third characteristic is *accuracy*. Accuracy simply means that the information is factually correct. Because it is impossible to be exhaustive, accuracy becomes all the more important since decisions will need to be made on whatever information is available.

The fourth characteristic is *timeliness*. Timeliness is so critical to good intelligence that the adage of "late is the same as absent" is often quoted to emphasize this aspect. Some types of information are so time sensitive that they are immediately relayed to decision makers without being thoroughly vetted. For example, reports of a suspect outside a containment may be relayed right to the incident commander prior to verification since if the information is correct actions must be taken immediately.

The fifth characteristic is that intelligence must be *usable*. While this may seem self-evident, it is becoming increasingly complicated as we rely more and more on electronic data. Besides the variety of portable storage devices like CDs, DVDs, USB flash drives, and so forth, are the number of incompatible software applications. Usable also means that it provides a decision maker with a clear and concise understanding without any additional investment in time and effort. At a minimum, this means that standard formats for intelligence reports and summaries should be mandatory, and ideally, text is augmented with graphics, maps, photographs, diagrams and charts.

The sixth characteristic is that it needs to be as *relevant* as possible. While it is easy to think of relevant in absolute terms, it is not that easy, especially with large and prolonged operations. Not all intelligence is equally significant to every organizational function or component. Moreover, even with the same intelligence, different echelons of the response organization are going to need different degrees of detail. Because an intrinsic attribute of information is that it is a consumer (in that it consumes human attention), overloading a decision maker with superfluous or immaterial information is not only distracting but counterproductive.

The seventh characteristic is that intelligence must be *available*. This means that it must be accessible and in a usable format to provide understanding for decision makers. Some intelligence is so sensitive that it must be kept secret; but secrecy is the antithesis to availability. Consequently, the intelligence apparatus must be designed to provide protection for sensitive information without denying access to decision makers who need it.

PRIORITY OF INTELLIGENCE CHARACTERISTICS

To a greater or lesser degree, each of these characteristics is required for good intelligence but they are not all equal all the time. For example, in some circumstances the importance of timeliness can trump the need for it to be objective and thorough. Similarly, when assessing information before it becomes intelligence the value can be greatly degraded, or even rendered worthless, when one of the characteristics is lacking. For example, what can be accurate can also be irrelevant and what can be objective can still be inaccurate. The process of vetting information before using it as intelligence requires a process in which the information is automatically corroborated, verified and validated. Corroboration means that it is available from more than one source without serious contradiction.[88] Verified identifies the need to examine it for accuracy. For example, an informant or witness can be telling the truth and still be mistaken. Validating the information may be thought of as an official stamp of approval by the agency or unit providing the intelligence. It is a declaration of the legitimacy, accuracy or worth of the information. It goes without saying that the reputation of the individual or unit validating the information is inherently and permanently associated with the intelligence.

It would seem that in this information age—when voluminous amounts of data are instantly available in any number of formats—that the difficulties in obtaining good intelligence would be greatly diminished. Such is not the case, however. In reality, the volume of available information has compounded the problem because what we have is information when what we need is understanding.

FIELD INTELLIGENCE REPORTS

All command posts rely heavily upon reports from field units for news about an incident. The larger the incident and the more spontaneous it occurs, the more heavily these field units are depended upon to provide firsthand information on the state of affairs. Sometimes called a "windshield survey," the raw but timely information is relayed back to a central collection point for evaluation and analysis. A problem arises however, when this information is received without an established format. Without some orderly arrangement, facts are jumbled together and the entire document must be read in its entirety to glean pertinent details. The problem is particularly acute when the operation is extremely large or prolonged because the relevant is obscured by the volume.

A term familiar to many military personnel but almost unknown in law enforcement circles is the "SALUTE Report." A **SALUTE report** is a field observation report that provides information about a specific occurrence in a standardized format. This allows an observer to go through a mental checklist when examining a situation and ensures that nothing of significance is omitted. It also makes it easier for an intelligence analyst to process a much greater amount of information, as well as make more accurate assessments and more precise forecasts.

Each of the six letters of the report represents a different factor in the observation and is arranged in the acronym "SALUTE" to make them easy to remember.

S stands for **size.** Size refers to the size, extent or magnitude of the event. In a civil disorder it might refer to the number of members of a mob. In a fire it might describe the number of acres or structures involved.

A identifies the particular **activity.** This is merely a description of the particular observation. It could be a fire, flood, looting or any combination.

L pinpoints the **location.** The location should always be given as precisely as possible. When addresses are not available, mile markers or distance and direction from prominent terrain features can be used. If the incident is dynamic, the direction and approximate speed it is moving should also be provided. For example, a report of a protest march would identify the location where the situation was first observed and then the direction and estimated speed the protesters are moving. Fires and floods are other examples of incidents that might require a direction.

U refers to **unit or uniform.** This section describes who or what is involved and what they look like. Whenever possible, a precise identification is preferred but when that is not possible a detailed description is substituted. For example, in a civil disorder, a particular gang might be recognized, or in a demonstration, a particular union or activist group. If it is a thing, it prompts the observer to identify it. In a flood, it might describe the origin of the water, e.g. a broken dam, overflowing river, reservoir, and so forth.

T defines the **time and duration** of the incident. This is the time that the observer first noticed the event or, if it is concluded, the time that it was observed. When an event is ongoing or continued for a period of time, the time it first was first noticed is provided with the duration of the observation. Time is critical to an intelligence analyst to avoid making assessments on "stale" information as well as to avoid confusing a single incident that is described more than once by a number of observers.

E identifies any **equipment or weapons** involved. An observer might note that a bunch of demonstrators were carrying placards, banners or flags during a protest. In an incident that didn't involve people this component may not be applicable but should be noted as such. No sections should be left blank. This avoids confusion as to whether something was not applicable or was just overlooked.

In large incidents, SALUTE reports may be categorized by the type of observation into separate intelligence logs; for example, road closures, damaged buildings, fires, broken water mains, gas leaks, etc. This greatly facilitates an intelligence analyst's task of compiling critical information and yields an abundance of useful "prepackaged" intelligence. The SALUTE report is easy to learn and is one of the most overlooked yet valuable tools a tactical commander can utilize to yield useful intelligence without an elaborate informational gathering mechanism.

---

82. Winston Churchill; Note to the Chief of the Imperial General Staff, 24 November 1940. Churchill wrote this in a note to General John Dill in the darkest hours of World War II. One important lesson learned here is that despite the expected bleak report, it was necessary to get an accurate picture. This lesson should likewise not be overlooked in modern times.

83. These terms may be considered antiquated in light of the adoption by the military community of terms like "Commander's Critical Information Requirements (CCIR)" and "Priority Information Requirement (PIR)," but in keeping with the goal of explaining the science in the simplest terms possible the original terms provide more clarity and understanding for an introductory text book.
84. For ease of understanding only four steps are described but many military texts identify five steps by separating the processing and production steps into separate components. Still others add a sixth step called "utilization," which refers to the exploitation of the intelligence.
85. "Loose data" refers to disjointed bits and pieces of information of undetermined value.
86. Not only can some information be useless, it can be a distraction.
87. Nearly all of this material is taken from "Intelligence," Marine Corps Doctrinal Publication 2, (MCDP-2) Headquarters United States Marine Corps, Department of the Navy, Washington D.C., 20380-1775
88. It is not unusual to have minor discrepancies between two more sources of information, especially when people are the observers.

LOGISTICS

Logistics comprises the means and arrangements which work out the plans of strategy and tactics. Strategy decides where to act; logistics brings the troops to this point.

—ANTOINE-HENRI JOMINI[89]

THE LOGISTICS FUNCTION IS RESPONSIBLE FOR THE ACQUISITION, identification, tracking, staging and recovery of all personnel, assets and resources. It provides the "service and support" function[90] for all operations. Additionally, this function determines future logistical needs, identifies and acquires resources and provides any required maintenance to ensure sustainment of the operation. Logistics answers operational questions like, "Who?" "What?" "How much?" "How far?" And, "How long?"

There is an old ditty that goes:

For want of a nail the shoe was lost,
for want of a shoe the horse was lost,
for want of a horse the general was lost,
for want of a general the battle was lost,
for want of a battle the war was lost.[91]

It clearly identifies and emphasizes the importance of logistics. Nevertheless, in law enforcement tactical operations, logistics is frequently the underdog when compared with more glamorous functions like operations or intelligence. Nevertheless, without a logistics capability tactical operations as a deliberate and organized activity become impossible because logistics sets the limits on what is operationally feasible. Cars can only go so far without gas and people can work only so long without food and rest. The most brilliantly planned and executed operation will be ultimately be stymied if the logistics function is neglected. This emphasizes the importance of sustaining operations, which is an implied responsibility of the logistics component. Sustainment refers to the responsibility to install, maintain and operate logistical support. This may require food, water, fuel, dedicated operators, technicians, mechanics, electricians or maintenance personnel and so forth. For example, when a commander calls for a helicopter, it should be assumed he or she also wants the pilot and fuel to fly it. Sustainment may also require making reliefs, assigning shifts and other essential planning measures to assure the continued support of a piece of equipment and deployed personnel. Once the operation reaches a conclusion, it is also responsible for servicing and returning equipment from lenders and/or staging areas.

Of all the functions in a tactical operation, logistics is the most scientific. Precise calculations are not only possible in logistics, but absolutely necessary. Items must be counted, distances must be measured and formulas and algorithms are necessary to predict things like the time it takes to move a given distance, the amount of food and fuel that will be necessary, and the number and types of equipment and weapons that must be available when needed. Consequently, the most valuable tools of logisticians are more likely to be spreadsheets, databases, status boards, and checklists rather than weapons.

THE LOGISTICAL PROCESS

The logistical function can be divided into four general roles, the fulfillment of each of which is necessary to achieve a satisfactory solution. The first is procurement. **Procurement** identifies the need to obtain the essential equipment, weapons, supplies, consumables and personnel. This will require a detailed knowledge of what tools and equipment will be necessary as well as where they are located and how to obtain them. Generically, the term used to describe this equipment is **materiel**, which identifies the aggregate of all things needed in a venture. Materiel is generally divided into two distinct groups, assets and resources. **Assets** identifies equipment, tools, weapons, personnel and the like, that are owned by an organization. **Resources**, on the other hand, identify those that are available but not owned by the organization. When materiel is needed but is unavailable, the logistics function is responsible for purchasing, leasing or borrowing it.

Arguably, the duties related to personnel are the most important, most complex and most labor-intensive of any of the logistical responsibilities. People are "high maintenance" items. They not only need to be fed, clothed, equipped, and paid, but they need rest and relief, not to mention matching their individual skills and abilities to appropriate tasks and assignments. Furthermore, the assignment of some personnel is integral with a request for equipment; for example, pilots with aircraft, paramedics with ambulances, bus drivers with buses, heavy equipment operators with bulldozers, and so forth.

Procurement is almost always a strategic function because much of the equipment needed in tactical operations is specialized in nature. Likewise, the necessity to pre-identify facilities and the use of pre-arranged loans, leases and contracts or the need to access reserve funds requires the efforts of personnel at the highest levels of the parent organization.

The second logistical role is distribution. Having the right equipment and personnel is not enough. It must also be at the right place and time to be of any use. **Distribution** involves the dispersing of equipment and personnel to where they are most needed and when. The distribution role is a diverse process that encompasses both strategic and tactical means since some equipment and supplies may require efforts at the highest level of the parent organization yet will be issued and used at the lowest levels. An important characteristic of the distribution role is that it competes with the recovery role at the end of an operation. Mistakes, inaccuracies and oversights made during distribution make it difficult, if not impossible, to correct when the logistical focus of effort shifts to recovery.

How distribution is accomplished tends to fall within two categories. **Centralized distribution** employs supply dumps, staging areas and issue points to which individuals and deployed units are expected to provide their own transportation to collect their supplies. Certain types of supplies will benefit from centralization. Fluids, like water and fuel, for one example, are more easily transported in large fuel or water trucks and then distributed in smaller containers and/or by refueling vehicles at a disaster scene. Likewise, specialized equipment, batteries or ammunition that are unique to a particular specialty or are only occasionally needed do not normally need wide dispersion.

Decentralized distribution issues equipment directly to an individual and/or a deployed unit. Like the centralized approach, some types of equipment are more amenable for individual issue. For example, equipment that comes in individual sizes or needs to be adjusted or modified for individual needs; like gun belts, gas masks and load bearing vests, become cumbersome and time consuming when they have to be readjusted for each new use. Similarly, those that have sanitary issues like ear plugs and protective masks are better issued to each individual. Serialized equipment that is specialized, fragile or expensive is another example, since the individual to whom they are issued becomes personally responsible for their safeguarding and return. Because the logistics component is responsible for disbursing the equipment this method has the inherent obligation of providing sufficient vehicles of the proper size and type to ensure that the right equipment is provided in a timely manner.

Sustainment is the third logistical role and ensures that the maintenance, replenishment and/or replacement of equipment, consumables and personnel are accomplished to ensure uninterrupted operations. The concept of sustainment has been understood as critical to success in tactical operations for nearly two millennia. Its importance was stated most succinctly by the Roman poet, Aulus Persius Flaccus as "He conquers who endures."[92] Failures here are usually as a result of either ignorance or neglect but manifest themselves in innumerable ways. Some of the most common in law enforcement operations include personnel assignments without scheduled relief, food or water, vehicles with no refueling available or radios and portable electronic equipment with no batteries or recharging capabilities. A lack of ability to sustain operations is also nearly always a critical vulnerability for suspects.

There are four main areas required to sustain operations. The first is **replenishment,** which refers to refilling or resupplying what is lacking. The most common area where this occurs in tactical operations is with consumables, such as fuel, food, batteries, ammunition and the like. The second is **replacement,** which refers to providing substitutes for damaged or destroyed equipment, vehicles and so forth. The third is **reliefs** of personnel and the fourth is **reconstitution** of units when degraded by injuries, fatigue, and the like.

The fourth and final logistical role is **recovery** and identifies those efforts focusing on the return of all equipment and personnel to their proper place and condition at the conclusion of the operation. This role will usually necessitate not only the efforts in collecting tools and equipment, but in repackaging, replenishing, replacing and/or restoring them to a place and condition so that they will be available for future operations. Mistakes made during distribution are manifested here and are sometimes irreversible. For example, many emergency expenses are reimbursable from disaster funds but failing to record fuel levels for equipment or collect mileage from vehicles used in an operation before they are deployed may forever forfeit the ability to make claim them. Likewise, extended operations with numerous personnel make it exceedingly difficult to recall and record individual hours and overtime expenses without earlier planning and preparation.

BASIC TASKS

The logistics function is always a work in progress. Demand will nearly always exceed supply. And, even when personnel, supplies and equipment are available, circumstances are always changing and the means to distribute and recover them must be continually refined. Friction is omnipresent and turmoil is always looming. To maintain order in the logistics function, the virtues are economy, accountability, standardization and regularity. In supporting the four logistical roles are six basic tasks.

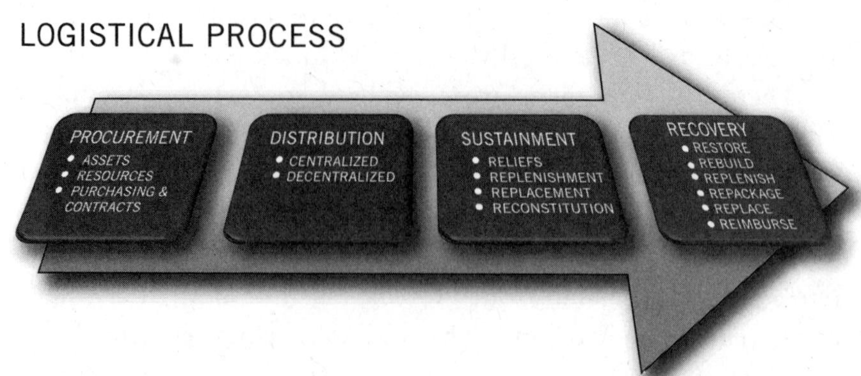

FIGURE 10-1 LOGISTICAL PROCESS: Of all the staff functions, logistics is the most scientific, so much so that it can be intimidating to those unfamiliar with it. This graphic depicts the logistical process in a simple manner. The four boxes in the center are the four essential roles. The procurement role is focused on gathering materiel by staging assets or borrowing resources. When necessary, it may also be purchased, rented, borrowed or leased. Distribution will then be needed to disperse the personnel and materiel to where they are needed. Whether it is more efficient to use a decentralized or centralized method of distribution depends on the nature of the equipment and type of supplies, as well as where, when and how they will be used. Once an operation is underway the logistics function is responsible for ensuring sustainment. This will always include the relief of tired personnel; replenishment of consumables, like food, water, batteries, and fuel; replacement of broken equipment or injured personnel; and reconstitution of units depleted by injuries and/or broken equipment. Finally, when the operation is completed, it is the logistics function that is responsible for the recovery of all equipment, ensuring it remains serviceable and either returning or staging it for future use.

Manning is directly supportive of activities involved with personnel. In the simplest terms, manning refers to the posting of people at the right place and time with the right equipment. It also requires that personnel be relieved when fatigued, hungry or hurt to avoid interruptions and stalling an operation. Lead time will need to be computed and applied to avoid tardiness and lag time will be needed to return equipment and travel to staging areas.

Arming refers to providing appropriate weapons, ammunition and related equipment. This always requires a "match-up" in both compatible equipment and trained personnel. Cartridge size, magazines, scopes, carrying cases and shipping containers must be appropriate for the particular weapon. Likewise, assigned personnel must be appropriately trained and currently qualified to use a particular weapon.

Fueling is necessary for all engines and is often referred to in the military as P-O-L, which stands for Petroleum, Oils and Lubricants. Like the arming task, fueling requires a match-up in that some engines are diesel, some take unleaded gas while some require aviation fuel. Besides the conventional fossil fuels, however, this task also includes all types of power sources, to include batteries for radios, flashlights, and night vision goggles.

Fixing is necessary to ensure that all equipment remains operational. Besides repairs, some types of equipment need calibration and maintenance to ensure continued operations. Equipment that has been deployed is often easier to fix in the field rather than bring to a garage or repair facility and so "contact teams" of mechanics, electricians, carpenters and other specialists may be necessary. In modern times, this task includes computer experts who are capable of onsite restoration of services.

Moving is a logistics task that refers to the necessity of moving personnel and equipment to where they are needed. Sometimes this will require dedicated vehicles, such as buses, trucks, aircraft, boats, and even individual radio cars; all of which are the responsibility of the logistics component. Some equipment requires specialized vessels and containers, such as water bulls (water trailers) and fuel trucks. Those vehicles and vessels that can be used for more than one task will require a prioritization of assignments. This task also includes medical evacuations and so ambulances and medevac helicopters may be necessary.

Protecting is a comprehensive logistical task that refers to safeguarding, shielding and preserving all materiel and personnel. It is comprised of two distinct duties. The first identifies the necessity for safeguarding all staged personnel and equipment. This includes protection from everything from adverse weather conditions to physical threats. Once deployed, this task falls naturally to the deployed unit but while they are being gathered, staged and assigned the logistics function is responsible. This duty also includes security for command posts and staging areas. The second duty is in protecting personnel from hazards and unnecessary risks. This means gathering and issuing safety equipment, such as earplugs, eye protection, hard hats, masks, sun screen, or whatever else is needed. Likewise, "comfort equipment" such as rain suits, warm clothing, hot food, portable toilets, and the like fall within this task.

IMPLIED LOGISTICAL TASKS

More than any of the other functions, logistics will require specialized equipment and subject matter experts, many of whom are not a part of any responding agency. While almost never explicitly assigned, the expectation (implied task) is that the logistics function provides a person qualified and capable of performing a given assignment. This requires a "reachback" capability. **Reachback** refers to the process of obtaining products, services, forces and equipment from organizations that are not deployed and may not even be otherwise involved in the operation or response. Well thought-out preparations are essential to an effective and efficient reachback capability and include memorandums of understanding, interagency agreements, prearranged contracts, reserve funds, preidentified subject matter experts, and so forth. Failing to consider these requirements ahead of time tremendously complicates the process and lengthens the time it will take when they are needed.

From a logistical standpoint, personnel account for the lion's share of logistical effort. Even when not being utilized, all personnel are consumers and will require food, water, rest and even comfort. As opposed to the military community, in the civilian world personnel also have to be paid, which complicates the assignment still further, especially since most responses to disasters and critical incidents will also include at least some personnel working overtime. In fact, it has been said that the first duty of the logistical component is the welfare of the troops. The success of the entire logistics component is often judged on this single factor.

Another implied task is finance. At higher echelons, finance is usually a separate function, in and of itself, but in the field it is an implied task for the logistics component. While most tactical operations will not require a separate finance assignment, nearly all responses to disaster will. This is because the expenses incurred

FIGURE 10-2 LOGISTICS TASKS: This graphic identifies the six most common tasks associated with the logistics function. Manning refers to all activities in support of personnel. It not only includes having the right person with the right tools at the right place at the right time, but feeding them when hungry and relieving them when tired. Arming identifies the need of matching the right ammunition with the right weapons, as well as any associated equipment. Fueling includes both the fuel for engines, but all necessary lubricants. Like the arming function, this also requires matching the types of fuels and lubricants to particular engines. Fixing will always be necessary because equipment doesn't break in storage. Accordingly, plans and preparations for repair and maintenance in the field are essential to ensure they remain serviceable. Moving identifies the need to have the appropriate people and equipment at the places and times needed. This can be extremely complicated in that it often involves disparate vehicles ranging from buses to pick-up trucks, or even boats and helicopters, which are also needed for other assignments. Protecting is a dual role. Besides identifying the need for safeguarding all personnel and equipment it also refers to protection from hazards encountered while deployed. Depending on the situation, this may require issuing gas masks or protective clothing.

from disaster are often recoverable from state and federal governments if properly tracked and documented. This is especially critical for those expenses that may not be later captured or reconstructed from data such as personnel overtime and vehicle mileage.

LOGISTICAL STRATEGIES

Strategies for logistics tend to fall into two categories. The first employs an active strategy by advocating a "push" system. A **logistical push system**[93] places responsibility on the logistics section for providing all necessary support to a deployed unit. Supplies and personnel reliefs are usually assigned, moved and distributed according to a schedule based upon an estimate of need by the logistics component. A push system has several advantages, not the least of which is that they relieve a busy commander involved at a disaster or crime scene from the burden of identifying what is needed and when. Accordingly, it works well at the initial stages of a major operation because the types and quantity of support can be more easily determined and provided without requiring detailed instructions. Notwithstanding, a push system tends to be inefficient in that the situational awareness for the logistics section is always somewhat lacking compared to the units at the scene where the supplies are actually needed. This makes accurate estimates difficult. Consequently, shortages of some kind are nearly inevitable. Conversely, too much or too many of something create their own problems.

The second strategy is reactive in nature and advocates a "pull" system. A **logistical pull system**[94] places responsibility on the supported unit for requesting logistical support. This means that all resupplies, maintenance, calibration, reliefs, and so forth, are "pulled" by requesting them as needed. A pull system enjoys the advantage of having the "issue owner" directly responsible for their own logistical support. While the logistics component is responsible for acquiring and delivering it, the deployed unit is wholly responsible for determining what or whom is needed and when. Because personnel and supplies are requested as needed this method tends to be more efficient because the estimates are based on actual consumption rates and the deployed unit gets only the support they need.

Because both strategies have their own drawbacks and advantages, effective logistical support will nearly always require a combination. Push systems are often preferred at the onset of large responses and later modified to pull systems when sufficient personnel arrive and can better estimate need. Moreover, after reliable communications have been established an amalgamation of the two methods can be accomplished with collaboration between the deployed unit and the logistics section. In fact, large operations often assign logistical specialists to a deployed unit to calculate need, coordinate support, make requests and even distribute supplies. In this manner, the disadvantages of both methods are greatly diminished.

---

89. General Antoine-Henri Jomini, *Precis de l'Art de la Guerre* (The Art of War), 1838
90. The term "service and support" is used by the U.S. Army to identify the fourth component in a tactical plan. The U.S. Marine Corps identifies it as the "administrative and logistics" section.
91. Although this poem has been around for hundreds of years and has been paraphrased many times the original author remains unknown. Tradition holds that it refers to Richard III of England at the Battle of Bosworth Field in 1485 during which his horse became mired in mud. It is reported that King Richard famously shouted, "A Horse! A Horse! My Kingdom for a horse!" as depicted in Act V, Scene 4 in Shakespeare's play, *Richard III*, written around 1591. Regardless, its relevance remains valid to this day.
92. Aulos Persius Flaccus, 34-62 A.D.
93. Sometimes referred to as a "supply-push system"
94. Sometimes referred to as a "demand-pull system"

COMMUNICATIONS

Congress makes a man a general but communications makes him a commander.

—GENERAL OMAR BRADLEY[95]

IT IS IMPOSSIBLE TO IMAGINE EVEN THE SIMPLEST TACTICAL operation or emergency response in which information is not shared in some manner. Indeed, in these types of situations lacking an ability to share information may render it completely useless! Communications is called the "voice of command" for good reason. You cannot command when you cannot communicate. Accordingly, communications is a command responsibility. In fact, communications is so essential to the success of any tactical operation that the military considers command, control and communications nearly inseparable and signifies their relationship with the abbreviation "C^3." Many a fiasco has been averted when communications enabled corrective measures in a rapidly changing situation.

Communications refers to any method of conveying information from one person or place to another to improve understanding. Thus the term is exhaustive and includes everything from speech and writing to signals and gestures.[96] How it is accomplished is secondary. There are many "moving parts" for even the most simple tactical organization and there is no doubt that command and control are the underpinnings of any successful response. Notwithstanding, communications is both the glue that binds everything together and the lubricant that reduces the friction between the many components. Commanders who neglect the importance of communications do so at their own peril. While communications has never been one of the components of a Napoleonic staff, per se, it has always been an inherent necessity. Nowadays, all modern military staffs have a separate communications component specifically assigned to establish and maintain communications throughout an operation.

COMMUNICATIONS OBJECTIVE

Communications may be thought of as a "data stream," and the "flow of information" varies in volume and direction depending on how it is to be used. Understandably, a greater volume flows through command posts than deployed units. Moreover, the volume and type of communications, as well as the means by which it is sent tends to change with the echelons of command. Even without an understanding of exactly what information is being transferred, headquarters units can be identified fairly easily by observing the volume of communications traffic routed through them.[97] Ideally, the information in the data stream can be tapped by any authorized person, whether specifically intended for them or not. This allows the information to become shared knowledge.[98] This is seldom practical, however, and efforts must be made to ensure the right information is routed to the right people.

It is not the amount of information that is important, however, but rather the amount of understanding. Gaining understanding is the objective of every communication. Nowadays information is available as emails, text messages, telephone conversations, letters, cards, briefings, reports, radio messages, ad infinitum. Too much information or information in an unusable format is a distraction. Information that doesn't directly contribute to understanding is often referred to as "noise" and the concept used to describe this situation is referred to as the "signal to noise ratio." The **signal to**

noise ratio compares the amount of useful information with the amount of useless information. The higher the ratio the more difficult it is to comprehend. As a general rule of thumb, any information that doesn't contribute to better understanding is noise and should be avoided.

REQUIREMENTS FOR COMMUNICATIONS

There are four fundamental and interrelated requirements for an effective communications system. These are reliability, security, speed and flexibility. **Reliability** assures that communications will function when needed and depends heavily on careful planning and dependable equipment. Reliability not only means that equipment must be in good repair and properly maintained but that batteries are fresh. Because no equipment or system is infallible this critical requirement may require redundancy; that is more than one means of moving information between the concerned parties.

Security refers to the precautions taken to deny unauthorized persons information of value that could be used to adversely affect an operation. Security measures are all encompassing and include anything that might expose information to unauthorized parties.[99] Thus, this requirement includes everything from encrypting sensitive messages during transmission to safeguarding messages and reports and even casual conversations in the presence of third parties.

Speed is somewhat relative in that it describes the time it takes to move a message from a sender to a recipient. While it would be nice to have every message instantaneously delivered from a sender to the recipients, in reality this is often impractical, especially when more than one method may be required to move the same information. This frequently occurs when the sender is at a command post and the recipient is deployed in the field. For example, a message may start as text, then be transmitted by radio or telephone, transcribed back to text, and then delivered by messenger. When more than one message must be sent using the same means it is sometimes necessary to prioritize which are more important and send those first. This concept is called "precedence," and with few exceptions is the responsibility of the sender to identify how rapidly a message must be delivered.[100] To be effective, information must arrive in time to be of value. Too late is the same as absent.

Flexibility is the ability to both support a wide dispersion of units as well as adapt to adverse and varying conditions. Like the reliability requirement, flexibility is often achieved with redundancy; that is by duplicating communications channels so that if one fails another is available. Moreover, some types of information are better suited for one type of transmission than another. For example, physical descriptions are better transmitted by a means that provides a photograph and directions are better understood when accompanied by a map. Likewise, while large sets of numbers can be transmitted by radio or telephone it is far easier and more accurate to provide them as an email or even a hard copy. Thus, a system that provides a variety of methods for passing messages is not only more versatile but more efficient.

While these four requirements are interrelated, they are not always compatible. Tactical conditions will almost always require some trade-offs, but of the four, reliability is the most critical. While compromises may be necessary with security, speed and flexibility, any tactical organization that cannot rely on its communications quickly loses confidence, cohesion and focus.

FORMS OF COMMUNICATION

Regardless of the method used to transfer information, there are only four forms of communication. These are signals, numbers, graphics and language. A **signal** is anything that serves to indicate, warn or direct some event or action. Signals come in all forms but the most common include sounds, lights and gestures. Unlike the other three methods of communicating, signals must almost always be pre-identified to avoid confusion. The rare exceptions are those gestures that are so common as to be considered "assertive conduct;" that is, conduct intended as communication. Examples include nodding or shaking the head for "yes" or "no" or shrug-

FIGURE 11-1 COMMUNICATION REQUIREMENTS: An effective communications system is vital for a successful tactical operation. In designing and operating such a system there are four essential and interrelated requirements. The first, and most important, is reliability. Reliability assures that communications will be available when needed. The second is security. Security is focused on the precautions to protect the information while it is being transmitted. Speed is the third requirement and is critical because in tactical operations, late is the same as absent. Last, but certainly not least, is flexibility. Flexibility refers to the ability to adapt and maintain communications through varying and adverse conditions.

ging the shoulders for "I don't know." Of note, however, is that many of these expressions are culturally contextual; indicating that they may mean something else in the context of another culture. Notwithstanding, signals are an instantaneous and powerful method to quickly convey information in chaotic circumstances.

The second form of communicating is with numbers. **Numbers** refer to the concept of quantity. Numbers have the advantage of conveying precision more than any other method or combination of methods because they impart a precise value. In tactical operations and emergency responses, numbers provide comparisons and answer questions like how long, how much, how far, and even when.

The third form of communicating is by the use of graphics. **Graphics** are images of all types. Images can be actual representations of objects or scenes or, just as useful, abstract expressions and ideas. Examples of actual representations in tactical operations include maps, drawings, diagrams, photographs and charts. Examples of abstract graphic representations often include representations of time, processes and/or sequences, such as time lines, matrices and flow charts. Words alone can be ambiguous or confusing and subject to individual interpretation but become far more lucid when augmented with graphics.

The fourth and most common form of communicating is with language. **Language** used for communicating includes all its forms but primarily expressions provided either as text or verbally. Language is more complex than most people imagine in that it includes not only words but how they are expressed. People routinely, and even unconsciously, convey meaning by how they utter words with a combination of volume, sounds, enunciations, facial expressions, and posture. It is for this reason that meaning is easier to convey "face to face" than over communication devices like radio, telephone, email and the like.

Some forms of communication easily lend themselves to transmission by one method of communications but not another. Computers, for example are excellent for text and graphics, but signals and language are more difficult. Radios and telephones are excellent for signals and language but poor for text and graphics. Furthermore, tactical situations will always dictate what type equipment is suitable. For instance, even the most portable laptop computer is awkward in tactical settings and radios in a busy command post can be distracting. Consequently, a good communications system uses the advantages of one method to offset the disadvantages of another.

COMMUNICATIONS SYSTEMS

A **communications system** is a group of independent but interrelated elements necessary for establishing, maintaining and operating communications that make up a unified whole. They include the various methods for transmitting information and the myriad configurations these take on and are limited only by the imagination and resourcefulness of the planner. Over the ages, information has been conveyed with smoke, bugles, drums, flags, messengers, and even birds. Nowadays, computers, radios, telephones, and fax machines are taken for granted. When designing a communications system for disaster management or a tactical operation it is important to understand the underlying needs.

One of the most fundamental questions to be answered is whether the system should be primarily a collaborative or noncollaborative system. A **collaborative system** is one that requires compatible equipment or software for both the sender and recipients. A system that uses radios is a good example. Both the sender and the recipients must be equipped with compatible equipment and a common frequency. Collaborative systems are the norm for emergency responders but frequently result in mismatches when one agency or discipline cannot communicate with another simply because of incompatible equipment, especially radios.

A **noncollaborative system** is one that allows communication without requiring compatible equipment. Noncollaborative systems are especially useful when impromptu communications are required. A public address system for crowd control is an example of a noncollaborative communications system since the recipients do not need to have any special equipment, or even need to cooperate to receive communications. Likewise, the stench added to natural gas to alert anyone of a gas leak[101] is a noncollaborative communication. Other examples include red lights and sirens on ambulances, fire engines and police cars, fire alarms and the verbal warnings at the ends of escalators and the ends of moving sidewalks.

Nowadays, a third system that is a hybrid of the collaborative and noncollaborative systems is appearing. This is because telephones, televisions, radios, and computers have become nearly ubiquitous in the modern world. While the requirement for having compatible equipment would meet the definition of a collaborative system, their near universal availability coupled with common conventions, protocols and standards have resulted in all similar equipment working in harmony with one another.

While one good example is cell phones, nowhere is this more evident than on the World Wide Web, which provides unlimited opportunities for sharing information. While a computer with an internet connection and web browsing software is necessary it matters not which computer hardware, operating system, or web browser software is used because of protocols and conventions like TCP/IP, FTP and HTML.[102] In the same manner, technology is now available to call thousands of telephones simultaneously with emergency information to broadcast storm warnings, tornado alerts, spreading fires, noxious plumes, and so forth. As software and computers become more powerful, subject matter experts will be able to participate ad hoc in crisis decisions while watching videos annotated with text, graphics and sound in real-time from anywhere in the world and at any time.

Likewise, participants will not always be available at the same time. Thus, some method must be established to ensure that essential information is available for those who may not be available at a particular time or place. A **synchronous system** is one that requires all participants to communicate at the same time. Radios and telephones are examples of communications devices that are synchronous since when a sender transmits a message all the receivers must be listening at the same time. Likewise, meetings and briefings are methods of communicating that are synchronous. An **asynchronous system** is one that provides communications but does not require all participants to be involved at the same time. The best example of an asynchronous communications system is an email or text message. Either of these can be sent to one or many people who can then read it at and reply at their convenience.

COMMUNICATIONS NETWORKS

There are almost no communications systems that are exclusively collaborative or synchronous but rather some combination. How a communications system is intended on being used will determine what types of equipment will be needed and how it will be used. A component of a communications system is a communications network. In simple terms, a **communications network** is a group of communication stations linked by a common means of communicating. One way to understand a communication network is that it manages information. This means that only those members who are a part of the network can receive and transmit information with one another. Information on a network is disseminated through one of two methods. The first method is by broadcasting. Information that is **broadcast** is simultaneously sent to a wide audience—anyone with access to the network in fact. The main advantage of broadcasting is that it gets the information to the widest audience in the shortest amount of time with the least effort. Commercial television and radio networks are examples of broadcasting, as are newspapers and magazines. With an audience that has the same informational needs, broadcasting is an extremely efficient means of communicating and this method is often used during tactical operations and disaster responses for situation reports, weather reports, and for disseminating plans. This method can easily lead to information overload, however, especially without some controls on what information is sent and how often.

When an audience has a need for different types of information broadcasting becomes problematic and a "point-to-point" transmission is more efficient. This method is also called narrowcasting. Information that is **narrowcast** is sent to specific users who have a need for it. It is not unusual for some information to be resent from one user to another depending on need. Narrowcasting has two advantages over broadcasting. First, the information can be customized to fit the needs of the recipients. Second, because information is often resent depending on the needs of the user, each sender becomes a filter to provide the information needed without retransmitting the entire message.

That said, narrowcasting also has two disadvantages. The first is that it takes much longer to "saturate" a group with the necessary information since it must be sent more than one time. Second, every time a message is resent it increases the possibility of error and distortion.

One workaround for some of the disadvantages of both broadcasting and narrowcasting networks is a method that "pushes" information to all those who need to know but in a format that allows recipients to ignore data they deem irrelevant while being able to "pull" just the types of information that they desire. One of the best examples is a website where information is published for everyone to view. If the information needs to exclude some recipients then an intranet or extranet[103] can be used also. For example, a disaster management website can be installed on the Internet to inform the public on the status of operations, refugee information, first-aid, notifications and so forth. An extranet can then link identified recipients to sensitive information that should not be shared. In this way, information can be stored in a "repository" to be accessed and referenced as needed without burdening busy planners and decision makers with irrelevant information.

Networks can further be divided into channels. For most purposes, a **communications channel**[104] is the route and medium that links two or more stations. Stations may share more than one channel; for example, it is not unusual to have multiple command posts linked by radio, telephone, email and messengers, each of which constitutes a separate communications channel. Because of the fact that different echelons of command share functional responsibilities, like logistics, intelligence and operations, each of these may have a different radio frequency (channel), all of which terminate in the same stations.

---

95. General Omar N. Bradley, 1893-1981 General Bradley was the last surviving officer who held a five-star rank and the first Chairman of the Joint Chiefs of Staff
96. For purposes of this book, the communications term is limited to con-

notations of sharing information. The distinction is necessary in that the military community also uses the term to describe a line of supply.

97. This is a foundation for the military's signal intelligence, or "SIGINT." Many an enemy headquarters has been identified and targeted by simply noting the volume of information flowing to and from them.
98. This shared knowledge is the most critical component of a "common operational picture." A common operational picture is one of the best ways to create synergy.
99. The military sometimes identifies this effort by the acronym COMSEC, which stands for Communications Security.
100. The U.S. military use four-step precedence. "Routine" is the default and is sent through normal channels as soon as practical. A message marked "priority" would be sent before a routine message. "Immediate" (sometimes called "Operational Immediate") is sent before priority messages and as soon as possible. "Flash" identifies those messages that are so urgent that they precede all other messages and will be sent as soon as possible by any available means.
101. Natural gas is colorless, tasteless and odorless but highly flammable, even explosive. A chemical called mercaptan, which smells like rotten eggs or sulphur, is added to alert people to a dangerous leak.
102. Transmission Control Protocol (TCP) and the Internet Protocol (IP) are networking protocols that have become standard in modern networking. Likewise, File Transfer Protocol (FTP) is a standard for transferring a file from one computer to another and Hyper Text Markup Language (HTML) is the building block of all web pages. These conventions have largely overcome many of the incompatibility issues that require specific computers, software and other equipment.
103. An intranet is a computer network within a single agency or discipline. An extranet is a term used for a secure network on an internet. Both limit access to the information with the use of user identifications and passwords.
104. The term "communications channel" actually has more than one meaning. As used in this book, it describes the pathway between two or more stations but is also used to describe the physical medium that carries a signal. For example, radios and cell phones travel on radio frequency waves, while regular telephones use wire or fiber optic cables.

SECTION 4

SECTION 4

PLANNING AND DECISION MAKING

You think out every possible development and decide on the way to deal with the situation created. One of these developments occurs; you put your plan in operation, and everyone says, "What genius. . ."whereas the credit is really due to the labor of preparation.

—FERDINAND FOCH[105]

THERE IS A HUMOROUS ADAGE CALLED THE "7PS" WHICH states that "Proper Prior Planning Prevents Pathetically Poor Performance." While personnel and equipment constitute the physical elements used for resolving crises, how they are used is far more important. Ultimately, plans and decisions are vital in providing the essential guidance and continuity for adapting to continually changing circumstances. Planning and decision making go hand in hand. All plans require decisions and decisions, in and of themselves, are always part of a plan, even if informal and incomplete. The success or failure of nearly every tactical operation or disaster response can be directly attributed to one or both of these. Accordingly, an understanding of the complex interplay of the factors and influences involved in planning and decision making is of great value.

This section begins by explaining that the process of planning is more important than the plan itself! It continues with a concise explanation of how to conduct an operational analysis and its contribution to gaining the critical comprehension necessary to design a satisfactory resolution. It emphasizes the critical role of the senior commander in the process and explains how to provide the necessary guidance without having to personally supervise the details. Finally, because plans will need to be adapted to fit changing circumstances it explains how to add flexibility to plans.

The second chapter focuses on the plan itself. It describes the three types of plans and how each is used before explaining the five indispensable components of every plan. It continues with how plans are implemented and how to monitor their progress after they are underway. The chapter concludes with the three most common attachments to avoid having a written plan become instantly out of date when changes are necessary or more information becomes available.

The section concludes with the peculiarities associated with making decisions in crisis conditions. In particular, information is provided on how expertise is acquired. It also looks at how experts think differently and use information more efficiently. Thus, experts aren't smarter and don't think harder, they just think in more productive ways. The chapter closes with a discussion of common methods to increase the retention and comprehension of information as well as methods for improving decisions, especially under conditions where certainty is not entirely possible.

---

105. Marshal Ferdinand Foch: Interview, April 1919 as quoted in *Command Concepts: A Theory Derived from the Practice of Command and Control*, National Defense Research Institute, Carl H. Builder, Steven C. Bankes, Richard Nordin, RAND, 1999, p. 17 Ferdinand Foch was a well-known French soldier and military theorist who was the supreme commander for the Allied armies at the end of World War I. His book, *The Principles of War* (1903) called attention to changes in warfare posed by the increased power, accuracy and lethality of modern weapons. This quote exemplifies his strong beliefs in the importance of planning.

PLANNING

Planning is everything—plans are nothing.
—FIELD MARSHAL HELMUTH VON MOLTKE[106]

SELDOM DOES A PLAN AT THE END OF AN OPERATION BEAR more than a vague resemblance to the one at the beginning. Situations change and so plans are frequently modified, and even discarded, before a satisfactory resolution is achieved. While a plan may become obsolete, the process used to craft it results in a great deal of insight and perspective that is invaluable for recognizing and adapting to changing circumstances. Factors and influences may have been underestimated but later become important. Potentialities that were thought to be remote may become likely, and vice versa. Options that were considered but not chosen might suddenly become viable. While a plan is static the process that created it is dynamic and the schemes that comprise a plan are in a constant state of review and revision. This results in the process being more important than the product!

TACTICAL PLANNING PROCESS

Planning is the art and science of envisioning a desired future and laying out effective ways of bringing it about. There are two dynamic and interrelated factors involved in any planning process. The first is preparing for anticipated contingencies. This involves identifying those events that are expected to occur and deciding what to do about them when they do. The second is recognizing that all planning attempts to alter the future. This means that a successful plan will result in a more favorable future. Thus, a planning process is simultaneously reacting to both a future that is expected and one that is desired.

With only one exception, the planning process benefits from the efforts and perspectives of more than one person. This is called **collective planning**. Collective planning has three major advantages. First, it reduces the impact of personal prejudices. Unreasonable opinions and attitudes are more likely to be challenged than accommodated. Second, it enhances perception and increases possibilities. Discernment and understanding are heightened when people discuss expectations and prospects. Third, it results in a more accurate assessment of risk. Suggestions that are overly timid or rash are less likely to be undisputed. Contrary to collective planning is individual planning. **Individual planning** is only advantageous when speed is more important than precision. Of necessity, this results in the acceptance of more risk and ambiguity but is sometimes necessary when handling rapidly evolving situations with potentially severe consequences for inaction. Understandably, experience and sound judgment are critical attributes for individual planning.

OPERATIONAL ANALYSIS

The law of entropy states that all natural processes tend to increase the measure of disorder in the universe. This is certainly the case in tactical operations when everything is going wrong, nothing seems to make sense and there appears no easy solution. Yet, if there is one common expectation for tactical commanders confronting these situations, it is to bring order from chaos. While the simple solution is to develop a plan, given the disorder and confusion inherent in these situations that is a most daunting prospect. An operational analysis is a valuable technique to gain sufficient insight and understanding to formulate an effective plan.

In the most simplistic terms, an **operational analysis** is just a method for developing a plan. It is a fundamental, but sometimes complex, prerequisite for any commander to gain the necessary understanding to formulate an effective strategy. Accordingly, it is a first step in gaining true situational awareness and is a valuable tool for translating operational requirements into tactical guidance.

While there may be any number of ways of conducting an operational analysis, one method has withstood the tests of time and trial and is routinely used by the U.S. military. It is known by the acronym **METT-T**, because it provides a mnemonic for identifying the five essential factors of Mission, Enemy (or obstacle), Terrain and weather, Troops and support available, and Time available. While it may seem that these factors are addressed sequentially, in reality, as more information becomes available, a deeper understanding of one factor often alters the perspective and anticipated influence of another. Consequently, the assessment process is one of nearly constant review, reinterpretation and revision.

The first step in an operational analysis is identifying the missions. This is because it provides the basis from which all planning must eventually follow and from which the essential tasks are derived. Fortunately, the ultimate objective is always apparent. For example, "restore the peace," "save the hostages," "capture the suspect," "put out the fire," "rescue the victims," and so forth. But there are any number of enabling objectives that must first be accomplished, such as containments, evacuations, traffic control, and the like; and these are not so obvious. Further, because of time constraints and limited resources and/or personnel, they are always competing with each other. Thus, a commander must develop a step by step process that will ultimately achieve the final objective. The **mission** portion of the operational analysis provides a clear, concise statement of what is to be done and for what purpose.

The second step is to determine the nature of the difficulty that prevents the attainment of a satisfactory end state. While domestic law enforcement does not encounter an enemy per se, this factor is readily adapted and just as useful by simply substituting the term "obstacle." In its most simple terms, the **enemy** (or obstacle) factor identifies the threat, which is whatever needs to be defeated, removed, circumvented or surmounted to achieve a satisfactory resolution to the problem. Many times this is an adversary, but it may just as likely be a flood, fire, earthquake, blizzard, train crash, hazmat spill, and so forth.

The third factor is **terrain and weather**. Both will impact operations, most commonly in the form of trafficability, visibility and sustainability. *Trafficability* refers to the condition of the soil or terrain with regard to being travelled over and is both terrain and weather dependent. Trafficability will impact everything from suitable modes of transportation to where they can go. While *visibility* can be terrain dependent, as with terrain shielding,[107] it is most often affected by weather and lighting conditions. Factors such as precipitation, sunrise and sunset, moonrise and moonset, percent illumination, winds, temperature and humidity[108] can all affect visibility. *Sustainability* identifies the need to maintain or endure. Weather effects like extreme heat or cold, rain, hail, or humidity will all affect how well and how long both equipment and personnel can operate effectively.

Troops and support available is critical for estimating the effectiveness, efficiency and sustainability of operations. Besides the numbers of available personnel, how they are trained and equipped is integral to planning as well as how, when and where they should be used. Likewise, specialized units, such as SWAT, canine, detectives, custody, explosive ordnance disposal, traffic, and so forth, are better utilized if their assignment exploits skills and equipment that are intrinsic to their routine assignments. In the words of one Marine Corps Colonel, "Our job is to put square pegs in square holes and round pegs in round holes. But that isn't as easy as it sounds because sometimes we have to look for square pegs to fit square holes and sometimes we have to make round holes for round pegs!"[109] Tactical situations will always fare better when they have the right person, with the right equipment, at the right place, and at the right time. Critical to this concept is the understanding that troops are always consumers. This means that in order to remain effective they must be regularly fed, rested and replenished.

Time always imposes prioritization requirements, especially when the time available and the time required may be irreconcilable. This factor is essential for determining prerequisites and defining priorities. Missions, tasks and assignments can be divided into two broad categories, those that are resource driven and those that are time driven. **Resource driven tasks** are those that are largely dependent upon the amount and type of resources that can be dedicated to them. For example, if it takes ten personnel two hours to evacuate one-hundred homes, twenty personnel should be able to accomplish it in one-half the time. Conversely, **Time driven tasks** are time dependent.[110] For example, if it takes five hours to drive to a location, adding more cars will not provide a faster arrival. It is important to remember that harsh time constraints always favor training. This is because well-trained personnel tend to be more efficient than those who are unfamiliar with what needs to be done and how. Consequently, enabling objectives, like fueling vehicles, selecting routes or staging in convoys, are accomplished without detailed instructions or advanced planning by personnel who intuitively understand what is needed.

CONCEPT OF OPERATIONS

While an operational analysis will help identify the nature of the problem and what personnel and equipment are available for resolving it, it stops short of breaking a problem into "bite-sized" chunks. Seldom do complex problems readily lend themselves to simple solutions and so a method of dividing a problem into more easily defined and manageable portions is valuable. One good method is with a tool called a situation assessment.

A **situation assessment** attempts to identify the various elements and dynamics at play, especially those that may influence a favorable outcome. This will require two distinctively different but interrelated approaches. The first is an "analysis." An **analysis** breaks a problem into its component parts. One good way is by using the "SWOT technique." The **SWOT technique** is a method of analysis that integrates the four factors that make up the acronym; strengths, weaknesses, opportunities and threats. Strengths and weaknesses are usually inward looking; meaning they examine factors related to the response organization such as available personnel, skill levels, logistical support, and other factors. Opportunities and threats are usually outward looking and attempt to identify favorable circumstances that can be exploited to advantage and threats or conditions that forewarn and call for caution to avoid increasing the risk or uncovering some pitfall. Examples include impending light, darkness, rain or fog and other environmental changes. In the same manner, changes in a suspect's disposition, prolonged fatigue, hunger, pain, and other factors may be advantageous or foretell threat. The second portion of a situation assessment is a "synthesis." A **synthesis** involves integrating the various components and activities into a cohesive whole so that the plan is both effective and efficient. It estimates the impact of the various dynamics and identifies intermediate objectives. In short, it puts the right parts in the right order.

From the situation assessment, a "concept of operations" evolves. A **concept of operations**[111] is simply a series of actions designed to progressively promote the accomplishment of strategic objectives. A concept of operations is not intended to be elaborate or detailed and may best be understood as a scheme for orienting activity without precisely prescribing what must be done. Once a concept of operations is identified subordinates use this guidance to develop the details to accomplish it. This always involves a number of missions, some of which may compete with one another; that is performing one impedes another because of the necessity of sharing resources, personnel, and the like. Furthermore, each mission will necessarily involve any number of tasks. Some of these tasks can be accomplished by almost anyone, while others may require teams or individuals with specialized skills. Consequently, the natural extension of the concept of operations is the prioritization and assignment of these missions and tasks.

In prioritizing and assigning missions, two important tools are "deconfliction" and "mission tasking." **Deconfliction** is the term used to identify those steps taken to reconcile potential conflicts, such as who will do what and when, as well as who and what will be assigned in support. This is a command responsibility and must be completed to avoid a plan that falters when subordinate units find themselves in competition for limited personnel and resources.

The other tool is called mission tasking. **Mission tasking** is often referred to as the "glue" that binds the concept of operations and the missions together and is especially critical in fast-moving situations that do not readily conform to detailed planning or expectation. Mission tasking works by recognizing that each mission actually consists of two parts; the task to be accomplished and the reason or intent it is necessary. Of the two, the intent is the most important. In the dynamic environment of tactical operations, circumstances and situations will change, often rendering a task unnecessary or even inappropriate, but the intent is more lasting and will continue to provide guidance for actions.

When it can be seen that an assigned task is unnecessary, ineffectual or even counterproductive, subordinates are free to exercise their own judgment and initiative to find other means of fulfilling the intent. This may require completing an assignment in a unique manner or even some other task altogether. In the midst of the chaos and confusion inherent in tactical operations, mission tasking provides subordinates a means to resolve problems by focusing on achieving the intent rather than dogmatic adherence to detailed instructions.

CONSTRAINTS VS. RESTRAINTS

Every plan is developed within certain guidelines. These limitations may involve political, environmental, tactical or economic considerations. Since no plan is entirely free of influencing factors, it is necessary to understand them in order to devise a safe and effective plan. Factors which are intended to direct planning and decision making can be categorized into two broad groups. Constraints are those things which a subordinate *must do* while restraints are those things he *must not do*.

Constraints are controls that demand some action. They may be requirements imposed by law or department policy. Examples may include the necessity to obtain a search warrant or to wear a certain uniform. Other constraints may be imposed by higher authority. These are almost always event specific; that is they are temporary requirements relating only to a single operation. A requirement to attempt to "call out" a suspect before forcing an entry or to have a prosecuting attorney present during the operation, are just some examples. Still other constraints may be imposed by the planner. These self-imposed constraints often relate to safety, such as requirements to have a fire truck and ambulance at the command post or for entry personnel to wear safety goggles.

The opposite of a constraint is a restraint. **Restraints** are controls which prohibit some action. These too may be imposed by law or department policy. For example, police are restrained from using excessive force, unnecessarily detaining bystanders or destroying private property. Likewise, they may be imposed by higher authority. Examples include prohibitions against the use of chemical agents in an apartment building or the use of diversionary devices in drug laboratories. Self-imposed restraints may prohibit firing on targets outside a sector of fire, leaving a containment position until relieved or prevention of traffic from entering an area.

RULES OF ENGAGEMENT

Effective tactical plans are never developed in a void. They must be adapted to meet the needs of all sorts of influences that are always somewhat unique to the particular operational activity, time and place. Good planners will consider not only what will be required to accomplish tactical objectives, but also whether the means used to achieve them will be acceptable. After all, every legitimate government serves at the pleasure of the people and must act within the scope and authority that has been granted. While tactical commanders are usually granted considerable leeway in handling situations, there are times when existing laws and policies do not provide sufficient guidance or they permit actions that may hinder, or even prevent, the attainment of strategic objectives. This is particularly the case in planning for civil disturbances, protests, demonstrations, walkouts, sit down strikes, job actions, and so forth. A useful tool for avoiding these problems is a set of rules, commonly called "rules of engagement."

Rules of engagement describe the circumstances, and set forth the conditions, under which law enforcement officers may initiate and/or continue actions against adversaries. They are crafted to address the specific situation for a particular operation, and are usually, but not always, more restrictive than existing policies generally permit. They prescribe acceptable actions, equipment and appropriate conduct for handling volatile situations. Examples of issues often addressed are the authority to arrest, authority and conditions to intervene, authority to negotiate, authorized weapons and munitions, employment of some types of weapons, especially chemical agents or nonlethal weapons.

Rules of engagement afford three major advantages. First, they provide a commander with an ability to maintain a higher measure of control of forces and events while focusing on strategic objectives. For example, they may forbid arrests for minor or unrelated offenses, or in sight of protestors. Thus, forces avoid being distracted and remain focused on the overall objectives. Conversely, they may compel arrests, such as a "zero tolerance" policy for public drunkenness or disorderly conduct during concerts and sporting events.

Second, they prevent a single individual from committing the entire tactical organization to an undesired course of action. Regardless of how unintentional or benign the action, in the context of emotion, nothing is so insignificant that it can't be blown out of proportion. A rash or impetuous act by a single individual could very well instigate an incident that requires intervention and support by the entire force to resolve. One common example is forbidding arrests without the approval of the on-scene supervisor.

Third, they provide clarification and guidance for decisions. Terms such as, "sufficient provocation," "riotous acts," or "reasonable and necessary," may require interpretation when applied specifically to the situation at hand and are too important to be taken for granted. Thus, rules of engagement can be used to impose constraints and restraints fitting to circumstances that are out of the ordinary.

When crafting rules of engagement, two principles are inviolate. The first is that rules of engagement can never violate law. When doubts arise, counsel should be sought from the city or prosecuting attorney. Second, rules of engagement can never remove the inherent right of self-defense. Indeed, people will act to save themselves regardless of imposed policies, so any rule that attempts to transcend a person's legitimate right to protect their own life will be immediately disregarded and is doomed from the onset.

In the presence of well thought-out policies, most plans will not benefit from including rules of engagement, but for those special situations that are especially susceptible for exploitation by adversaries, rules of engagement provide a greater assurance of achieving success and avoiding a loss of public confidence and esteem.

COMMANDER'S INTENT

The commander's guidance is vital to planning. It is an indispensable tool for communicating essential guidance to staff and subordinate commanders alike. Accordingly, as a plan becomes more mature and comprehensive, subordinate commanders can then issue their own guidance for enabling objectives in respect to their particular units and assignments. An effective operational plan focuses the efforts of each individual toward a common objective.

This unity of effort is the most crucial aspect of any tactical operation and the responsibility falls squarely on the senior commander. Because most tactical operations in law enforcement are spontaneously reactive to an unfolding set of circumstances, the response is oriented, initially at least, to tried and true procedures rather than a detailed plan crafted specifically for the particular circumstances. In these cases the principal objective—for a response to a foot pursuit, say, or a robbery in progress or officer requesting assistance—can be reliably inferred from the nature of the incident.

When an operation is more complex, however, the precise objective may be neither clearly understood nor universally shared. In these situations it is essential that everyone fully comprehends what is required. The method used to express this concept is called the commander's guidance, or more formally, commander's intent.[112]

Simply put, the **commander's intent** may be defined as a concise expression of the purpose of the operation and the desired end state. It provides the essential focus to concentrate activities and facilitate coordination. Accordingly, it serves as the initial impetus and provides a foundation for the planning process to follow. Even when changing circumstances render a plan or concept of operations no longer appropriate the commander's intent provides a direction for what needs to be done to achieve a satisfactory end state and subordinates can improvise, adapt and overcome obstacles without burdening superiors with endless details.

The commander's intent is formed and provided during the earliest stages of planning and is based upon a commander's estimate of the situation. In law enforcement operations it is more often than not issued verbally. Nevertheless, complex operations are those which most benefit from a written plan and in like manner, a written statement of commander's intent is even more important when a written plan is also required. When providing a written commander's intent, it is done in "free form" (without a standard format), and describes both the commander's vision of an acceptable end state and a concept of operations to achieve it. An example of a verbal commander's intent might be: "It is my intent that the demonstrators will be allowed to protest without interference from counterdemonstrators or the authorities. Intervention will only be authorized to prevent personal injury or destruction of property. The operation will be concluded when the demonstrators voluntarily disperse at the conclusion of their march."

Additionally, the commander's guidance may also include "follow-on actions." **Follow-on actions** are those intended procedures and activities that follow others. It is important to note that follow on actions are often contributory to a desirable end state but are not necessarily prerequisites. They are typically preparatory in nature in that they anticipate and prepare for additional requirements. An example of an order for a follow-on action might be, "Upon completion of your mission, move to location A and prepare to support unit B."

To illustrate how a commander's intent is used for planning, consider the following scenario. A law enforcement agency is called upon to handle the security for a large political rally concerning a highly controversial election issue. The rally will undoubtedly draw activists on both sides of the issue and in past incidents violence has erupted between the two groups. Typical control measures for mobs and riots have included dispersing the mob, isolating and containing the rioters or early intervention by identifying and arresting the provocateurs. Needless to say, each of these strategies requires different tools and methodologies and the choice of one will affect everything from the selection of personnel to the logistical support required. Furthermore, they are often in competition with one another. In this scenario for example, a strategy that advocates mass arrests and another that promotes dispersing a mob cannot both be simultaneously implemented, and in fact, preparations for one may actually hinder the other. The decision for the preferred course of action rightfully lies with the senior commander and failing to provide the necessary guidance not only unduly complicates planning but cedes the essential decisions to subordinates. To avoid this untenable situation, the senior commander issues guidance on the preferred course of action. This allows planners to develop strategies, identify enabling objectives, gather logistical support, select and stage equipment, and so forth.

BRANCHES, SEQUELS AND COUPLINGS

One of the most critical requirements for effective tactical planning is to allow for flexibility. Situations requiring tactical intervention are not amenable to dogmatic adherence to rigid schemes. Tactical plans must continually adapt to perpetually and rapidly changing circumstances. In order to remain viable, even the best laid plans must allow for changing situations. This is often done with branches and sequels.

Branches identify those courses of action that may be necessary, dependent upon the changing circumstances, while **sequels** refer to actions that follow other actions. Branches and sequels address the central points of "if" and "what." Examples of branches may include plans to evacuate a subdivision during a large fire if the winds shift toward it. A sequel would include plans of what to do with the evacuees after they leave, or what to do to prevent looting while the homeowners are absent. An easy way to understand the significance of branches and sequels is by remembering that

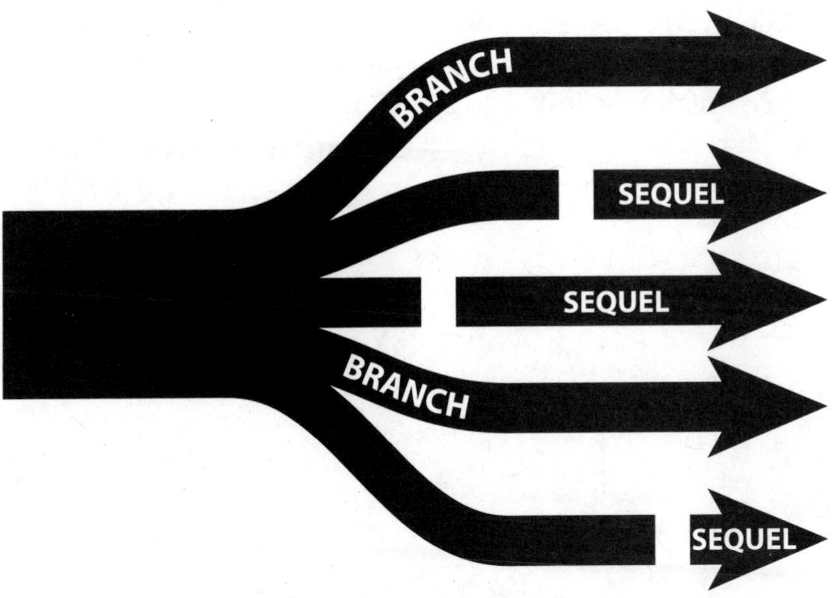

FIGURE 12-1 BRANCHES & SEQUELS: Branches in a plan identify courses of actions that may be necessary because of changing circumstances. Sequels are actions that follow other actions. For example, a fire that suddenly changes direction will require a different course of action than the one originally intended. The new course of action would be a branch. If evacuations become necessary what to do with the refugees would be a sequel. One easy way to remember the differences is that branches ask questions of "What if?" while sequels answer questions as to "What next?"

they each answer a different type of question. Branches answer questions of "What if?" while sequels answer questions of "What next?" Together they provide an ability to anticipate and plan for contingencies.

How the actions along branches or between sequels interact with one another is called coupling. **Coupling** is a relative term used to describe how two or more components in a plan interact. If actions must occur at specific times or in a specific sequence for the plan to be effective, it is said to be tightly coupled. **Tightly coupled** plans are closely coordinated and have more time-dependent processes. These types of plans are useful when incorporating resources not entirely controlled by the incident commander. A plan that relies on public transportation such as planes or buses, for example, would necessitate tight coupling to the departure and arrival schedules. Another example is when the allocation and integration of scarce resources is necessary, as in the temporary use of a helicopter. Tightly coupled plans are efficient but not very flexible and tend to be easily damaged and difficult to repair because changing one part necessitates changing other parts.[113]

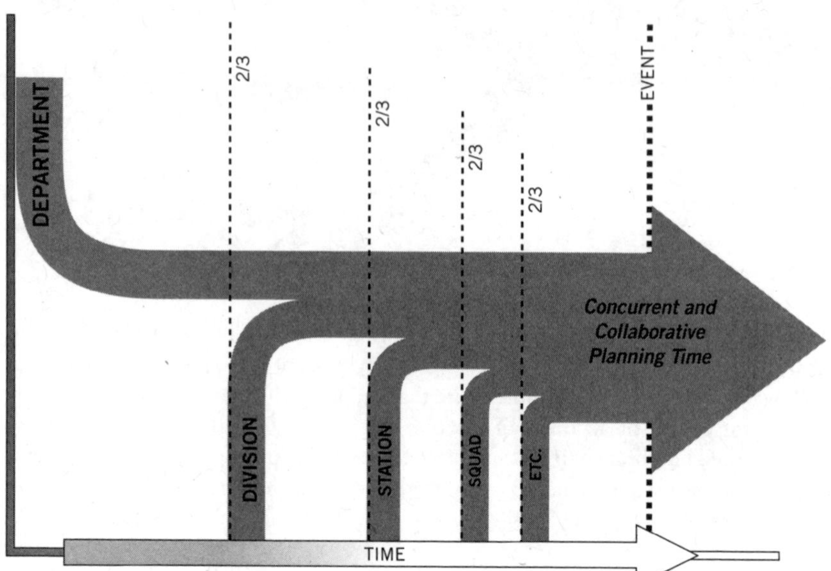

FIGURE 12-2 TWO-THIRDS RULE: Planning time is never limitless and complicating things still further is that the time available for preparation is often shortened to compensate when a plan is tardy. Either an incomplete plan or lack of preparation can be a recipe for disaster. One way of alleviating this problem is by adherence to the "2/3 Rule," which states that two-thirds of available planning time belongs to the next subordinate unit. If a department has three-weeks to prepare for security at a major sporting event, for example, they are allowed one week to provide sufficient guidance so that the concerned subordinate division can begin planning. The division then has about 5 days before providing guidance for the concerned stations, and so forth. This doesn't mean planning stops with the higher units, however, it simply means that planning is conducted concurrently as a group after their allocated time is expended. This method ensures that even the smallest units and individuals will have time to plan and prepare for their particular roles.

In the figure above, the horizontal arrow represents the total planning time available. As each subordinate element begins their own planning, the planning effort becomes both concurrent and collaborative. Notice also, that this planning time does not stop at the event but rather continues to adapt to the changing circumstances throughout the conduct of the operation

When close coordination is not required, loosely coupled plans are used. A **loosely coupled** plan is one in which the interactions between the various components do not require close coordination. Parts can be modified without seriously affecting others. Although they are not as efficient as one that is tightly coupled, they are more flexible and not as easily disrupted. An example of a loosely coupled plan would include the interaction between a fire department and a police department involved in fighting a large brush fire. While the fire department is engaged in fighting the fire, the police department is providing traffic control and making evacuations. Although they interact with each other (are coupled), neither is likely to be greatly hindered should the other encounter difficulties. Loosely coupled plans tolerate more friction and are more quickly amended.

One way to understand the difference between tightly and loosely coupled plans is by comparing the games of football and soccer. Football is a game with tightly coupled plans. There are frequent time-outs and a huddle is required before every play. A player who misses an assignment may single-handedly ruin a play. In contrast, soccer players are required to constantly adapt to new situations without elaborate planning. The overall objective provides the focus of effort and each player is expected to exploit opportunities as they appear. Detailed planning is almost impossible because time-outs are prohibited and the players are often too far apart for efficient communication.

Whether a plan should be tightly or loosely coupled depends upon the circumstances. When concerns regarding precise timing or the integration and allocation of scarce resources predominate, tightly coupled plans are better. In unpredictable situations, or when there are likely to be high levels of friction and chance, loosely coupled plans allow for more flexibility.

Planning for contingencies is a critical aspect in effective tactical planning because it provides for an organized response to a somewhat unpredictable change in circumstances while still maintaining continuity with the preferred course of action. An understanding of the critical role of branches, sequels and couplings is an invaluable planning aid.

TIME FOR PLANNING

Because tactical plans are most often contrived with harsh time constraints a dilemma occurs. The problem is that detailed planning is time consuming but time is not usually available. Consequently, some compromise is necessary. To save time, planning is usually done by a single individual, or better, a small highly-skilled group who have a thorough understanding of the factors involved, coupled with experience in dealing with similar situations. Because planning time is never limitless, a good rule of thumb is called the "2/3 Rule." The **2/3 Rule** states that two-thirds of available planning time always belongs to the next subordinate unit. This increases participation and enhances troubleshooting. Further, it ensures subordinates have time for preparation and implementation. This does not relieve the senior units from planning, however, rather planning continues concurrently with subordinate units. This ensure that the planning effort is comprehensively distributed throughout the organization and while senior echelons will remain focused on strategies and broad-based objectives, lower echelons have an ability to provide the critical details related to their specific assignments. This method not only makes the planning process participatory but enhances troubleshooting.

---

106. The saying is attributed to Field Marshal Helmuth Karl Bernhard Graf von Moltke (the elder) 1800-1891, but has almost certainly been paraphrased from the original "No battle plan survives contact with the enemy." The expression is so poignant in military planning circles it is used as a slogan and is frequently cited as "Moltke's Dictum." It has hung on a sign over the entrance to the Joint Staff at the Pentagon and was reportedly on General Dwight Eisenhower's desk. Notwithstanding, it is probably best known in a humorous version as one of "Murphy's Laws of Combat."
107. Terrain shielding is a term used to describe using terrain features, such as hills, valleys, ridges, buildings, and so forth, to provide cover and concealment.
108. Percent illumination is used to describe the amount of ambient light at night, as from the stars, phases of the moon, etc. Likewise, winds

routinely carry dust, smoke and other obscurants and fog is a combined result of temperature and humidity.

109. Col. Timothy G. Anderson, 1 MACE, Camp Pendleton, CA, during a staff meeting in 1996
110. A more evocative way of understanding the difference between resource and time driven tasks is with human pregnancy. No matter how many doctors or women are involved, it still takes nine months to have a baby.
111. This concept is often abbreviated in military circles to "CONOPS."
112. For the remainder of this chapter, the terms "commander's guidance" and "commander's intent" will be used interchangeably.
113. This condition is commonly referred to as the "domino" or "snowball" effect. It describes a condition in which one event will affect a number of other events.

PLANS

The main thing is to have a plan; if it is not the best plan, it is at least better than no plan at all.

—GENERAL SIR JOHN MONASH[114]

SHORTLY AFTER NAPOLEON BONAPARTE HAD ESTABLISHED himself as Emperor of France, he wrote a letter to his brother Joseph stating, "Everything that is not soundly planned in its details yields no result."[115] So it was then and so it remains to this day. The most indispensable part of any successful tactical operation is the operational plan. The business community describes it as a "blueprint for success." In tactical operations, the command and control architecture may provide the support for decisions, but it is the operational plan that binds the disparate parts of an organization into a cohesive whole. Plans not only ensure that each decision is supportive of the next but that the aggregate will eventually lead to a satisfactory resolution. It is hard to imagine any significant human undertaking that does not involve some sort of a plan, and plans are the pivotal factor for a successful tactical intervention.

THREE TYPES OF PLANS

In the simplest terms, a **plan** is "a structured configuration of actions in time and space envisioned for the future."[116] Therefore, every plan is a design to change the future to something better than anticipated. The momentousness of this concept cannot be more blatant than when involved in operations where lives are at stake.

Tactical plans fall into three distinct categories. These are deliberate plans, hasty plans and contingency plans. Each type serves a different purpose but it is common to have all three types in the same operation. All three are guided by the commander's intent, which in turn is focused on the desired end state for the event.

The most commonly recognized plan is a deliberate plan. A **deliberate plan** is a comprehensive and detailed method for accomplishing an objective. It is as comprehensive as time will permit, and is frequently referred to as the "master plan," since it serves as a baseline for all related plans and operations and describes the preferred course of action. Deliberate plans are especially useful for problems that reoccur and disasters that fall into categories. When used in this manner they are intended to provide an organized and thoughtful approach when the unthinkable happens and are sometimes referred to as "standing plans."[117]

Every disaster management agency worthy of the name has standing plans for classes of disasters, such as flood inundation, fire evacuation, earthquake recovery, hurricanes, tornadoes, riots, and so forth. Deliberate plans are most often authored collectively, over time, and incorporate the perspectives, knowledge, and experience of all participants. It is not unusual for deliberate plans to be prepared weeks or months, and sometimes even years, before being implemented.

A **hasty plan** is used to provide an organized response for spontaneous or unintentional events and which are so impromptu that detailed planning is not possible, or so remote that comprehensive planning is not justified. In simpler terms, hasty plans provide an organized response to surprise. They are used when timeliness and a quick response are paramount. Examples include the killing or escape of a hostage, the unexpected surrender of a suspect, the sighting of a tornado, or a change in direction of a fire.

A hasty plan provides a tailored response to immediate concerns and allows the much more detailed and time-consuming deliberate plan to continue to be developed. In this manner, hasty plans perform the duties of a "sentry" while continuing development of the deliberate plan. Sometimes a hasty plan is necessary even when a deliberate plan has been completed. This occurs when some critical factor is preventing the deliberate plan from being immediately implemented, such as shortage of logistical support, lack of transportation, or while awaiting the arrival of personnel. When used in this manner, hasty plans act as a "fail safe" to ensure that efforts to resolve an emergency are not deferred while waiting for conditions to improve.

In either case, hasty plans may be considered a substitute for deliberate plans, which though they describe the preferred course of action take longer to prepare and implement. They provide a temporary solution by adhering to the tactical adage, "A good plan implemented now, is better than a perfect plan executed later."[118]

A **contingency plan** is an alternate plan that focuses thought and effort on anticipated problems that may arise during the conduct of an operation. Because a contingency plan is a branch from the deliberate plan, it is often referred to as "Plan B." Contingency plans allow for operational deviation while maintaining continuity with the preferred course of action and guard against operations being stymied by confusion caused by a sudden change in the situation. Contingency plans differ from hasty plans because they are frequently authored in advance of an operation, often as part of the deliberate plan, to prepare for a potential deviation from the expected. In fact, sometimes hasty plans are viewed as a subset of contingency plans rather than a separate type altogether. Like hasty plans, however, contingency plans never describe the preferred course of action and are intended to provide guidance for deviations from the more probable chain of events. Therefore, they usually alter only the concept of operations or execution portions of the deliberate plan rather than committing actions to an entirely new direction or purpose.

COMPONENTS OF A TACTICAL PLAN

Not all tactical operations require a written plan. In fact, the vast majority of law enforcement tactical operations are successful with no written plan whatever. Police officers are daily called upon to conduct building searches, foot and vehicle pursuits, investigations and arrests without written instructions. As a general rule, however, written plans should be considered mandatory whenever an operation is multi-disciplinary[119] or multi-jurisdictional in nature, or extends through two or more operational periods.[120]

While there is normally no required standard format for a plan, five components should always be present. The military frequently reduces these five components to an acronym called "**SMEAC**," which stands for **S**ituation, **M**ission, **E**xecution, **A**dministrative and Logistics, and **C**ommand and Signal (or Coordination).

These five components provide a quick and concise format for developing an effective plan, whether it is reduced to writing or not. The format is especially useful when severe time constraints do not allow for detailed comprehensive planning. Furthermore, it provides a mental checklist for briefing so that information is presented in an orderly fashion and nothing of importance is accidentally omitted.

The first component deals with the **situation** at hand. This portion provides a brief summary of all that has transpired and any mitigating or aggravating circumstances that can affect the operation. At a minimum this should consist of a statement comprehensive enough to provide personnel with a situational awareness but concise enough to avoid confusion with unessential details.

The **mission** is the second component and must precisely identify the objective to be accomplished. This is the most important component because it provides the basis for which all planning must eventually follow. Every situation involves more than one mission. For example, a hostage situation would certainly have a mission of securing the safe release of the hostages, but the operation would not be complete if the suspect was then allowed to escape. Furthermore, the victim will want her property recovered, detectives will want to preserve the crime scene, prosecutors will want witnesses identified and interviewed, and so forth. Not only is there always more than one mission, they are often competing. That is, attempting to achieve one mission impedes the attainment of another. This is a frequent occurrence when rescue efforts are destroying a crime scene or tactical deployments are jeopardizing negotiation efforts. Thus, it is critical that the incident commander be able to precisely define and clearly articulate each mission, as well as which will have priority.

The **execution** component is usually the most voluminous and time consuming of the five components because it not only assigns missions to each unit, but also describes how they are expected to be achieved. Thus, it explains "why" as well as "how." The first part begins with a *concept of operations*, which explains the commander's intent or purpose for accomplishing the objectives. By explaining why something is important, subordinates are more likely to recognize and exploit opportunities to accomplish their assignment while serving the commander's intent. In this manner, resourcefulness, ingenuity and imagination can be incorporated into a plan.

The second part deals with how each assignment is expected to be achieved and contributes to the attainment of the overall objective. Because some assignments are more critical than others, the commander should specify one as the focus of effort. All other assignments are then secondary. Likewise, the main effort identifies the individual or unit responsible for accomplishing the primary assignment and other units are expected to render necessary aid. Together, the focus of effort and the main effort, seen through the prism of the commander's intent, provide an operational harmony since disagreements and conflicts can be resolved without further involving the commander.[121]

The **administrative and logistics**[122] component is often referred to as the "beans, bandages and bullets" section. This component provides instructions for logistical support, such as how personnel are to be fed, equipped, transported and relieved. Other critical logistical issues may include how and where to obtain replacement batteries, where casualties are to be medevacked, what to do with detained suspects, procedures for handling juveniles, female searches, recovered evidence, field booking, refugees, and so forth. This component also provides administrative instructions such as recording mileage of vehicles, overtime and payroll issues, capturing lessons learned, turn-in procedures for equipment, and so forth.

The last component is **command and signal**. This component identifies and describes the critical command and control personnel and facilities and provides information on how the various units will communicate. It includes their locations, telephone and fax numbers, radio frequencies, email addresses and any other essential information to ensure reliable communications. This component also identifies alternate means of communication when failures occur. When a plan is written, this component benefits immensely from a graphic table of organization that clearly identifies the major component parts of the tactical organization.

IMPLEMENTING PLANS

Plans can be implemented in one of three ways; on order, by time or sequence and contemporaneously to an unfolding incident. A plan implemented **on order** is one that is executed upon receipt of a command. Plans that are implemented in this manner have been prepared but not yet carried out and await only the order to put them into action. Standing plans are commonly implemented on order.

The second method is by time or sequence. A plan implemented **by time or sequence** is one that is awaiting a scheduled event or when one event is a precursor for another. A predetermined time or event then becomes a tripwire for implementing the plan. Events such as championship games, concerts, parties, elections, protests, and demonstrations, for example, are highly predictable and lend themselves to scheduling. Likewise, some natural occurrences are nearly as predictable in that if one event occurs other subsequent events are likely to follow. Examples include road closures during floods or blizzards, traffic accidents from ice storms, or power outages during thunderstorms and windstorms.

The third method is contemporaneously to an unfolding incident. A plan implemented **contemporaneously** is one that is reacting to a developing situation. This method is the most common for both fire and law enforcement in that they are the two most common disciplines called upon to intervene in deteriorating circumstances. Examples include residential and brush fires, traffic accidents, train wrecks, hazardous material spills, crimes in progress, and the like.

MONITORING PROGRESS

Effective plans provide a progression of actions to accomplish the end state. They provide guidance throughout situations that are inherently fraught with risk and uncertainty. Because of the time and effort required to prepare them, some commanders are reluctant to deviate from the prescribed course of action, insisting instead that the plan be followed punctiliously. This is almost always a recipe for disaster. In the words of one USMC officer, "Never fall in love with a plan."[123] This is because the situation will change faster than the plan.

This is not a recent phenomenon. More than 2,000 years ago Publilius Syrus—a Roman writer in the 1st century BC—stated that, "It is a bad plan that admits of no modification."[124] Regardless of the brilliance and insight of the author(s), no plan can predict future actions and reactions precise enough to be completely inerrant. Consequently, a rigid or dogmatic adherence to any plan is a recipe for disaster. Lt. General Patton once wrote in his diary, "It may be of interest to future generals to realize that one makes plans to fit circumstances and does not try to create circumstances to fit plans."[125] It stands to reason then, that plans must be continually reviewed and constantly revised to ensure that they remain relevant and adequate to accomplish their purpose.

One of the most useful tools for organizing, coordinating, and tracking components of an organization and specific assignments, tasks and missions is a matrix. A matrix is simply a rectangular array of rows and columns that form boxes when the lines cross. Thus, it becomes a chart that can be used to plot and track data as well as the relationships between the column and row headings. Matrices have an ability of organizing a large amount of information in such a manner that gaps and duplications are obvious. They are particularly valuable for handling tactical operations and disaster responses because they can easily expand as the operation progresses.

The most common matrix used for tactical operations and disaster responses is called an event matrix. An **event matrix** is a chart designed to identify what units have been assigned to which tasks. This ensures that valuable resources are appropriately assigned and that critical functions are not overlooked. It is especially useful for gaining and maintaining control of large tactical operations because it simultaneously tracks multiple units combined with multiple tasks. It can be used for preplanned operations such as parades, sporting events, concerts and the like, or it can be used for spontaneous operations such as barricaded suspects, hostage situations, riots, fires and so forth.

The construction of an event matrix is extremely simple. It can be preformatted and provided on blank forms or it can be constructed at the scene. To construct an event matrix simply draw a matrix listing the units, agencies or individuals available along the left side and the tasks or missions needed to be accomplished

This can be any function task, mission or assignment that will be performed during the incident.

This can be any individual, unit or agency assigned to the operation.

Unused resources have blank cells.

Unit / Event	Saturation Patrol	Field Booking	Traffic Control	Looting Suppression	Crowd Control	Tactical Intervention	Press Liaison	Intelligence	Fire Suppression
East Patrol	X								
West Patrol			X						
East Traffic				X					
SWAT						X			
Custody									
Aero Bureau								X	
Detectives					X			X	
Fire Department									X
Public Works			X						X

FIGURE 13-1 EVENT MATRIX

across the top. When a unit is assigned a mission, an "X" is placed in the box where the unit row and the mission column intersect. As the matrix is filled in, it graphically and clearly displays which units have been assigned to which missions. Unused units or unassigned missions are very conspicuous because their particular row or column is blank. As more units arrive and more tasks become identified, they are listed and assigned as appropriate.

When used in this manner the event matrix is two-dimensional; that is, it tracks only which units have been assigned what tasks. The matrix can be made even more insightful by assigning a value to the box instead of simply checking it with an "X." Because of the depth this adds, a matrix used this way is often called a three-dimensional matrix. For tactical operations, the most useful value is normally time. To use an event matrix in 3D fashion, simply sub-

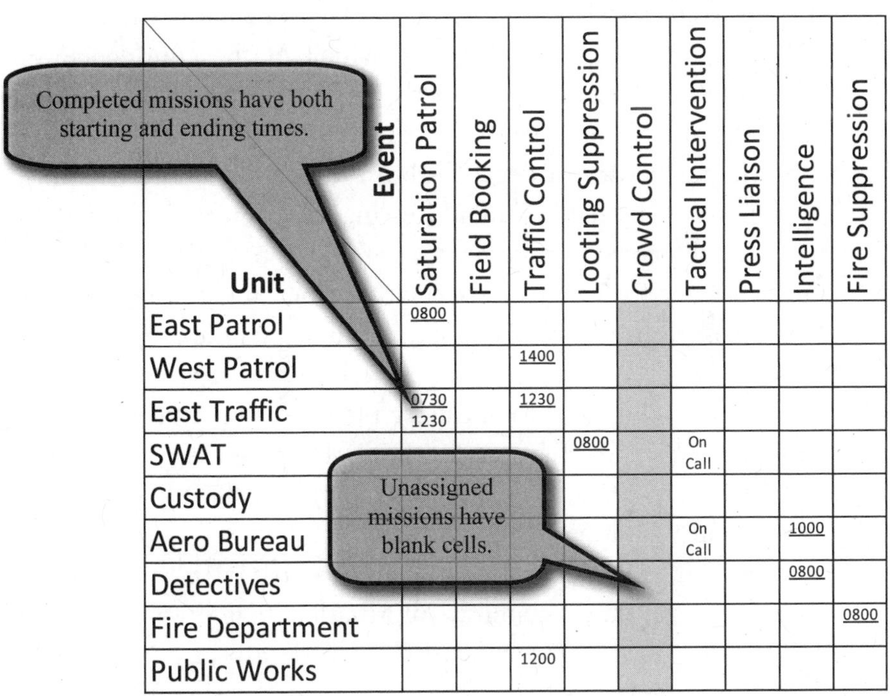

Unit \ Event	Saturation Patrol	Field Booking	Traffic Control	Looting Suppression	Crowd Control	Tactical Intervention	Press Liaison	Intelligence	Fire Suppression
East Patrol	0800								
West Patrol			1400						
East Traffic	0730 1230		1230						
SWAT				0800		On Call			
Custody									
Aero Bureau						On Call		1000	
Detectives								0800	
Fire Department									0800
Public Works			1200						

FIGURE 13-2 EVENT MATRIX 3D

stitute the time of assignment for the "X" in the box. Now a commander can view the matrix and see with a glance not only which units have been assigned to which tasks but how long they have been involved. This allows additional information to be extrapolated such as when reliefs should be considered or whether a unit needs to be resupplied. When a mission is complete, an ending time can be added under the starting time. This tells a commander that a unit is available for reassignment. Because an event matrix is so simple to construct and use it serves as a sort of "cheat sheet" for a commander to oversee a much larger and complex operation than human memory alone will allow.

ATTACHMENTS

Writing a plan is time-consuming and labor-intensive and is complicated by the fact that changes, additions and deletions are frequently necessary. This is especially problematic after a plan has been copied and distributed. Much of the confidence and reliability of a plan can be directly attributed to how current and accurate it is. Consequently, a plan that has information that is out of date or in error degrades both its reliability and its value.

One excellent method of addressing this problem is through the use of attachments. Attachments contain important details that are not necessary for every person involved but are still important to the success of the effort. They simplify understanding by providing a structure for organizing information so that it is readily available without cluttering the primary plan. Because attachments can be discarded in their entirety without changing the primary plan, updates are more easily achieved by simply replacing a particular attachment with a new version.

There are three common attachments to a plan.[126] The first is an annex. An **annex** contains information that provides specific and detailed instructions related to a single aspect or function of a plan. An annex may focus on a particular function, like logistics and communications, or a particular problem, like evacuations and traffic control. The greater the scope of a plan, the more likely it will benefit from one or more annexes. An annex is written as a comprehensive document so that it functions nearly as a standalone component of the overall plan. In fact, an annex is often a plan, in and of itself, but with a supporting role to the overall plan to which it is attached. Because of the comprehensive and specific nature of annexes it is not unusual for each one to have a separate author.

The second common attachment to a plan is called an appendix. An **appendix** contains detailed supplemental information that adds clarity or precision to an overall plan. Unlike an annex, an appendix has little meaning out of the larger context. The information contained in an appendix facilitates or explains some other activity. Consequently, it is not unusual to have one or more appendices attached to an annex. Examples of information commonly provided in appendices include checklists, graphs, charts, tables, forms, inventories, schedules, and the like.

An enclosure is a third common attachment to a plan. An **enclosure** contains specific information on a single subject that is used for reference. It is not unusual to have information provided as enclosures that was originally prepared and intended for another purpose. Common examples of information in enclosures are photographs, maps, sketches, overlays, diagrams, addresses, and contact information.

While there are no requirements in the law enforcement community for where to place attachments or what to name them, by custom and convention, all attachments are placed at the end of the parent document (written operations plan). Annexes are typically identified with a capital letter followed by a name based on their subject. For example, Annex A (Explosive Ordnance Disposal), Annex B (Radio Communications), and so forth. Appendices follow annexes in order and are identified by an Arabic number followed by a name based on their predominate subject. For example, Appendix 1 (Robot Checklist), Appendix 2 (Schedule of Events), etc. Enclosures follow appendices and are usually identified with an Arabic number followed by a name identifying their specific topic. For example, Enclosure 1 (Precinct Map), Enclosure 2 (Suspect Photograph), etc. When an appendix and/or enclosure is attached to an annex rather than directly to the operations plan it is listed according to the order of the parent documents. For example, Enclosure 2 (Missing Child Photograph) to Appendix 1 (Mountain Search Team) to Annex A (Search and Rescue Operations) to Operation Plan (name or other designation).

---

114. In spite of the fact that he was never trained to be a professional soldier (he was a civil engineer), General Sir John Monash was the commander of the Australian Army in World War I. He participated in a number of major engagements, including the disastrous campaign at Gallipoli and led the final major assault before the evacuation. He was a strong proponent of combined arms and was known for his organizational and planning abilities and is reported to have written these sentiments in a letter in 1918. Note the resemblance of his career to that of Union General Ulysses S. Grant, who was also trained as an engineer and never envisioned as an infantry officer. Both gained fame as a result of their deep understanding of logistics and planning.
115. Napoleon, September 18, 1806, *Correspondence*, No 10809, Vol. XIII. Joseph was Napoleon Bonaparte's older brother and was involved in French and Italian politics for many years, and for a time was King of Naples. It was about this time that his brother penned this guidance on planning to him.
116. This definition is taken verbatim from *Planning*, Marine Corps Doctrinal Publication 5, U.S. Marine Corps, 1997, p. 5
117. It is important to note that "standing plans" are fundamentally and distinctively different than "standing operating procedures." For more information on standing operating procedures (SOP), see Chapter 8—Operations.
118. This adage is one of the many "Murphy's Laws of Combat," but is paraphrased from General George S. Patton, Jr's book, *War As I Knew It.* (Houghton Mifflin Company, NY, NY, 1947) The verbatim passage reads, "A good plan violently executed now is better than a perfect plan executed next week."
119. Multi-disciplinary means that it pertains to more than one discipline, such as a combination of law enforcement and medical, fire, or rescue personnel.
120. An operational period refers to the length of a deployment cycle. Since tactical operations frequently require personnel to work beyond the normal eight-hour shift, the term "operational period" is used and

identifies the typical tour of duty for the operation. This is frequently twelve hours.

121. For more information on a concept of operations, focus of effort and main effort, see Chapter 7—Command. For more information on commander's intent, see Chapter 12—Planning.
122. Some military texts identify this component as the "Service and Support" or "Service and Supply" section.
123. Col. "Wild Phil" Tracy during a briefing in preparation for Operation United Shield, on the USS *Ogden*, off the shores of Mogadishu, Somalia, late-January 1995. It was after weeks of detailed planning and countless changes when frustration was beginning to set in that he was admonishing those involved to be prepared to continually adapt and improvise to an ever-changing set of circumstances.
124. Publilius Syrus, *Moral Sayings*, circa 1st Century B.C. translated by Darius Lyman. Publilius Syrus was well-known in his time and famous for his insightful wit. He is known to have so captivated Julius Caesar that he was awarded a prize in recognition for his improvisations. He wrote a number of maxims that have been translated into various languages. The quote here is Maxim 469.
125. Lt. Gen. George S. Patton, Jr., diary entry from February 26, 1945, as quoted in *The Patton Papers*, Volume II, 1974. It is particularly poignant in that this entry was one month after the Battle of the Bulge in which Patton distinguished himself by turning his Third Army north to relieve U.S. troops at Bastogne, Belgium.
126. Military operation plans use a hierarchal system of attachments. In order, these are; annexes, appendices, tabs and enclosures. Tabs are used so seldom in civilian operations that they do not merit mention here.

CRISIS DECISION MAKING

In all operations a moment arrives when brave decisions have to be made if an enterprise is to be carried through.

—SIR ROGER KEYES[127]

WHEN TACTICAL OPERATIONS ARE ANALYZED THE MOST conspicuous elements are the decisions. Even novices are quick to notice that the direction and tempo of every action began with a decision. Decisions are the pivot points in these types of situations and at some point every person involved is required to make them. For obvious reasons, even a basic understanding in what is involved is advantageous.

More has been learned about how humans make decisions in the last twenty-five years than in all previous history. One of the most ambitious efforts has been with the U.S. Navy's TADMUS Program. The TADMUS program (Tactical Decision Making Under Stress) stemmed from two highly publicized incidents. The first was in March 1987 when the USS *Stark* was struck by two Exocet missiles fired from an Iraqi Mirage fighter jet, killing 37 American seamen. Despite the fact that the aircraft had been detected some 200 miles away the Stark's captain decided not to engage it. The following year the guided missile cruiser USS *Vincennes* was confronted with a similar situation in July of 1988 when it detected an aircraft heading directly for it. This time the captain ordered the aircraft shot down only to learn that it was a civilian airliner. All 290 people on board were killed.

As a result of these incidents the U.S. Navy instituted a lengthy study on the factors involved in making decisions that continues to this day. The knowledge gained from this and other studies is just as applicable for domestic tactical operations and responses to disasters as for military operations.

CRISIS DECISIONS

In the simplest terms a decision means to solve a question and provide a conclusion. In the chaotic conditions surrounding tactical operations and disaster responses decisions are always encumbered with uncertainty, harsh time constraints and risk. Moreover, a mistake can lead to a calamity. This type of decision making is far more risky and tense than those in other circumstances but is the norm for crises, hence the term "crisis decision making." **Crisis decision making** is best understood as the mental process of reaching a conclusion during a time of instability and danger relevant to resolving the situation.

As might be expected, the methods and procedures that render good decisions in other conditions can be problematic for crisis decision making for one fundamental reason; speed is more important than precision. Tactical operations and disasters are dynamic and a decision delayed is often rendered worthless because the situation will have changed. The best solution for handling these types of situations is one that is timely even though it may not be the optimal.[128] The most common method for making crisis decisions is called "satisficing." **Satisficing** is a method for making decisions that opts for a prompt search for adequacy over a prolonged one for the optimal.

To understand how satisficing works and why it is important, consider the following example. Some campers watch as a spark from their campfire ignites some dry leaves. They quickly jump up and one begins to stomp out the fire while another tries covering it with loose dirt and the third camper removes any flammable material. Only later do they note that the water they were boiling on the campfire would have been an even better solution. The critical importance of solving the problem quickly was more important than searching for an ideal solution that a delay may have rendered ineffective anyway. In situations like these perfect is the enemy of good enough.

Naturally, if the situation repeated itself their first thought would be to douse the flames with the water they were boiling. They might even keep water available for just such a reoccurrence. This illustrates the value of experience. **Experience** is practical wisdom comprised of knowledge and skills attained through personal participation or observation. People who make decisions based on experience don't start at the beginning of a problem but rather where they left off the last time. They mentally dismiss actions that have proven inadequate or unproductive on previous occasions and seek better alternatives.

The value of experience in crisis decision making cannot be underestimated. Persons who have experienced a similar situation make better decisions faster than those who have not. In fact, the greater the repertoire of experiences the more likely a decision maker will be able to contrive or adapt a solution that has worked previously. Moreover, they tend to be more imaginative in problem solving because they have a greater depth of understanding than those experiencing a situation for the first time.

This method of decision making is called "Recognition-Primed Decision Making" often abbreviated to just "RPDM."[129] To a greater or lesser extent, everyone faced with a decision in an atmosphere of uncertainty and accompanied with harsh time constraints will use some derivation of this method. It is a natural way of thinking when the circumstances will simply not permit detailed analysis with prolonged conclusions.

While not everything about RPDM is wholly understood, some generalizations can explain how it works. When a decision maker is faced with a situation in which a rapid decision is required he or she mentally generates alternatives and then imagines which one will provide a satisfactory solution. The first alternative that appears to offer a solution is then selected and/or adapted to fit the particular circumstances encountered. Experienced people have the advantage of being able to draw upon previous problems that are similar while novices must continue to cycle through possibilities to find one they think will suffice. As can be seen, a similar experience provides a substantial advantage in both speed and effectiveness.

The value of training and education in gaining insight and understanding from personal participation and observation is critical. A decision maker is not even required to have experienced a similar problem in reality because all that is necessary is that they have thought through the problem at least once. The value of training and education for enhanced decision making then is to create "artificial experience."[130] Experience makes the knowledge gained in training and educational activities practical.

Arguably, the best training and education is not the knowledge on how decisions are made but rather the principles on which they are based. For disaster responses and tactical operations this refers to tactical science. In the most general understanding **tactical science** is that body of knowledge focused on how crises emerge, evolve and are resolved. It emphasizes the fundamental doctrinal principles and time honored concepts that have been gleaned over thousands of years. Some outstanding advice on this issue comes from USMC General Al Gray who commented, "The most formidable warriors are students of their profession."[131] Only those who possess the knowledge and experience, coupled with an understanding of the factors and influences in play, will be fully capable of coping with the scope of the possibilities and depth of the consequences because a perfect solution requires an infinite wait.

REACTIONS VS. DECISIONS

One of the amazing things about the human brain is its capability for "multi-tasking;" that is, the ability of simultaneously doing more than one thing. Take driving for example. It has been estimated that when you drive you are consciously and unconsciously making as many as 300 decisions a minute! These involve steering, braking, accelerating, estimating distance, anticipating actions of other drivers, and so forth. At the same time you may also be listening to the radio, carrying on a conversation with your passenger and drinking a cup of coffee. In order to appropriately handle these many decisions the brain must prioritize which decisions are more important and when they must be made. Say for instance you are talking with your passenger when you suddenly notice the car immediately in front of you is braking hard and you are in danger of hitting it. This creates unbelievable stress and your brain immediately focuses on identifying an appropriate response, such as taking an evasive maneuver or braking hard. When this occurs you do not even have the ability to finish your sentence, much less carry on the conversation. This is because the brain processes safety decisions faster than cognitive ones.[132] You react before thinking.

Like driving, many situations arising in a tactical operation also require near instantaneous responses. A delay of even a split-second can be calamitous. During depositions and testimony, however, officers are expected to relate in great detail those factors that caused them to act. Because they usually can, it appears that these factors were all known and considered before the action. Herein lays the root of one of the most common misconceptions in tactical decision making. Decisions and reactions are distinctly and fundamentally different but are easily confused with one another because stressful events are so easily imprinted in memory.

Decisions are conscientious choices between alternatives. They involve the portion of the brain[133] where intellect and memory provide the basis for a cognitive judgment. At the risk of oversimplification, decisions involve three separate, but interrelated, factors. The first is reason or judgment. This aspect may be most simply thought of as an examination of the "cold, hard facts." It is an objective and rational comparison and selection between alternatives. If reasoning were the only factor involved, tactical decisions could be reduced to mathematical computations and computer models. In truth, how information is evaluated and judged to be relevant, as well as the degree of importance it is accorded, is just as crucial.

The second factor is the inclusion of emotions. **Emotions** are subjective feelings and influences that occur without conscious effort and are affected by such things as anxiety, fatigue, hunger and pain. Emotions also influence decisions from personal dispositions, biases, and prejudices. That they can also evoke physical feelings should not come as a surprise either. Our language is rich with descriptions of "gut-wrenching" anguish and "heartbreaking" sorrow. To a greater or lesser extent, emotions are always present and significantly influence how we receive and process information. Contemporary thinking equates emotions to "decision making shortcuts." It is believed that, lacking sufficient, reliable information, emotions serve to heighten awareness and vigilance to prevent inappropriate decisions. Emotions are why a salesman saying things too good to be true is disbelieved.

The third factor, perceptions, determines how we assimilate information. **Perceptions** refers to how the mind interprets a sensory stimulus. For example, the same word carries a different interpretation depending on whether it is whispered or screamed. This is because how we interpret information and determine its importance is a complex and interrelated process of culture, values and experience, embedded in context. These create a frame of reference we use to sort through a jumble of seemingly incomprehensible factors and reach a decision. Likewise, even information from unimpeachable sources will be immediately suspect, or even disregarded, if it contradicts existing beliefs. Before information can be incorporated into the human decision making process it must first be accepted. The truth is not enough; we must also believe it!

To a greater or lesser degree, these three factors (reason, emotions and perceptions) are always present and strongly affect how people make decisions. They also unequivocally demonstrate that decisions are an intellectual process that occurs almost completely in the brain itself.

In contrast, **reactions** are responses to some treatment, situation, or stimulus. One of those most often encountered during tactical operations is fear. Unlike decisions, mental reactions are processed in a more primitive portion of the brain that is incapable of conscious thought.[134] When a threat is perceived, this portion of the brain sounds a kind of general alarm. The adrenal system quickly floods the body with adrenaline and nonessential physiological processes, such as digestion, are switched off. Our heart races, breathing quickens and blood pressure increases, saturating the body with oxygen. At the same time the liver releases glucose for quick energy. The entire body is instantly at a high state of arousal. These are primarily physiological reactions and require no intellectual activity whatsoever.

As can be seen, reactions are distinctly and fundamentally different than decisions. What is not well known, however, is that while both reactions and decisions originate in the brain, the sensory data from which they are derived have taken two different paths to two different locations and arrived at two different times.

It happens like this.

When we encounter a threat, the sensory data from our eyes, ears and other senses are simultaneously transmitted to different parts of the brain. One data stream is directed to a place where it will be integrated with other real-time sensory data, memories and other more elaborate associations. This often takes several seconds to complete. The other, with far less detail and almost no processing, is sent to an area where an alarm is sounded to mobilize the body to meet the threat. This takes only a fraction of a second. Thus, the same sensory data follows parallel pathways to the brain but at different speeds. This is why a person who is startled by a figure in a dark hallway may freeze, flinch, scream, or even attack, before recognizing the face of a loved one that frightened them.

And, because fear evokes memories that are easily triggered and hard to shake, people who encounter these situations can often recall them in great detail long afterwards even though the events may have unfolded in only a few seconds time. Consequently, the impression that conscious thought was involved is easy to believe. Even the person experiencing the threat may be confused. Because people who can "think on their feet" are held in high esteem, their ability to recall details and explain their reasoning is reinforced with praise. Thus, our own human nature adds to the confusion.

EXPERT THINKING

Expertise refers to the advanced skills and knowledge people use for decisions and actions. All expertise is contextual; that is it is limited to a specific discipline, subject or field of study. Every tactical operation requires a seamless integration of the skills, knowledge and abilities of any number of subject matter experts. Courts recognize the value of experts and they are allowed greater latitude in testimony than a lay witness because they are not limited to their personal observations but are allowed to present their expert opinions.

Not surprisingly, experts make better decisions than novices. What is more, they do it faster and often with less information. This is because experts work not so much by seeking the relevant but rather by eliminating the irrelevant. This allows them to spend more time thinking about a smaller sample of possibilities. Because they already know what won't work, or won't work very well, they are able to quickly dismiss these options to better concentrate on those that seem more feasible. Thus, experts are not necessarily smarter and they don't think harder, they just think in more productive ways.

There are four factors necessary for an effective tactical decision. The first three, training, education and experience, are an individual's personal contribution. They take considerable time and effort to acquire and are vested in the individual; meaning that they accompany them and are completely and permanently held by that person. The fourth, and most important factor, is situational awareness. Without an understanding of the nature of the situation even the most accomplished expert is powerless to comprehend what is needed. Nevertheless, while situational awareness is crucial, a person lacking the essential training, education and experience is poorly equipped to discern critical factors and influences in play.

The knowledge needed to become an expert is largely a result of personal determination. There are many who attend formal and lengthy schools but lack the personal initiative or ambition to move beyond the level of graduation.[135] More to the point, becoming an expert is a personal decision and not one that can be forced upon someone. Regardless of how knowledge is attained, the distinguishing feature of experts is how they make it practical. Subject matter experts are better at organizing information that they need to make decisions relating to their specialty. Any method that increases a person's ability to recall useful information then becomes a valuable tool to quickly gain perspective and suggest useful solutions. Studies have shown that there are at least eight factors that distinguish how an expert approaches a problem that differ from others.[136]

First, experts discern patterns and relationships that escape an amateur. This allows them to identify similarities and make comparisons with previous situations, which are accompanied by memories of what worked and didn't.

Second, experts are quick to notice deviations and anomalies, which create expectancies of what should follow. Of particular note is that experts are also quick to detect the absence of something that should be present. Thus, an expert is surprised when an expectancy is not fulfilled and reacts by examining the situation more closely.

Third, experts tend to view a situation holistically rather than get bogged down in the myriad factors, influences and permutations that capture the attention of a novice. In this manner they have a better grasp of the situation in its entirety, which in turn makes it easier to identify the major dynamics involved and estimate their impact.

Fourth, experts understand the way things work (or should work) and how they relate to one another. In the tactical domain this factor is often identified as the coup d'oiel concept. **Coup d'oeil** (pronounced koo dwee) is a French expression which, loosely translated, means the "strike of the eye" or the "vision behind the eye." The closest translation to English is as "perceptive insight" or "the power to discern the true nature of a situation." It explains an expert's ability to envision everything from who is doing what, in what manner, and how it contributes to the overall solution, to what is needed, why and when. Thus, experts tend to think in all three aspects of time when they use the past to make comparisons, the present to what is ongoing and the future expectancies.

Fifth, experts more readily recognize opportunities and tend to be more imaginative in their problem solving. In particular, experts tend to be more adept at identifying leverage points. A **leverage point** is a critical time, place, step or event in a system where force can be applied to make a change. An ability to quickly identify leverage points is particularly advantageous in tactical operations and disaster responses because a little effort applied at the right time and place can have far-reaching positive consequences. For example, recognizing that evacuations may be necessary at an early stage of an operation provides an ability to prepare for everything from evacuation routes, temporary housing, medical care, feeding, family notification, etc., all of which are greatly facilitated when not required in haste. Understandably, every leverage point presents an opportunity of some sort.

Sixth, experts tend to examine a situation from the perspectives of both the past and the future. They understand how things came to be and develop a set of expectancies of what they can become. The fundamental common denominator for this factor is an understanding of cause. Once a cause is recognized efforts can be focused on encouraging or discouraging it depending on the expected consequence. This is extremely valuable in tactical operations and disaster responses in that those difficulties that can be anticipated can oftentimes be averted, or at least attenuated.

Seventh, experts are able to detect subtle differences that are not obvious to the less knowledgeable. Many harmful factors in tactical situations are insidious and become obvious only after damage is done. Experts tend to be more perceptive in recognizing and understanding the significance of everything from faint smells to unlikely events.

Eighth, experts understand and manage their own limitations. They understand their own thought processes, estimate time and effort, establish priorities and make revisions. In short, they critique themselves and are quicker to notice when they are doing a poor job.

USING INFORMATION

People with expertise not only possess greater knowledge they also use information more efficiently. Experts are able to recall with clarity and precision facts and concepts that provide immediate value. While people use all sorts of methods to retain, recall and arrange information, some methods are so valuable that they merit special attention.

One good method of organizing and remembering information is through the use of mnemonics. A **mnemonic** is any technique that aids memory. Mnemonics often take the form of verses, acronyms, stories, and anecdotes. Mnemonics work by linking the information with other information so that is

HOW EXPERTS THINK

THOUGHT PROCESS	ADVANTAGE
Discern patterns and relationships that escape others	Identify similarities and make comparisons with previous situations and recognize what worked and what didn't
Notice deviations and anomalies	Creates expectations of what is to follow
View situations holistically	Don't get bogged down with trivia which allows major dynamics to become more conspicuous
Understand the way things work and how they relate to one another	Provides insight and a deeper understanding of the situation
Readily recognize opportunities and be imaginative in problem solving	Better at identifying and exploiting leverage points
Examine situations from both past and future perspectives	Provides ability to recognize opportunities and detect dangers
Detect subtle differences	Allows recognition of insidious influences before serious damage occurs
Understand and manage their own limitations	Quick to note when things are beyond their own abilities

FIGURE 14-1 EXPERT THOUGHT: Experts are not necessarily smarter than others, nor do they think harder; rather they think in more productive ways. This allows them not only to make better decisions but also faster. The matrix above identifies eight fundamental ways that experts think about a problem that gives them an advantage over a novice.

easier to retain. For example, nonsensical names and phrases can be used to remember complicated sequences, such as "Roy G. Biv" to remember the spectrum of colors of visible light in order—red, orange, yellow, green, blue, indigo and violet, and "My very earnest mother just served us nine pickles" to remember the planets in order from the sun—Mercury, Venus, Earth, Mars, Jupiter, Saturn, Uranus, Neptune and Pluto. In the same manner, an acronym that makes up a word, like MOOSE MUSS for the nine principles of war (Maneuver, Objective, Offense, Simplicity, Economy of force, Mass, Unity of command, Surprise and Security) or SALUTE for the six elements in a field intelligence report (Size, Activity, Location, Unit or uniform, Time and Equipment), provide a mental checklist not only for what is needed but also in what order.

While most mnemonic devices are text or verbal, a visual mnemonic with which everyone is familiar is highlighting text with a vivid but translucent color. Highlighting text not only makes important information more conspicuous it also makes it easier to remember. This is due to the **isolation effect**, which describes the fact that the more information stands out the more likely it is to be remembered.[137]

Another method people use to make decisions is with the use of heuristics. In the most general terms, a **heuristic** is a mental shortcut; that is a procedure or technique that increases the probability of finding solutions with less time and effort than that required by a random or exhaustive search. Whether they are aware of them or not, everyone uses heuristic devices to make decisions. The principle advantage of a heuristic is that it speeds up good decisions. The principle disadvantage is that they provide a bias that may not be accurate. Consequently, the knowledge and experience of an expert assists in ensuring that the circumstances that make a general precept or principle valid are also present in the situation under consideration.

There are all kinds of heuristics but one of the most common is a "rule of thumb." A **rule of thumb** is a principle with broad application that gets a decision maker close to a solution. It is not precise enough to identify a solution but it helps provide a focus to avoid pitfalls and unproductive efforts. Heuristics are especially valuable in resolving problems for which no formula exists. Tactical rules of thumb are often expressed as axioms, principles, precepts, sayings and other expressions that suggest caution or provide advice. For example, "Murphy's Laws of Combat" provides a list of humorous but poignant observations or admonitions that emphasize important tactical considerations.[138]

Another heuristic device is similarity. A **similarity heuristic** is one that provides clues to solutions based upon what has worked in the past in similar situations. Similarity heuristics rely on pattern recognition; that is, the decision maker is able to classify the current problem as fundamentally the same as one in memory, either from training and education or from personal experience. Because each tactical situation is always somewhat unique, it is just as critical to identify those factors and influences that do not fit the pattern, which in turn makes an expert more suspicious and cautious. Needless to say, the value of the similarity heuristic is tightly coupled to the personal knowledge and experience of the decision maker.

Experts also use intuition. **Intuition** refers to the "thoughts and preferences that come to mind quickly and without much reflection."[139] Intuition allows a decision maker to quickly grasp the essence of a situation, sort through a vast amount of ambiguous and uncertain information and find an acceptable solution. Experts do not use intuition in place of reasoning but rather to supplement it. Because experts have a wealth of knowledge and experience, they are able to identify classic patterns that provide insight and understanding when compared with an unfolding one. Once the principle factors and influences are discerned an expert is able to ignore those that are inconsequential and concentrate on those that require more scrutiny.

GRAPPLING WITH UNCERTAINTY

No matter how capable a decision maker, there are some issues that will severely tax his or her abilities, not the least of which is uncertainty. Uncertainty pervades tactical situations and is generally attributed to two major factors. One of them is the element of chance. For better or worse, every situation has a number of unpredictable and unknowable factors that will influence a favorable outcome. The other is unreliable information. Every decision is based upon information that is always somewhat incomplete, confusing, ambiguous, or even conflicting. Because neither of these elements can be completely eliminated, some method of coping with them becomes essential.

There are many different methods of managing uncertainty and experts tend to be more adaptable and efficient than others because they have a larger repertoire of methods to draw from. While each expert tends to prefer some methods over others, some have proven so reliable in tactical operations and disaster responses that they are used by nearly all.

One method of dealing with uncertainty is to insist on recommendations by trusted subordinates. This not only relieves a commander of the necessity of personal effort to determine the merit of information but gains the perspective of another person whose insight is already valued by the decision maker.

Another method for handling uncertainty is to push decision making to the lowest possible level. In many cases this will be all the way to the issue owner. The **issue owner**[140] is the person most accountable for performing a specific function or solving a particular problem. The closer a person is to a problem the more likely they are to be familiar with the specific factors and influences in play. It is not necessary, nor even advantageous, for senior commanders to make every decision, and in fact, this tends to mire them in unessential details that actively compete for their attention.

A third method is to delay the decision. While this is not always possible, not every problem needs to be solved when it first becomes apparent. In some cases a problem diminishes in importance or complexity over time. In others, more information is needed to diminish the uncertain aspects before a reliable decision can be made. Experts are adept at separating the urgent from the important and prioritizing what must be done and when.

A fourth method is by increasing attention. This means that the decision maker gets personally involved in vetting the information, determining relevance, seeking solutions and so forth. This becomes problematic when the effort it takes to solve one problem competes with the necessity of solving others. In these cases the use of a decision point allows a harried commander to focus on more important issues without losing control of another situation of concern.[141]

A fifth method is through the use of incremental decisions. An **incremental decision** is one that offers a partial solution and involves little risk but with the expectation that subsequent decisions will progressively promote a satisfactory resolution. This method allows a decision maker to avoid having to simultaneously resolve all the issues involved by addressing them a few at a time. Experts are acutely aware, however, that there is a natural human reluctance to abandon the effort when a failure occurs even when another course of action looks promising.[142] One adage describes this problem with "Exploit success—don't reinforce failure."[143] The greater the reluctance of a decision maker to admit mistakes and failures, the more incremental decision making loses its value.

A sixth method is to simplify the plan. Simplicity reduces the chances for misunderstanding and confusion and allows critical actions to be more conspicuous. This allows component parts of a plan to be modified without seriously affecting others. It also illustrates the value of pushing decision making to the lowest possible level because the semi-autonomy granted to subordinate commanders provides them an ability to adapt and improvise to ensure their particular assignment remains supportive of the overall objectives.

---

127. Sir Roger Keyes, *Letter from the Dardanelles*, 1915. Keyes was a noted British Admiral and good friends with Britain's Prime Minister, Winston Churchill. He was eventually promoted to Admiral of the Fleet and later elected to Parliament. At the time he expressed these thoughts, Keyes was Chief of Staff for the campaign to take the Dardanelles Straight, between the Aegean and Black Seas in eastern Turkey, as part of the ill-fated Gallipoli campaign during World War I.
128. It is a bitter irony that the optimal solution is often cited as definitive by naïve "experts" testifying against law enforcement officers after the fact and with little understanding or appreciation for the dynamic and stressful conditions under which such a decision was actually made.
129. It is also commonly referred to as Recognition-Primed Decisions or "RPD."
130. A good example of this is the Mercury spaceflight program, which was unique in that staff were training astronauts for an experience no one had ever had (as opposed to passing along experience already learned.) This is the reason the Mercury astronauts spent so many hours in simulators: NASA was trying to precondition these men to ignore small issues that might otherwise be distracting. This allowed them to focus

with limited time and mental effort in space onto larger problems. When the first astronauts returned they noted watching the launch gantry fall away from the capsule window and the vertigo this induced; this stimulus was thus cranked into the simulators to prevent such distractions from affecting the next astronauts by preconditioning them to expect it. (as described in *The Right Stuff*, by Tom Wolfe, published by Farrar, Straus & Giroux, Inc., New York, New York, 1979, p. 317)

131. General Alfred M. Gray, 29th Commandant of the United States Marine Corps. Upon assuming his role as Commandant of the Marine Corps in 1987, General Gray insisted that all Marines become knowledgeable in the moral and physical characteristics of war. To that end he initiated a series of doctrinal publications that succinctly explain some of the lessons learned throughout history and how they apply in modern situations. Recognizing his contributions, the research library of the Marine Corps University in Quantico, VA is known as the Alfred M. Gray Research Center.
132. This phenomenon is often called the "amygdala hijack," because of the portion of the brain that "overrides" the cognitive portion. In reality, the process more closely approximates a faster processing time. Because it is largely based on a chemical process, the effects dissipate in about three to six seconds. The effect on cognitive thinking is devastating, however, and if sufficiently stressed (scared in this case) the person will not even remember what they were talking about. The amygdala takes its name from the Greek word for the appearance of an almond.
133. While not everything is known about how decisions are reached or precisely how they are formed in the brain, the portion most actively involved is the hippocampus. It takes its name from its Greek word for the appearance of a seahorse.
134. This portion of the brain is the central nucleus of the amygdala and links the key brain stem areas with the autonomic (involuntary) functions of the body.
135. Expertise is always relative; that is someone is always more or less knowledgeable or skillful. Notwithstanding, no one would accept a pilot or doctor, or even a baker or carpenter, as an expert who hadn't done considerable work beyond the formal study of a particular field under the tutelage of a master instructor.
136. The subject of how people gain expertise and make decisions is far more complex than can be adequately explained in a single chapter, or even a single book. Most of this material has been taken from the excellent works of Dr. Gary Klein, who has not only been personally involved in many of the groundbreaking studies but writes clearly and simply so that it is understandable by laypeople. In particular, I would

recommend his books, *Sources of Power: How People Make Decisions, The Power of Intuition: How to Use Your Gut Feelings to Make Better Decisions at Work and Streetlights and Shadows: Searching for the Keys to Adaptive Decision Making.*

137. It is sometimes called the "Von Restorff Effect," named after the German psychologist Hedwig von Restorff who first reported it in 1933. Anything that makes information stand out tends to make it easier to remember. This not only includes how the information is presented, such as color, contrast, and format, but the nature of the information itself, such as that which is absurd, vulgar or funny. You will note that this text exploits these phenomena by providing acronyms to remember procedures or components, by the use of examples to highlight critical points and by bold printing a concept to make it stand out when it is first introduced.
138. While the exact lineage of the fictional sage "Murphy," is unclear, the pithy and amusing proverbs now include virtually every subject and discipline. Regardless of the authorship, they often humorously encapsulate an important aspect of some subject. Their value in gaining insight and understanding during the chaotic and dynamic circumstances inherent in tactical operations and disaster responses speaks for itself. Likewise, the quotes used throughout this text and at the beginning of every chapter are intended to succinctly elucidate critical concepts.
139. Kahneman, Daniel, "Maps of Bounded Rationality: A Perspective on Intuitive Judgment and Choice," Nobel Prize Lecture, December 8, 2002 p. 449
140. While the issue owner has a responsibility for performing an assigned function or solving a problem, the ultimate responsibility always lies with the senior commander. This is based upon the precept that "you can delegate authority but you cannot delegate responsibility."
141. For more a more complete description of decision points, see Chapter 8—Operations.
142. This natural proclivity is called the "sunk cost effect." In brief, it refers to an unwillingness to abandon an investment after a mistake or failure.
143. This is a common expression in both the business and tactical communities. While at first glance it might seem to advocate timidity, in actuality it encourages developing a strong and resilient self-assessment which removes decisions from self-image, and thus provides more clarity in decision making.

SECTION 5

SECTION 5

MULTI-DIMENSIONAL BATTLESPACE

Battle should no longer resemble a bludgeon fight, but should be a test of skill, a maneuver combat, in which is fulfilled the great principle of surprise by striking 'from the unexpected direction againstan unguarded spot.'

—CAPTAIN SIR BASIL LIDDELL HART[144]

ALL TACTICS INVOLVE SOME TYPE OF MANEUVER. IN FACT, THE term "getting flanked" or "blindsided" refers to being put at a disadvantage by some maneuver of an opponent and maneuver of an opponent and is used in business and sport settings as well as tactical. The advantage of any flanking maneuver is that it avoids the opponent's front, which is where they are usually focused and prepared. Likewise, maneuvers can be defensive in nature, as when an opponent moves out of range of a weapon or behind cover to avoid injury. Maneuver of any kind benefits with surprise and once a commander recognizes a vulnerable flank they take steps to reinforce it. In times gone by this might be accomplished by building fortifications or providing reinforcements. Nowadays, however, conflict is multi-dimensional and weak flanks may lie entirely outside the realm of space.

This section is focused on multi-dimensional battlespace. It begins with the realm of space and how to conduct a terrain analysis and continues with a discussion on how to gain an appreciation of terrain and the anticipated effects it will have on operations. Because the usefulness of terrain is highly dependent upon weather conditions it also provides a brief description on the most common ways weather affects the use of terrain. The chapter concludes with a discussion of the four most common methods for navigating in tactical situations and why they are nearly always used in combination during movements and maneuvers.

The second chapter deals with the dimension of time. While time is a notional dimension it is possible to maneuver through it. Timing alone can, and often does, have a decisive impact in resolving conflicts. It explains what the maneuver objective is and why. This chapter concludes with a concept called the Boyd Cycle, which has proven to be one of the most useful tools for understanding how to effectively maneuver in time.

The section concludes with a description of the fifth dimension—cyberspace. This dimension is not only far more expansive and complex than most people understand but has far ranging implications. After explaining how the dimension of cyberspace interacts in tactical operations and disaster responses the discussion continues with explaining how to maneuver in cyberspace. In particular, the significance of humanspace and cyberspace and how they interact. The section concludes by explaining how to dominate cyberspace, particularly the capabilities provided by new technologies.

---

144. Captain Sir Basil Liddell Hart, *Thoughts on War*, 1944. Hart was a British soldier who became a military journalist and historian and was eventually knighted. In spite of his lack of experience of actual combat (less than two months in World War I) he became a life-long student of conflict and generalship and advocated the use of mobility and surprise to achieve decisive results. Ironically, it is felt that his thoughts were more influential in Germany than in his own country and was a basis for the successful German blitzkrieg warfare early in World War II. The quote summarizes his thoughts and is particularly apropos in any discussion on battlespace.

TERRAIN

The nature of the ground is often of more consequence than courage.

—FLAVIUS VEGETIUS RENATUS[145]

IT IS NEARLY IMPOSSIBLE TO OVERESTIMATE THE effect of terrain on tactical operations, and it has been well-understood and documented throughout history. More than 3,000 years ago the story of the Israelite prophetess, Deborah, is documented in the 4th chapter of the book of *Judges* with details of how she lured the Canaanite army with "900 chariots of iron" into the mucky terrain of the Kishon Valley in modern-day Israel where the dismounted Israelites overwhelmed the mired charioteers.[146] Some seven hundred years afterward, in his seminal work, *The Art of War,*[147] Sun Tzu provides some of the earliest tactical references of how the various types of terrain will affect movement across it. Several centuries later still, Alexander the Great used rough ground to defeat the Persian chariots at the Battle of Gaugamela.[148] Moreover, he routinely assigned geographers to augment his intelligence and planning. More than two-thousand years later, Frederick the Great stated, "...terrain for the military man is the same as the chess board for the player who wants to deploy and move his pawns, knights and elephants in the most effective way."[149]

Terrain is just as significant for tactical operations and disaster responses. Because some types of terrain may hinder or help the movement of persons across it, a prediction of their movements is possible. In operations attempting to resolve problems resulting from natural disasters, such as fires and floods, terrain also plays a critical role. For example, fires burn better uphill with many waterways as barriers, while floods are entirely terrain dependent. Moreover, regardless of the nature of the operation, to a greater or lesser extent, all responses are restricted by terrain. Accordingly, an understanding of terrain provides valuable insight for responding to and handling both natural disasters and conflicts.

TERRAIN ANALYSIS

One of the best ways of determining the impact terrain will have on an operation is by conducting a terrain analysis. A **terrain analysis** refers to the process by which important terrain features are identified and evaluated for their impact on a tactical operation. A terrain analysis may be as simple as a mental survey of the likely influence of various terrain features or as sophisticated as a written, comprehensive and detailed analysis that includes the effects of lighting and weather.[150] Regardless of the amount of detail required, every terrain analysis is focused on five considerations. These are:

- **K**ey Terrain Features
- **O**bservation and Fields of Fire
- **C**over and Concealment
- **O**bstacles
- **A**venues of Approach and Escape

To help remember them, these factors are often arranged as an acronym. The most common is "KOCOA."[151] Each of the factors serves as a pointer to help identify and determine the influence of a particular terrain feature on an operation.

A **key terrain feature** is any locality or area, the control of which affords a marked advantage to either the suspect or police. There are plenty of features that offer marginal advantages but it is not a key terrain feature unless it offers a marked advantage. Key terrain features can be natural or man-made. Thus, conducting a terrain analysis is just as appropriate in the urban environment as the rural.[152] While many people think of key terrain as being the "high ground" this is not always the case. Terrain is only important to the degree that it provides some sort of advantage. For example, a ravine may provide a protected avenue of approach or a lake may prevent a suspect from escaping and could provide significant advantages when incorporated into a plan.

It is also important to understand that key terrain features need not be occupied to be controlled. It is only necessary that the terrain is appropriately exploited. It may not be possible, for example, to physically occupy the upper story of a house, but it may be possible to prevent a suspect from using it by filling it with tear gas.

Some terrain is so critical that the success of an operation may hinge on who controls it. This is a special kind of key terrain called "commanding terrain." **Commanding terrain** is any terrain that offers a decisive advantage. Perhaps one of the best known examples is the tower at the University of Texas occupied by Charles Whitman when he killed 15 people and wounded 31 others. In order to defeat Whitman, the police were required to physically seize control of the tower.[153]

The second consideration is observation and fields of fire. These two factors are so closely related that they are examined together. **Observation** refers to the ability to view an area or other feature. It includes any ability gained with visual enhancements such as binoculars, spotting scopes, telescopes, night vision goggles, thermal imagers, etc. Accordingly, the most appealing terrain features that provide an ability to view are nearly always some type of vantage point that provides a wide, long or advantageous perspective. Vantage points are frequently located on some type of high ground, as from a hill, mound or ridge or even the upper floors or roof of a building. Notwithstanding, they might also be on the same or lower elevation if a terrain feature provides concealment for an observer. The only necessity is that the terrain feature provides an ability to view an area that has tactical significance.

A **field of fire** refers to the area that a weapon can cover effectively from a given position. There are two factors that define a field of fire. The first is where a weapon is positioned. A shooter firing from the top of a tall building, for example, can fire at targets in all directions but if he shoots from a window in the same building he is limited in both vertical and lateral limits by the building itself. The second factor is the type of weapon. Because a rifle can shoot farther than a pistol it has a greater field of fire.

A related, but distinctly different concept is a sector of fire. A **sector of fire** is a designated zone to be protected by an individual, team, or unit. Any target within a sector of fire is the responsibility of the person or unit assigned, and conversely, no individual is allowed to shoot outside their assigned sector of fire. They can take on any shape, including three dimensional. A rifleman positioned inside a skyscraper, for example, might well be given vertical as well as lateral limits.

Sectors of fire provide three major advantages. The first, and most important, is to prevent friendly casualties. Even when they can't be observed, innocent personnel may be on gun-target lines. Second, it increases the effectiveness of weapons fires. This is usually done by overlapping sectors of fire so every area is covered by at least two individuals or teams. Third, they ensure that there are no gaps in weapons coverage that might provide a break or opening that could be exploited by an adversary.

The third consideration is identifying cover and concealment. **Cover** is defined as anything that protects against weapons fire and their effects. In order for something to be considered as cover it must not only protect from the projectiles but any of their effects. While exploding projectiles are rare in law enforcement, many objects can throw shrapnel, or its equivalent. A brick wall, for example, may stop a projectile but throws a cone-shaped chip (usually called a spall) that often weighs more than the projectile and for a short distance is travelling just as fast, and accordingly, is just as lethal. Likewise, a propane tank may stop a projectile but the ensuing explosion may be even more deadly. It should be also be understood that cover is dependent upon the nature of the weapon. What may provide cover for pistol bullets or shotgun pellets may be completely inadequate against more powerful rifle bullets.

In summary, where a field of fire is limited only by the nature of a weapon and how it is employed, a sector of fire is an assignment. Accordingly, a field of fire is concerned with capability while a sector of fire is concerned with permission. A field of fire is a factor to be considered during a terrain analysis; a sector of fire is a factor to be considered during planning.

Distinct in both concept and application is concealment. **Concealment** refers to anything that prevents observation. A feature may conceal without providing cover, and conversely, a feature may provide cover without concealment. Vegetation, for example, commonly provides concealment without cover and bullet-proof glass may provide cover without concealment. Furthermore, some types of concealment, such as darkness and fog, are temporary. For this reason it is important to understand that a prolonged operation will require review of the practicality of terrain features used for concealment.

The fourth consideration involves searching for obstacles. An **obstacle** is any object that stops, impedes or diverts the movement of forces. Like all terrain features, obstacles favor neither friend nor foe. Those that encumber friendly forces are disadvantageous but obstacles that impede a suspect are advantageous. An operation commander who recognizes the significance of obstacles can exploit them to great advantage and thus more effectively utilize personnel and predict a suspect's movements. Examples of obstacles often encountered in police operations are fences, (particularly when topped with razor ribbon), walls, flood control channels and the like.

Some obstacles are so formidable that they prevent movement. These obstacles are called **barriers.** Barriers are especially critical in the urban environment because of the nature of terrain. A fifty-foot cliff in a rural environment may be a formidable obstacle but can usually be traversed. A two-story wall in an urban area, however, is oftentimes a barrier and must be circumvented.

The fifth consideration is identifying avenues of approach and escape. An **avenue of approach** is simply a route by which friendly forces can reach an objective. Vice versa, an **avenue of escape** is simply a route by which a suspect can maneuver to a better position or evade attempts to capture him. A good avenue of approach supports the movement of personnel while providing cover and concealment. Avenues must also be broad enough to permit necessary maneuver and bypassing of any obstacles. When an avenue of approach is too narrow a tactical team may become constricted and channelized. This makes mutually supporting actions difficult and inhibits the ability to take advantage of available cover and concealment. Likewise, avenues of approach and escape are strongly affected by the nature of how they are expected to be traversed. What may be a barrier to a vehicle may not even be an obstacle for a pedestrian. This in turn affects the significance of terrain features for different echelons of the tactical organization since the higher levels of the organization are more dependent on large machinery and vehicles while the lower levels may not use vehicles at all.

The effects of terrain are one of the earliest known influences in tactical operations and were described in Sun Tzu's *The Art of War*, written around 500 B.C. Accordingly, a terrain analysis will help reveal how terrain will affect a particular course of action.

TERRAIN APPRECIATION

Terrain is rarely flat or bare. With very few exceptions it has buildings, roads, trees, vegetation and other features. Furthermore, terrain that is disadvantageous for one opponent can be favorable for the other. Thus, it goes without saying that any assessment must consider both perspectives. **Terrain appreciation** is the process used to glean insight from how terrain will affect an operation. Because it is a process, it is never fully complete and when conditions change, especially with lighting and weather, earlier versions may be rendered obsolete. Consequently, these factors must be incorporated into the process, especially as to their anticipated effects on visibility and trafficability.

There is no standard procedure or methodology for terrain appreciation but there are some commonalities. For example, nearly every one begins with some type of map reconnaissance. A **map reconnaissance** is simply an inspection of one or more maps of an area in question to gain a general perspective. This provides a commander a quick and easy orientation of the major features and serves as a basis for the more detailed terrain analysis that often follows. Aerial photographs provide even more insight because they depict micro-terrain. **Micro-terrain** is terrain that is tactically

FIGURE 15-1 TERRAIN: Most law enforcement operations take place on urban terrain. It is important to understand that urban terrain is not just rural terrain with structures. In point of fact, there are at least six fundamental differences that will influence how operations unfold. As can be seen in this picture of Los Angeles, the terrain is channelized and compartmented by things like buildings and roads. Thus, movement is restricted and more predictable. Second, there is an uneven ambient light. The urban environment is characterized by harsh shadows and dazzling lights which makes consistent night vision nearly impossible to attain. Third, confrontations occur at extremely close ranges with 90% occurring at less than twenty-five yards. Moreover, the targets are moving and fleeting. Fourth, it has a three-dimensional characteristic which requires planners and decision makers to consider factors above and below the plane of operation. Fifth, it offers a defensive advantage. Even the most uneducated adversaries quickly discover how to use buildings, balconies, sewers, crawl spaces, and other terrain features to their advantage. Finally, civilians are always present. This complicates matters because they may be supportive, adversarial or passive but their mere presence requires consideration of their involvement.

significant because it will have an impact on an operation but is too small or insignificant to be depicted on a map. Examples of micro-terrain may include ditches and small hills, sheds and other small buildings, or even fences, trees and hedges. When micro-terrain is particularly important, diagrams and sketches will be required to augment commercial maps. The reverse of micro-terrain is prominent terrain. **Prominent terrain** is any terrain feature that can be easily identified and is displayed on a map. Prominent terrain may include features such as large hills, road intersections, rivers, bridges and cultural landmarks such as churches or schools. Prominent terrain is especially beneficial for orientation as to direction and distance.

Some terrain naturally protects personnel and equipment as they move across it. For example, a tactical unit that moves along the "backside" of a hill or behind a building to avoid entering a suspect's field of fire uses the elevated terrain between them for cover and concealment. This concept is called terrain shielding. **Terrain shielding** describes the utilization of terrain, including the vegetation and structures on it, as protection from a threat. Understandably, the same unit on the other side of the same hill would be exposed to the threat. Terrain that increases the vulnerability of personnel and equipment because it exposes them to observation or hazard is called **enfilade terrain**. Conversely, terrain that is used so that it provides increased protection from observation or hazard is called **defilade terrain**. Gaining an appreciation of how terrain will benefit or impair tactical objectives, especially maneuver, is of great value for tactical commanders at all echelons.

When possible, a reconnaissance of the terrain may be conducted. Sometimes called a "pre-battle walk through" or "leader's reconnaissance;" commanders attempt to personally walk over the terrain or at least view it from a safe vantage point.[154] When time or circumstances prevent an actual walk through, it is often done from the air, especially in helicopters. While not as effective, an ability to actually view the terrain is so valuable that when unable to personally conduct one, many commanders assign the mission to reconnaissance teams.

Understandably, certain regions merit more attention than others. Generally, there are three operational regions that merit particular interest. The most important region is that area where an operation is actually being conducted, or is planned on being conducted. This is called the area of operations, [155] frequently identified by the abbreviation, "AO." An **area of operations** refers to the geographical area associated within a single command where the commander has the authority to plan and conduct operations. In large disaster responses, there may be more than one AO, especially if the disaster scenes are not contiguous.

Another region that merits closer scrutiny, although not usually to the same extent as an AO, is the region wherein a commander may not be in control of an area, but has an ability to influence actions on it. Accordingly, this region is called the area of influence. An **area of influence** identifies a geographical region in which a commander may influence an operation, even indirectly, without being in command. Unlike an area of operation, which is usually quite conspicuous, an area of influence is always somewhat subjective because what can be controlled is far more distinctive than what and how much it may be influenced. An example might be during a flood or hazmat spill where the runoff is leaving a commander's AO and entering into another jurisdiction. While the commander may not be able to affect the area of influence directly, there are many possibilities for indirectly influencing it, such as damming or diverting the runoff, diluting it, and so forth. Together, an area of operations and an area of influence may be referred to as the **zone of action** since this is where a commander is actively attempting to influence the outcome of an operation.

The third region is called an area of interest. **Areas of interest** are those geographical regions of concern to a commander, either because of the impact on current operations or those that are planned, but that are unable to be controlled. The most common reasons that areas of interest are unable to be controlled is either because of a lack of personnel and resources, or more commonly in law enforcement, because of a lack of authority. While a commander may not be able to directly influence the actions within this area, they nevertheless merit concern and consideration as to how, and to what degree, they may impact a successful outcome of an operation. A good example might be a raging fire burning in one jurisdiction but with an expanding, and dangerous plume cloud drifting toward another. While the responsibility for putting out the fire remains with one jurisdiction, the consequences resulting from the plume cloud cannot be ignored.

Terrain appreciation provides insight and understanding for planning and organizing tactical and disaster responses of all types.

As with all assessments, however, how comprehensive it is often depends upon the time and resources available. Nevertheless, a commander who makes the effort will gain a substantial advantage over one who does not.

WEATHER ANALYSIS

In the simplest terms, **weather** is the state of the atmosphere at any given time and place with respect to such things as temperature, wind speed and direction, humidity, precipitation, and so forth. The effects of weather on tactical operations have been irrefutable. Indeed, the outcomes of many historical events that may have changed the world as we know it have been determined by weather. History records the destruction of the Spanish Armada by a storm in the North Atlantic in 1588 that left England as the undisputed "Queen of the Seas;" the defeat of Napoleon's army in Russia in 1812 when severe winter weather reduced the attacking French force to less than two percent of their initial strength; and the use of darkness and inclement weather by General George Washington to cross the Delaware River in 1776 in the Battle of Trenton was a turning point in the American Revolution. In more recent times, calm waters in the English Channel and rainy weather on the French shore allowed the allies to escape from Dunkirk in 1940 and when a favorable "weather window" was forecast by a young Scottish meteorologist General Eisenhower gave the order for Normandy landing to proceed on the 6th of June in 1944. Each of these incidents played a decisive role in each of their settings, and indeed, almost certainly changed the course of history. The study of weather and its effects on tactical operations has been a critical part of tactical planning since prehistoric times and is no less important today.

The three most common effects of weather on tactical operations are those that affect visibility, trafficability or sustainability. **Visibility** refers to the clarity and distance something can be seen with or without visual aids. Weather conditions like fog, rain, snow, smog, dust, and the like, strongly influence our ability to detect and identify objects at various ranges. **Trafficability** refers to the ability of moving something from one place to another, especially in a conveyance of some sort. Weather effects like rain, snow, ice, and wind quite commonly interfere with everything from flying, driving or even walking. **Sustainability** refers to an ability to maintain or endure. Weather effects like extreme heat or cold, sleet, dust, or humidity will all affect how well and how long both equipment and personnel can operate effectively.

Weather also affects how terrain is used. For example, open terrain that would permit observation in daylight might be safely traversed in darkness. Consequently, factors such as moon rise, moon set, percent illumination,[156] and cloud cover become critical planning factors. Likewise, terrain must also be considered in conjunction with weather since bright moonlight on sand or snow will tremendously attenuate the effects of darkness and a heavy rain may be just an inconvenience for vehicles on paved roads but can be a "showstopper" for dirt roads and trails. This is why weather and terrain are always considered together.

Military organizations throughout the world consider a weather analysis as an integral part of the planning process. Law enforcement agencies, however, especially those in the milder climates, seldom do more than a cursory review. A **weather analysis** refers to the process by which atmospheric conditions are identified and evaluated for their impact on a tactical operation. Because the use of terrain is so dependent on weather, a weather analysis is most often conducted in conjunction with a terrain analysis. Some aspects of a weather analysis, such as sunrise, sunset, moonrise, moonset and tides can be precisely determined with near absolute certainty months and years in advance. Nearly all others, however, require a forecast to determine a range of possibilities, coupled with a continual reassessment as weather conditions change.

Unlike the algorithmic process involved in a terrain analysis, a weather analysis more closely approximates a prognosis in that it is a calculated projection based upon factors that can be reasonably determined. There is an intuitive aspect to weather forecasting that computers simply cannot completely replicate. Weather analysis incorporates the technical expertise of professional meteorologists with the tactical acumen of operational planners. Both disciplines are critical to a reliable assessment since both an accurate forecast of weather conditions and a realistic appraisal of their effects on personnel and equipment are necessary for planning and preparation. All the same, even the most general instructions as simple as "Expect rain," provide personnel a warning to plan and prepare.

In spite of the fact that there is no established algorithm for conducting a weather analysis, a methodical approach will provide a more precise and reliable assessment. The assessment usually begins shortly after the concept of operations is developed. In the simplest understanding, a concept of operation provides a general scheme for orienting activity and a direction for planning. Likewise, this is when the effects of terrain begin to be considered. In understanding the impact of weather, the first step is usually estimating the amount of illumination. Thus, the time and expected duration of the operation are the initial compelling criteria. The analysis continues with other weather factors, especially temperature and precipitation. Needless to say, if the use of chemical agents or smoke is expected, wind speed and direction are vitally important. The process continues by estimating the influence of the expected weather conditions on each of the tactical maneuvers. Understandably, the expected time and duration of an activity coupled with the anticipated weather conditions become inseparable and are considered together.

When evaluating the effects of weather, some general rules provide clues to the type and amount of influence weather factors can exert. First of all, weather affects all parties but not all equally. For example, a driving hail storm may be nearly intolerable for individuals in the open but not even an inconvenience for a suspect inside a building. Second, inclement weather generally favors offense. This is because it provides a cover for movement. A driving rain or howling wind storm may not only obscure a barricaded suspect's ability to see, but to hear. Third, because nearly all domestic law enforcement operations are of short duration, and most artificial urban lighting[157] exceeds nighttime terrestrial illumination, a local weather forecast provides ample information for planning purposes.

It's been said that, "Weather is never important until it's important and then it's too late."[158] Finding out that a plan relying on darkness failed to account for a full moon or a sudden rainstorm made an avenue of approach too muddy to traverse is inexcusable in this day of ubiquitous weather forecasts. As with terrain, a commander who understands and plans for the impact of weather gains a substantial advantage over one who does not.

NAVIGATION

Accurate navigation across terrain is an indispensable element of maneuver. It is essential that individuals and units are at the right place at the right time. Navigating around threats and hazardous areas complicates the process in disaster responses and tactical operations. Compounding the problem still further is the fact that there is no single navigation system that provides sufficient accuracy, ease of use and precision to enable guidance in all locales and circumstances. Typically, the law enforcement community employs four different navigation methods.

The most well-known system is with the use of a compass. **Cardinal directions** is a system of navigation that uses the cardinal points of a compass for steering. Directions are given with one of the four cardinal points of a compass; north, south, east and west. When more precision is necessary the intermediate points of northwest, northeast, southwest and southeast are provided.[159]

While relatively rare in urban applications, this system can be made more precise by providing an azimuth. An **azimuth** is an angle of deviation measured clockwise from north, nearly always given in degrees.[160] Cardinal directions have two major disadvantages. First, they are difficult in urban environments because compasses are affected by magnetic fields and steel objects, both of which are plentiful in built-up areas. Second, without a lensatic compass and an ability to use it, cardinal directions don't provide enough precision for close coordination.

The oldest known navigation system known is called shift from a known point. **Shift from a known point** is a navigation system that calls attention to an easily identifiable terrain feature or man-made object and then provides a direction and distance from it. This method is easy to learn and use and requires only that everyone involved is focused on the known point. This is done with the use of a steering mark. A **steering mark** is any well-defined object on the ground that can be used for orientation. Prominent terrain is often used for this method because it is easy to identify on both a map and the actual terrain. When prominent terrain is not practical a substitute is used. Examples in the rural environment include distinctively shaped or colored rocks or hills or lone trees in a field or on the horizon. In the urban environment they may take the form of brightly colored roofs, signs, lights or unusually shaped buildings. The only necessity is that the feature be so clearly distinguishable that it won't be confused with something else. To use this method the guide identifies the steering mark and then gives a direction (usually a cardinal direction) and distance from it. A typical example might sound like, "From the tall building with the radio antenna on top, move east 500 feet." The major disadvantage with this navigation method is that it requires either prior knowledge of the known point or detailed descriptions and directions to ensure that nothing is confused.

A third method is with the use of coordinates, most often referred to as a grid system. A **grid system** of navigation consists of a map, diagram or aerial photograph superimposed with straight lines intersecting at right angles over it. The squares formed by the lines are called "grid squares" and the lines are assigned either numbers or letters to identify a particular square. The grids can be mentally divided into even smaller girds for more precision.

This method is used globally as the Universe Transverse Mercator coordinate system with horizontal lines following latitudes and the vertical lines following longitudes. Military units use a similar system called the Military Grid Reference System. This system is also very popular with commercially available road atlases and maps. Grid navigation systems are also adaptable as an ad hoc method by simply drawing grid lines over an aerial photograph or diagram. Directions are always given by first identifying a particular grid and then describing the feature sought. More precise measurements are possible by mentally dividing each grid into ten increments and then estimating the precise location of a particular feature within a designated grid square. The major disadvantage of the grid system is that everyone involved must use the identical system. This requires both planning and preparation. Furthermore, maps and aerial photographs that depict large areas are valuable for helicopters and convoys but nearly impossible to use for navigation with micro-terrain. Conversely, aerial photographs that provide enough detail to maneuver through micro-terrain are so large they become cumbersome for traversing over long distances.

One common tactical adaptation for navigation with micro-terrain is called the tactical numbering system. A **numbering system** of navigation assigns a number or letter to each side of a building to enable clear and precise directions with a minimum of confusion or conversation. While there are a number of variations, one of the simplest assigns the front of the location, usually determined by the entrance door, as the "1-side" and then moves clockwise around the structure with each side getting the next number in sequence. Hence, the "2-side" would be the side to the left when facing the

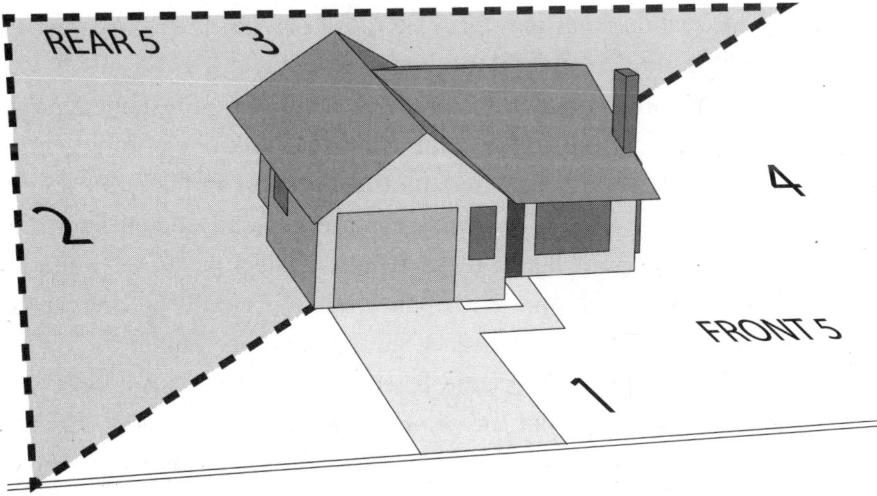

FIGURE 15-1 NUMBERING SYSTEM: Navigation in urban environments often requires more precision than is possible with coordinate or grid systems. A useful "work around" is a numbering system in which each side of a building is identified with a letter, color or number. As depicted above, this system identifies the front of the house with the letter one and continues clockwise around the building. This allows corners to be identified as a combination. Of example, the "1-2 Corner" is on the left side of the house at the front of the garage. This system is readily adaptable for immediate deployments by mentally dividing the house in half diagonally. The "front 5" includes sides 1 and 4 and the "rear 5" includes sides 2 and 3. As personnel hastily take up a position they can take their radio call sign from the particular side of the building they face. This allows everyone listening an ability to identify the particular assignment but the perspective they have on the building.

front and the "3-side" would be the back of the location, and so forth. Corners can be designated as the "2-3 Corner" or the "1-4 Corner." This system works even though buildings are seldom perfectly rectangular because small alcoves and walls perpendicular to the primary side are considered as part of that side.

This system will work for almost all buildings up to about three or four floors. When multiple-story buildings are encountered, letters are used to designate a specific story. This is only necessary when there are more than three-stories, since "plain text" is preferred for clarity and ease of understanding. Letters are used only when clarity and brevity suffer by requiring an elaborate description. For example, a sniper firing from a window of the sixth floor at the back of a large apartment building can be identified as "3F3," meaning that he is at the back of the building, firing from the sixth floor and the third window from the extreme left corner of that side. While there are other systems that may provide more precision, they usually do so at the sacrifice of clarity and understanding.

A team confronted with a situation requiring immediate deployment simply responds to the scene with one component taking positions along the "front five" and another component taking positions along the "back five." The call-signs are generally taken from the side of the building where a team member is deployed. For example, a sniper deployed at the rear of the building would be designated "Sniper #3" and one along the "4-Side" would be "Sniper #4." Once the team is in place, everyone listening can identify not only the particular assignment but the perspective they have on the building.

Like the other methods, the numbering system is not without disadvantages. While it is highly effective for micro-terrain it is inappropriate for longer distances. Consequently, a combination of navigation methods is the norm for tactical operations and disaster responses. In fact, it is not uncommon to use all four methods in the same operation.

---

145. Publius Flavius Vegetius Renatus, *The Military Institutions of the Romans*, circa AD 378, translated by Lt. John Clarke, 1767. (The quote

is taken from Book III) Not much is known about the life of Renatus beyond what he personally reveals in his writings. He is thought to have written from the western portion of the Roman Empire during a time when it was in a state of decline with continuous pressure from local tribes. Many Roman military men of the time were advocating reform in the Roman Army and Renatus apparently had no small influence on the thoughts and ideas of his readers in that he is first quoted by a writer in Constantinople in 450 AD. The book became a foundational text for the medieval conduct of war and was widely read and distributed throughout Western Europe. It was eventually translated from the original Latin into English by Lt. John Clarke.

146. Most historians place this battle around 1200 BC. Two interesting aspects are the historical portrayal of a woman leading warriors in a discipline and era completely dominated by males. Likewise, her staging of the Israelite army on the slopes of Mount Tabor, out of reach of the Canaanite chariots, and then attacking the chariots with her infantry while they were mired along the shores of the Kishon River, shows considerable acumen and understanding of the effects of terrain on the movement and capabilities of troops.

147. There are more than thirty tactical books entitled *The Art of War*, and while some of them have gained considerable attention, none is as renowned as the one by Sun Tzu written around 500 BC. This work is widely considered one of the earliest focused specifically on strategy and concepts of tactical operations. It remains relevant to this day and is required reading at many military institutions.

148. The Battle of Gaugamela (also called the Battle of Arbela) took place in 331 BC and was a decisive Macedonian victory. The Persians enjoyed a substantial numerical advantage and chose a flat plain where they could deploy their chariots for maximum effectiveness. Recognizing how the terrain would work to the Persians advantage, Alexander moved his army to uneven and rocky ground, flanked the Persians and defeated them. It is estimated that Alexander lost 390 men to as many as 40,000 Persians.

149. Frederick the Great, *Testament Politique*, 1768. At the time of this writing Frederick II (the Great) was King of Prussia and had already gained a reputation as a military strategist. He is particularly famous for employing a tactic which intentionally weakens one flank in order to concentrate strength on another (Oblique Order or Declined Flank), which showed the depth of his understanding of the principles of economy of force and mass. Likewise, Frederick had a keen appreciation of the significance of terrain in an era that emphasized warfare as mathematical and scientific algorithms. He also commented, "I approve of

all methods of attacking provided they are directed at the point where the enemy's army is weakest and where terrain favors them least."

150. Detailed terrain analyses are often part of a methodology called "Intelligence Preparation of the Battlefield"—IPB), which is intended to reduce uncertainties related to the terrain and weather for all types of operations. In the law enforcement community it is normally reserved for the higher echelons of an emergency response organization, especially emergency operations centers, and is referred to as "Intelligence Preparation for Operations"—IPO.
151. KOCOA is a military acronym. Others use OCOKA and some law enforcement texts use "COCOA" which substitutes the term "Critical terrain features" for "key terrain features."
152. While not as common, a terrain analysis can also be useful for large buildings and complexes, such as office buildings, factories, auditoriums, hotels, airport terminals, shopping malls and custodial facilities.
153. Widely known as the "Texas Tower Incident," Charles Whitman occupied the tower for 99 minutes and was only defeated when police stormed the tower and killed him. This incident occurred on August 1, 1966, and is largely credited as the impetus for the formation of SWAT teams.
154. An historical sidelight is that during the American Civil War, Confederate General Thomas "Stonewall" Jackson was accidentally killed by his own troops while conducting a terrain reconnaissance during the battle of Chancellorsville in 1863. After a huge victory earlier in the day, Jackson took an entourage to determine if a night attack would be feasible and upon his return he and his staff were thought to be Union cavalry and fired upon by his on troops. Several of the party were killed outright and Jackson was severely wounded and died a week later.
155. Sometimes called an "operational area"
156. Generally speaking, "percent illumination" refers to the amount of illumination on the ground from the moon compared with the amount of interference from clouds, fog, dust and the like.
157. Understandably, the presumption is that the operation is in an urban environment. If not, factors such as percent illumination, moonrise and moonset, sunrise and sunset, should be evaluated for their impact.
158. Anonymous.
159. These are called "intercardinal" directions. An intercardinal direction is any of the four directions midway between the cardinal points.
160. While degrees are normally the standard of measurement for domestic law enforcement applications, military units, especially those using indirect fires, normally use mils for more accuracy. Where there are 360 degrees in a circle there are 6,400 mils.

TIME

It is better to be at the right place with ten men than absent with ten thousand.

—TAMERLANE[161]

NO ONE IS PROBABLY MORE AWARE OF THE SIGNIFICANCE OF time than a traveller. Regardless of how well a person prepares for a trip, if he misses the departure of his plane or train by even a minute their entire plan immediately collapses. All the preparations, no matter how thorough, are for naught. In order to reach his destination he must make new plans and preparations; all for a minute lost. So it is with tactical operations.

Tactical operations always unfold in at least four dimensions. In fact, the older term "battlefield" has been replaced in modern military discourse by the more descriptive "battlespace"[162] to provide a more descriptive understanding of this concept. In the simplest terms, **battlespace** is the area, dimension or environment determined by the maximum capabilities to acquire and engage an adversary.

The first three dimensions—length, width and height/depth—make up the realm of space. Space is a physical dimension and so the maneuver elements are also physical. They can be seen and felt; they take up room and have position and weight. Examples include personnel, vehicles, supplies, equipment, and so forth. The fourth dimension is time. No one disputes the importance of time, but what they often miss is that time is not just a critical factor, it is an entirely different dimension altogether! The recognition of this concept is more critical than it might seem at first appearance. For example, without an understanding of the concept of time a clock has no purpose or meaning. Likewise, understanding how it works or what it is used for becomes equally impossible. So it with is with tactical operations and disaster responses.

A **dimension** may be understood as an environment, realm or domain which defines the state and conditions of the predominate influences. While **space** may be defined simply as a three-dimensional realm in which matter exists, the dimension of **time** is a non-space continuum where events occur in an irreversible succession from the past through the present to the future. While the maneuver elements involving time are just as intrinsic, they are intangible. They exist only as a mental image. Where space is a physical dimension, time is a notional dimension. Examples include actions, events, circumstances and opportunities. Nevertheless, they are just as real as those in the physical realm and just as critical in achieving a satisfactory resolution. Furthermore, the rules that govern one dimension are completely irrelevant for another. For example, where distance can be measured in space it is completely irrelevant in time. Conversely, circumstances are wholly time oriented and completely irrelevant in space. In order to handle disasters and tactical operations effectively, commanders must fully understand the impact of time.

MANEUVERING IN TIME

The importance of maneuvering in time can scarcely be exaggerated and has long been recognized by military strategists. In the words of one, "Strategy is the science of making use of space and time. I am more jealous of the latter than of the former. We can always recover lost ground, but never lost time."[163] Maneuver is one of the nine principles of war and refers to the movement of troops and equipment to gain an advantage. While this definition is easily understood when applied in space, it is also applicable in time. Every tactical operation is the result of a unique and temporary set of circumstances. Unique, because each circumstance is dependent only upon those factors that are present at a particular time and place. Temporary, because an outcome, of any kind, affects the next set of circumstances in an irreversible succession. Because tactical operations unfold in time as well as space, it becomes clear that they are in a constant and never-ending state of change. This dynamic nature makes them inherently time-sensitive because they are easily altered by actions. The actions may be intentional, such as those deliberate attempts at attaining a favorable outcome, or they may be unintentional, such as with accidents or misfortune. This is why a decision or action delayed may be rendered ineffective because the circumstances will have changed. While all tactical operations are dynamic, the problem is especially acute when suspects are involved because they provide an opposing interest that is actively attempting to exploit the circumstances for their own benefit. Conflicts are not only time-sensitive; they are time-competitive, because an adversary who can most quickly exploit the circumstances for their own benefit gains an advantage. In short, time or opportunity neglected by one adversary can be exploited by the other.

Unlike maneuver in space, which can be in any of the three directions of forward or backward, left or right, up or down; maneuver in time is always linear. This is because time is defined as a succession of events moving from the past toward the future. Thus, while we can think in the past all actions are in the future. Thus, maneuver in time is always toward the future. Notwithstanding, maneuver in time is possible because time can be divided and events can be retarded or accelerated.

Time can be divided in three ways. The first is with fixed time. A **fixed time** is definitively and unequivocally set and not dependent upon external factors. Perhaps the most well-known example of a fixed time is a deadline, which refers to a point in time that must not be passed without the completion or submission of something. Other examples include curfews, D-Day, H-Hour,[164] birthdays, anniversaries, noon, midnight, and so forth. Time can also be divided into periods. **Periodic time** refers to a specified division, portion or interval identified by a distinctive characteristic. For example, the month of June is a division of a year between May and

July, and an hour is identified as an interval of 60 minutes. Other examples include daytime, nighttime, afternoon, autumn, weekend, lead time, and lag time. The third way time can be divided is in relation to something. This is referred to as relative time. **Relative time** is a point or period of time having significance only in relation to something else. Two of the most common examples are yesterday and tomorrow, but others include designations of before, afterwards, again, between, concurrent, consecutive, continual, formerly, temporary, subsequent, and thereafter.

Maneuver in space is measured in distance, while maneuver in time is measured in speed. In tactical operations and competitive games, this is often referred to as tempo. **Tempo** refers to the speed, rhythm or rate of movement of something. In a tactical operation it describes the rapidity at which events are unfolding. The impact that tempo has on tactical operations can be easily illustrated by recalling the advantage of the "fast break" in basketball or the "breakaway" in hockey. The team that moves faster gains a considerable advantage. It is not new tactics that provide the advantage, it is the same tactics applied at a faster rate. Tempo is relative. A rapid tempo is only beneficial when compared with how fast an opponent can react because sheer speed is not the critical factor. It is only relevant in that whatever is done is done faster than the adversary. As an example, consider a game of football with a running back carrying the ball toward the goal line. In order to succeed, he doesn't need to be the fastest man on the field, nor does he even need to run as fast as he can. It is only necessary that he is running fast enough not to be caught.

Closely associated with tempo is initiative. **Initiative** refers to the power or ability to begin and follow through with some plan or task. Initiative lies entirely in the dimension of time. It is not action, per se, but rather the freedom of action; the ability to choose when and how to act, or in some cases, not to act. It is important to understand that deciding not to act and doing nothing are not the same. Doing nothing is passively abandoning the responsibility for handling a situation, while not acting is a conscious decision to continue to observe and gain understanding before acting. A good analogy to understand this concept is revving an engine before

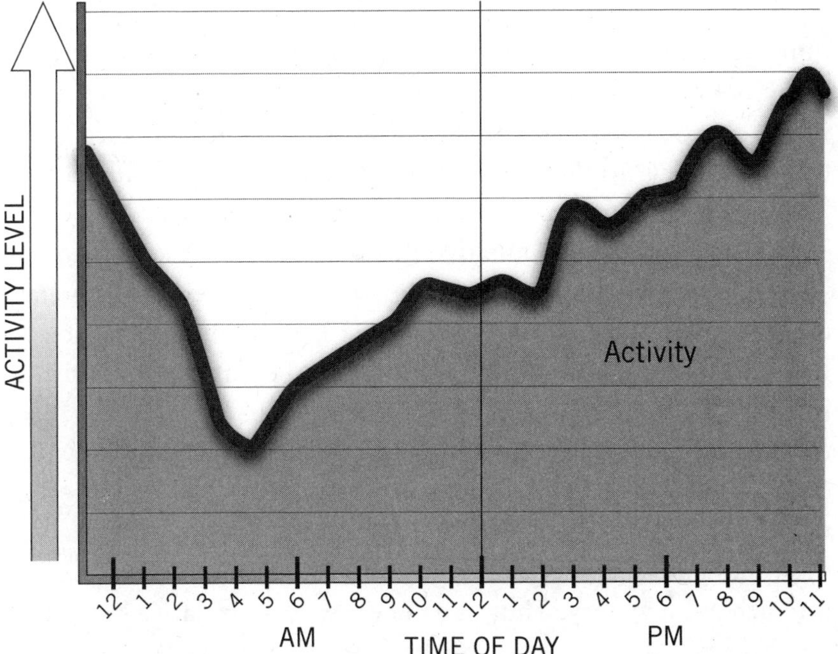

FIGURE 16-1 OP TEMPO: The amount of activity during a crisis is never static but rather ebbs and flows. Those of short duration are usually characterized by an initial period of intense activity followed by a lull and concluding with a higher level. While not fully understood, those of longer duration follow somewhat predictable patterns over time. Because of these patterns they are said to "pulse." The term used to describe this phenomenon is "tempo" which refers to the speed, rhythm or rate of activity. An effective response must necessarily adjust to these changing tempos. The rate of activity of a response effort is called the "operational tempo," or often just "op tempo" for short.

The chart above depicts one of the most common patterns for law enforcement tactical operations that exceed one day. Typical lulls are early in the morning while the most intense activities occur just before midnight. Knowing how a particular situation "pulses" facilitates all sorts of activities such as assignment of personnel, shift changes, resupplies, and the like. What is more, functioning at a higher op tempo than an adversary provides an advantage that is decisive in nature.

engaging the transmission. The preparation makes the subsequent action all the more effective.

To better understand the concept of initiative imagine a game of chess. The game board displays sixteen white pieces opposed by sixteen black pieces on the other side of the board. Neither side has moved. Everything is identically arranged in every respect with the only distinguishing feature the different colors of the opposing pieces. Why then do chess players choose who has white? If everything is identical then what difference should it make? It is because white is first to move and thereby gains an immediate advantage. Black cannot move without first observing white and then must effectively react to the move lest white gain even more advantage. Initiative then, refers to which side has the ability to act.

The importance of initiative can be easily and clearly demonstrated in other competitive games. In football, what difference does it make who receives the kick-off? It is because possession of the ball is necessary to score and thus, to be fair, the initiative is initially determined by chance—a coin toss. In board games, like Monopoly™, it is determined by a throw of a die or in chess, by choosing in which hand a pawn is hidden. As a game progresses, the initiative may revert back and forth among the players numerous times until one succeeds in gaining, maintaining and exploiting it to achieve a victory. Thus, it can be seen that initiative has value. Some games, like hockey and basketball, compete for initiative from the onset by throwing the ball up in the air or dropping a hockey puck. So it is with tactical operations where initiative is always contested. A tactical commander who has the initiative places the suspect in a reactionary mode and forces him to respond rather than act. Thus, *an implied objective of every operation is to gain and maintain the initiative*.

In a tactical operation without an opposing will, such as a response to natural disasters like fires, floods, earthquakes, storms, and the like, initiative may not be competitive but is still critical to success. The "opponent" may simply be the arbitrary and capricious whims of nature but to achieve a satisfactory resolution, a tactical commander must overcome the effects or attenuate the consequences in some manner to succeed. While there is no necessity (or capability) to "outwit" an opponent, there is a physical logic that must be understood to the best degree possible. For example, fires have "behaviors" that are subject to wind, humidity and terrain. Likewise, floods have characteristics that are entirely predictable; as in gravity holding water to the lower elevations, and so forth.

Another important maneuver factor in time is density.[165] When maneuvering in space, density refers to the number of personnel, citizens, vehicles and the like, per unit of space. When maneuvering in time, **density** refers to the quantity of activities per unit of time. Generally, humans generate most of the actions that are relevant for tactical operations. This results in situations in the more densely populated urban environments changing faster than those in rural areas. It also means that there are more factors that need to be considered and more decisions that need to be made. Thus, operations in urban environments tend to be more complex than similar operations in a rural area.

When maneuvering in space the early identification and control of key terrain takes on critical importance. In the same manner, when maneuvering in time, an ability to recognize (or create) and exploit opportunities is paramount. An **opportunity** is simply a brief interval in time in which circumstances are temporarily favorable. Opportunities in tactical situations tend to be elusive, sporadic and fleeting. They are elusive in that they are seldom clear and unequivocal but instead difficult to define, describe or anticipate. They are sporadic in the sense that they occur at irregular intervals without any pattern or order and are often isolated from predictable precursors. They are fleeting because they pass quickly. Consequently, time may provide for opportunities, but ignoring an opportunity always requires that it be abandoned forever. Opportunities that seem to be repetitive are each unique in that the conditions in which they reappear always differ to some extent from those in the past. The importance of being able to recognize and exploit one when it occurs can hardly be overestimated.

WINDOWS OF OPPORTUNITY

Because an opportunity is always an interval in time it is frequently likened to a window and sometimes even referred to as a "window of opportunity." While the more naïve often attribute these opportunities to chance or good fortune, in reality there has never been a tactical situation in which one or more of these windows were not present, albeit sometimes only recognized in hindsight.

Accordingly, the better tactical commanders attempt to identify and anticipate them in advance and prepare to exploit them when they occur.

In tactical situations, some windows of opportunity are more predictable than others and can even be intentionally created; so much so that they have been given names. The most familiar is probably the exploitation window. An **exploitation window** is a period of time in which an individual or unit is at some sort of disadvantage as a result of an intentional action by their opponent. One of the most common methods for creating an exploitation window is by dividing attention, frequently with a distraction of some sort. When a suspect's attention is temporarily diverted, even briefly, they are less capable of quickly employing effective countermeasures. It hardly needs to be emphasized, but when creating an exploitation window any expansion of the duration or increase in the effect provides a greater advantage. An aggregate of even minor distractions or multiple stimuli at close intervals can be confusing to the point of stupefying.

Another method is by creating a competing interest. A competing interest is anything that engages the attention and results in a division of attention or resources. To be effective, a competing interest need not be so startling that it diverts attention. It is sufficient that it just can't be completely ignored. Competing interests occur naturally, as when a suspect is torn between defending a location and preventing the interference and escape of hostages. Moreover, these natural competing interests occur to both sides of a conflict, and so routinely that commanders of tactical situations are required to prioritize them to avoid the adverse effects on their own organization.

While a competing interest is not usually as powerful as an intentional distraction, their principal advantage is that they last longer. Indeed, some will be present throughout the entire operation, causing continual and fatiguing internal strife and confusion. One of the most common methods for creating a competing interest is when a deployment of personnel creates a situation in which a suspect is vulnerable from more than one avenue of approach. Regardless of how a competing interest is accomplished, the stronger the challenges, and the more of them, the more difficult they are to effectively oppose.

Closely related to an exploitation window is another type of window of opportunity called the window of vulnerability. A **window of vulnerability** occurs when conditions exist that place a tactical team at a disadvantage. Some windows of vulnerability are nearly inseparable with certain activities. This is especially true for those involving movement of some kind, such as movements to contact, and during entries and assaults. Because windows of vulnerability are difficult to completely eliminate, efforts are usually directed toward diminishing their duration or reducing their effects.

One of the great ironies is that while opportunities are always elusive, sporadic and fleeting, they are also omnipresent. There has never been a tactical operation in which opportunities were not available. Once this fact is accepted, an ability to exploit them becomes a tactical imperative; it is not that we can take advantage, it is that we must. As in exploiting terrain, this requires flexibility in thought and plans coupled with mobility to enable prompt actions and reactions. While it has been said that time and chance favor no one, an ability to take advantage of a temporary set of favorable circumstances has momentous tactical significance and at times has been decisive. All things considered, both time and chance favor the prepared mind.

OBE

Like space, time can be congested and cumbersome in which to operate. Congestion in time ensues because the human mind is incapable of endlessly processing an infinite amount of information. A large number of events requiring decisions occurring in close succession means there is less time to analyze the situations and alternatives and more anxiety over the most appropriate course of action. In spite of the fact that successful tactical commanders are often judged by their ability to simultaneously handle multiple issues, human intellect, memory and attention are finite. It is simply not humanly possible to continually appraise an endless amount of information. As more information is presented than can be comprehended, older information is either deleted (forgotten), reprioritized (jumbled) or neglected (overlooked). The term used to describe this condition is usually identified by its acronym "**OBE**," which stands for "Overwhelmed By Events."[166]

Common symptoms of a decision maker experiencing OBE are manifested with behavior such as shouting at subordinates, continually countermanding previous orders or displays of temper. Other, more subtle, symptoms include headaches, confusion and anxiety. A commander afflicted with OBE is ineffective and, without some remedy, will inevitably reach a point where they simply "implode." When maneuvering through a congested time period, it will be necessary to "clear the landscape" by removing distractions, demanding standard formats, insisting on recommendations by trusted subordinates and delaying nonessential decisions.

There are two situations which are particularly prone to the OBE condition. The first is when a commander acquires an inordinate span of control. This is particularly significant since operations often grow faster than a commander's ability to handle them. The commander soon becomes inundated with decisions that should be made by subordinates. Commanders lose the ability to direct the efforts of the organization as a whole when they become overwhelmed with the details of one or two functions.

Generally, the span of control for individuals with emergency management responsibilities should be smaller than those conducting routine operations. Factors such as the kind of incident, hazards and safety factors, complexity of the task and physical proximity to supervisors all have considerable influence on the number of subordinates an individual can effectively supervise. The early identification of a maximum span of control will aid in assigning subordinate commanders and avoid the OBE condition. Generally, this has been determined to be about five subordinates.

The second situation occurs when a commander feels a need for excessive control. While most everyone will recognize the futility of attempting to control every facet of even small tactical operations, some commanders are extremely uncomfortable with relinquishing any authority. This not only encumbers the commander with trivial details but inhibits the initiative of subordinates. Further, since this requires virtually every decision to be passed up the chain of command, the tempo of the operation is reduced to a snail's pace in order to accommodate the limitations of a single human, regardless of personal skill, knowledge or ability.

Without exception, every commander will at some time experience the OBE condition. All the same, early recognition and avoiding the circumstances which are most predisposed for it to occur can dramatically reduce its impact.

THE BOYD CYCLE (OODA LOOP)

A useful tool for understanding the importance of tempo is the "OODA Loop." The **OODA Loop**, often called the Boyd Cycle, is a creation of the late Colonel John Boyd, USAF (Ret.). Colonel Boyd was a student of tactical operations and observed a similarity in many battles and campaigns. He noted that in many of the engagements, one opponent had presented the other with a series of unexpected and threatening situations with which they had not been able to keep pace. The slower side was eventually defeated. What Colonel Boyd had observed was the fact that conflicts are time-competitive.

In its simplest form, the **Boyd Cycle** views conflict as an overlapping series of time-competitive, **O**bservation-**O**rientation-**D**ecision-**A**ction (OODA) cycles. Each party to a conflict begins with **observation.** This step scans the environment and includes all aspects, such as the physical surroundings, lighting conditions, weather, terrain, the adversary and even themselves. Understandably, the better the observation the clearer will be the perspective gained by the observer. Observation is the first step in separating the factors relevant to a situation from the volume of all the information available.

Next, they orient themselves. **Orientation** identifies the need to gain perspective and provides a foundation for understanding. This phase is necessary because the fluid, chaotic nature of conflicts makes it impossible to process information as fast as we can observe it. This requires a "freeze-frame" concept and provides a perspective that would otherwise be lacking.

Once an orientation is gained, a decision is necessary. **Decisions** must be made to influence the outcome. Based upon the decision maker's understanding of the situation, hypotheses are developed and conclusions are drawn. The resulting decision takes into account all the known factors present at the time of the orientation.

Last comes the implementation of the decision. This requires **action.**[167] Actions are always necessary to affect those factors that influence a favorable outcome, whether by making adverse influences less likely to occur or less damaging when they do, or conversely, to encourage those that are favorable. Though the very word "action" seems decisive and final, it in fact represents simply a test of the hypothesis. In this manner it works as feedback to confirm or deny our desired outcome and provides information to begin the cycle anew with both the change in our perspective and the change in the situation caused by the action. The cycle continues to repeat itself throughout a tactical operation.

THE BOYD CYCLE (OODA LOOP)

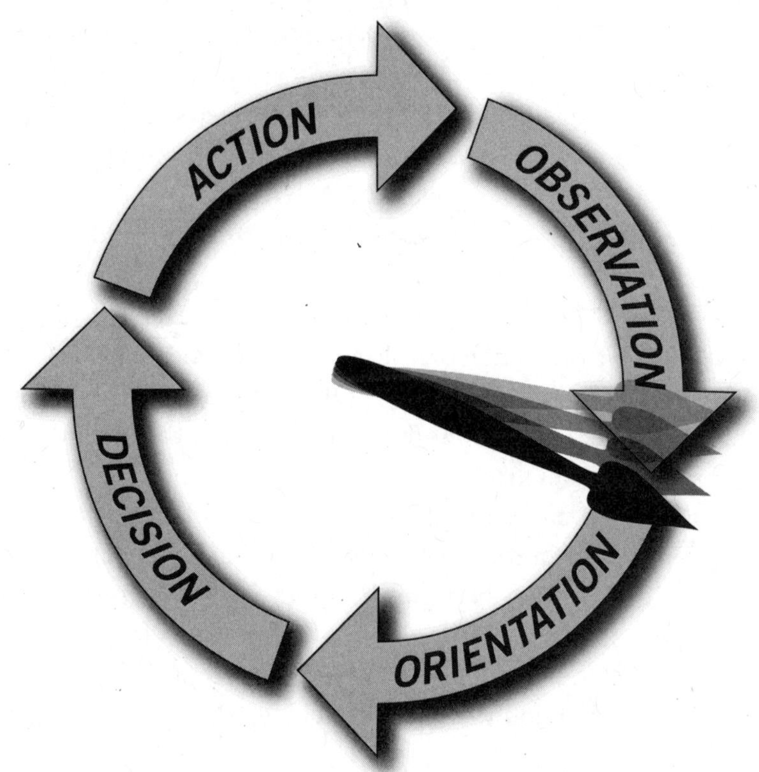

Whichever opponent can consistently go through the Boyd Cycle faster than the other gains a tremendous advantage. By the time the slower adversary reacts, the faster one is doing something different and the slower action becomes less effective because it is now addressing a new situation. With each cycle, the slower party's action is less effective by a larger and larger margin. The aggregate resolution of these episodes will eventually determine the outcome of the conflict. This demonstrates that the initiative follows the faster adversary because tempo is a force multiplier in and of itself.

The Boyd Cycle demonstrates the value of gaining and maintaining the initiative. A commander may decide to initiate an action simply to cause a suspect to respond. By forcing a response, the commander maintains freedom of action while requiring the suspect to react. Once gained, the initiative can be maintained by compelling the suspect to respond in some manner that consumes so much time or resources that it is not practical to do anything but react. This eventually results in exposing a critical, sometimes even decisive, vulnerability that can be exploited.

While Boyd's cycle is a great descriptive tool, it has even richer and deeper applications as a tool of analysis. The ability to gain

FIGURE 16-2 BOYD'S CYCLE (*OPPOSITE*): Maneuver in space is measured in distance but maneuver in time is measured in speed. One method of understanding tempo is with the Boyd Cycle, which is just as often identified as the "OODA loop." The concept was used by USAF Colonel John R. Boyd to explain how a faster tempo can be used to create opportunities in the dimension of time.

In the simplest terms, the Boyd Cycle is an organism's or organization's method of interacting with the environment. The cycle begins by trying to understand the environment by means of the senses, followed by an examination of the information to provide a perspective, which in turn helps choose a promising course of action followed by putting it into action. Each of these processes overlaps the others and because the action will change the circumstances, the cycle begins anew. Each iteration of the cycle allows an adversary to adapt to a new set of circumstances and if conducted faster than an adversary will create an accumulation of advantage until the final action is decisive. The concept has been demonstrated in a wide range of activities to include competitive games and business.

Of particular note is the fact that when it is not possible to speed up your own tempo it is often possible to slow down that of the adversary which has the same effect. In law enforcement operations this can often be done by interrupting an adversary's plan or action or interfering with some activity that provides him an advantage. This is often referred to as "getting inside the loop."

speed in deciding and acting relies heavily on a deep and intuitive understanding of the rapidly changing circumstances. For this reason, Boyd believed that the orientation phase of the cycle was the most important in that the knowledge, experience, insight and understanding of the combatant decision maker was necessary to fully comprehend what was actually occurring and why. This orientation provided not only the guidance of what should be done and when but a focus for the observation phase of the next iteration of the cycle. In this manner, every iteration of the loop is shaped by a previous one and in turn, shapes the next. The faster this can be achieved the more advantage it provides. Boyd refers to this concept as a "fast transient." A **fast transient** refers to the capability of rapidly changing from one maneuver state to another. The four most common methods are changing speed, direction, location or attitude.[168] An ability to employ fast transients provides a unit with agility that enables rapid exploitation of opportunities. Each opportunity that is seized and exploited provides an advantage that increases each time it is repeated. The football example described previously is a good example of how fast transients can provide advantages. For example, raw speed is nearly useless on a football field in that someone is nearly always in a position to intercept the ball carrier. Better than speed, per se, is an ability to stop quickly, change direction and quickly reaccelerate. This makes it far more difficult to anticipate intentions, adjust to the changing circumstances and outpace the opponent.

There are two important factors that must be understood when attempting to gain advantages with fast transients. First, speed—in and of itself—is not the objective. It is only important that whatever is done is faster than the opponent can effectively react. Thus, the necessary speed is always relative when compared with how fast an adversary can or will respond. An understanding of this concept provides alternatives to speeding up actions because slowing down the adversary accomplishes the same thing. This has momentous significance in that creating delays can provide time for reinforcements to arrive, establish containments, conduct evacuations, seize key terrain and a host of other actions.

Second, an ability to think faster and clearer than an adversary provides even greater advantages than speed of action because it provides an ability to anticipate actions. This ability must come from a thorough understanding of the factors and influences involved. Decision makers with expertise are more perceptive and insightful when examining a situation and more readily recognize what is likely and intended. They also tend to be imaginative and clever in their plans and actions, especially with deceptions and delays. This is often referred to as "getting inside the loop." Returning to the football example, an experienced runner is quicker to assess the situation, anticipate the actions of the opponents and move to avoid defenders. Moreover, actions like a feint, cause even more confusion and provide still greater advantages.

---

161. Tamerlane (AD 1336-1405), quoted in Lamb, *Tamerlane, The Earth Shaker*, 1928. Tamerlane was a descendant of Genghis Khan and was one of the most influential rulers in Central Asia during the middle ages. He engaged in nearly constant warfare throughout his life and gained a reputation as a ruthless military genius. His name is reportedly derived from "Timur Lang" or "Timur the Lame" because he was partially paralyzed on his left side from a battle injury. He was known as an opportunist and perhaps that is the basis of his understanding of time in the conduct of tactical operations.
162. At the risk of oversimplification, battlespace is defined as the area, dimension or environment determined by the maximum capabilities to acquire and engage an adversary. While time is critical in all operations, it is competitive in conflicts because adversaries are contending for advantages at the same time.
163. Field Marshal August Graf von Gneisenau, (1761-1831), quoted in Foertsch, *The Art of Modern War*, 1940. Gneisenau was born into abject poverty but rose to become a Prussian Field Marshal. Although not well-known outside military circles, he was considered the greatest Prussian general since Frederick the Great. In his early career he was part of the mercenary regiments that fought against the Americans in the Revolution but distinguished himself in the Napoleonic wars and was a major factor in the defeat of Napoleon in the Battle of Waterloo. Another little known fact is that the famous Carl von Clausewitz served as Gneisenau's personal aide for two years between 1813 and 1815 and later his Chief of Staff (1830) and Gneisenau undoubtedly contributed to much of Clausewitz's understanding of the nature of war.

164. D-Day is a military term which identifies the unnamed day on which a particular operation commences or is to commence. H-Hour refers to the specific hour on D-Day at which a particular operation commences or is to commence. While seldom used in law enforcement tactical operations, the concept of a particular point in time, even though unscheduled, allows planning to develop with time apportioned and in sequence.
165. For more information on density, the author highly recommends the book, *Heavy Matter, Urban Operations' Density of Challenges*, by Russell W. Glenn, RAND Corporation, Santa Monica, CA, 2000 (310-451-6915 or order@rand.org). Dr. Glenn served 22 years with the U.S. Army with combat in Operation Desert Storm. He is a graduate of the U.S. Military Academy at West Point and qualified as a Ranger, Pathfinder and Airborne (parachutist). He is a learned scholar with a wide array of experience and a renowned expert in counterinsurgency and urban operations. More to the point here is that he is also one of those scholars who expresses his thoughts with clarity and simplicity and so even a novice reader can readily understand the concepts.
166. Sometimes called "*Overcome* By Events." Whichever term is used, it is most often identified by the acronym, OBE, in which each letter is usually pronounced separately.
167. One tactical adage states that, "Decisions without actions are pointless. Actions without decisions are reckless."
168. As used here, attitude refers to the orientation, disposition or state of a thing. For example, a unit that quickly changes from a defensive posture to an offensive one, from an exhausted state to a refreshed state, from a discouraged disposition to a determined one, and so forth.

CYBERSPACE

We lack dominance in cyberspace and could grow increasingly vulnerable if we do not fundamentally change how we view this battlespace.

—GENERAL JAMES CARTWRIGHT[169]

NO ONE WILLINGLY TAKES A BEATING. LACKING an effective means of resisting, flight is the natural and understandable alternative. This reveals an axiom that holds true in all conflicts; the weaker adversary always seeks refuge. Escape in the realm of space is usually accomplished by either moving beyond the range of the offending force or seeking protective cover which shields from injury. Escape in the realm of time is almost always some type of avoidance. There are other sanctuaries, however. For example, criminals (and terrorists) depend on remaining undetected. Once identified and located they are virtually powerless to continue their anti-social behaviors and are extremely vulnerable to arrest and prosecution. This concept is called the **sanctuary of anonymity**. What is revealing here, however, is that anonymity is dependent on neither time nor space. It lies in an entirely different dimension altogether.

The fifth dimension is cyberspace.[170] **Cyberspace** is an intangible information space where people interact with one another and with machines. While most people think of cyberspace as the online world of computer networks it is actually a much richer and deeper environment. It is better understood as a domain of information.

Besides information transferred between computers; such as email, file transfer protocols (FTP), web browsing and the like; it includes all types of information like that transferred from wireless cell phones, text messaging, pagers, and even electronic door locks, TV tuners or garage door openers.

Like all dimensions, the rules for one are completely irrelevant for another. Neither space nor time is applicable in cyberspace for one simple reason; information can reside in more than one place at the same time. For example, a mother purchases a combination padlock for her young son's school locker because when he inevitably loses the key she can unlock it over the telephone by giving him the combination. When that happens the information needed to unlock the padlock is simultaneously at home with the mother and at school with the son. So it is with all information. Only the medium used to store and transmit it occupies space.

In law enforcement applications, five-dimensional battlespace can be readily understood in the stark reality of every day examples. For instance, it is not an uncommon occurrence to stop a vehicle for a traffic violation only to discover after leaving the scene that the driver was just involved in a crime. It is a vivid example that the suspect was trapped in both time and place during the stop but the lack of knowledge left him immune from arrest and prosecution. So it is with tactical operations. No good commander ignores an unprotected flank and a lack of knowledge can be every bit as devastating as being in the wrong place or at the wrong time. It would seem prudent then to understand the implications of a multidimensional battlespace.

MANEUVERING IN CYBERSPACE

Maneuver in cyberspace requires a new paradigm because the defining characteristic is information. Whether it is needed to locate a criminal hiding in darkness or to identify a terrorist concealed by anonymity, it is information that is necessary to acquire and effectively engage him. Consequently, the maneuver elements in cyberspace are informational, often obtained as the "fruits" of devices designed to allow humans to interact in this dimension. Examples

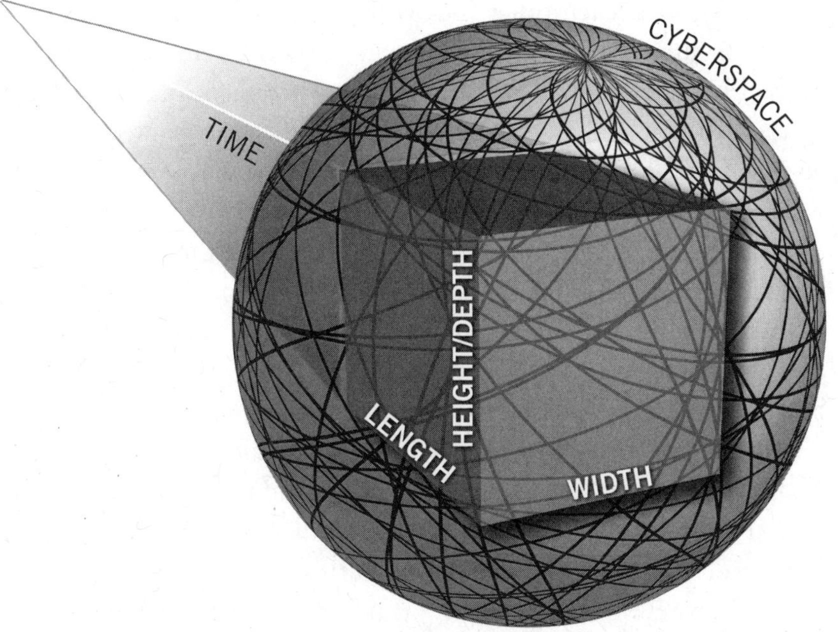

FIGURE 17-1 VISUALIZING BATTLESPACE: If it were possible to see battlespace, it might look something like this. Length, width and depth/height comprise the dimension of space. In space the maneuver elements are physical in that they take up space, have weight and volume. The fourth dimension is time. Time is a notional dimension in that the maneuver elements are conceptional and exist only as a mental image. Each tactical situation is a temporary and unique combination of circumstances and as such, is dissimilar at different times. Together, space and time comprise humanspace. Humanspace is where humans live and interact. The fifth dimension is cyberspace. Like time, in cyberspace the maneuver elements are intangible and the maneuver elements are informational in nature, often as a means of communication between people and other people or people and their machines. Information has one critical aspect that distinguishes it from others in that it can reside in more than one place at the same time. Thus, both time and space become irrelevant. An adversary in cyberspace is thus immune from attack because his identity and/or location are unknown. Commanders who ignore the vagaries of multi-dimensional battlespace surrender the advantage to their adversary.

include the information obtained from cell phone conversations, pager messages, location reports from global positioning systems, or that taken from email, web sites and other on-line transactions. It also includes the information gleaned from sensors, such as motion detectors, surveillance cameras, thermal imaging devices and night vision goggles. This interaction not only includes humans interacting with each other, but with machines. Examples include television tuners, garage door openers and even remotely operated automobile alarms and locks. No law enforcement officer is likely to miss the tactical significance of being able to remotely open a garage door, lock a criminal out of his car or prevent him from watching a live TV broadcast.

Despite their fundamental differences all five dimensions interact with one another with humans as the common "go between" or element. Every disaster or tactical situation is a result of a unique and temporary set of circumstances unfolding in space. Unseen, but ever present, is the intrinsic information, including that of the authorities, victims, bystanders, witnesses, and even suspects. It also includes information between people and things, like a suspect remotely opening or closing a garage door or setting off a bomb. For actions in time and space, some of this information is valuable, and some is even crucial. Thus, all five dimensions are an integral part of battlespace.

When attempting to gain an advantage it is important to understand that two adversaries need not be in each other's battlespace at the same time. In the previous example of the traffic stop the officer's lack of knowledge of the driver's criminal conduct was a critical vulnerability which resulted in the suspect's escape. Conversely, the knowledge possessed by the suspect provided him with an ability to manipulate a situation to make getting caught even more difficult, to include the use of surprise. Tragically, this has resulted in the deaths of officers who stopped criminals unaware of the danger and were attacked, and even killed. As can be seen, because of a lack of knowledge the officer was in the suspect's battlespace but the suspect was not in the officer's battlespace—which provided a decisive advantage.

Understandably, maneuver in cyberspace is measured in knowledge, and the ability to acquire, deprive and manipulate information is critical. The two most commonly sought after facts in law enforcement are usually the identity of culprits and their location. Similarly, an ability to manipulate information is of great value. Many a fugitive has been arrested as part of a sting operation after having been lured to a location with false information.

While the maneuver objective in space is gaining and controlling key terrain and in time it is identifying, creating and exploiting opportunities; in cyberspace the goal is gaining understanding. Information is only useful if it contributes to identifying and comprehending the factors and influences involved. Information that does not provide better understanding is distracting. In some cases this necessitates acquiring new information but in many cases the same thing can be accomplished by rearranging and interpreting information that is already available. Once a fact has been determined to be relevant to some concern, a second fact can not only be used to corroborate the first but also to extrapolate a wealth of information. Just two sightings of a fleeing suspect, for example, provide such things as a direction of travel, approximate speed and may even indicate intentions with a potential destination.[171]

MULTI-DIMENSIONAL BATTLESPACE

DIMENSION	MANEUVER ELEMENTS	MEASURED IN	OBJECTIVE
Space	Physical	Distance	Gain and maintain control of key terrain
Time	Notional	Speed	Identify, create and exploit opportunities
Cyberspace	Informational	Knowledge	Acquire and apply understanding

FIGURE 17-2 MULTI-DIMENSIONAL BATTLESPACE: Multi-dimensional battlespace is not as complex as it might seem. In fact, adversaries with no understanding whatsoever move seamlessly between them. A commander with a thorough understanding of the nature of battlespace can understand and anticipate actions and counteractions. The matrix above compares each of the five dimensions with the major factors that differentiate each of them.

NATURE OF KNOWLEDGE

The maneuver elements in cyberspace are informational; meaning that they are related to the nature of information. Gains and losses are measured in knowledge and the objective is to acquire and apply understanding. Accordingly, it is of great benefit to have some understanding of the nature of knowledge and comprehension.

The rawest form of information is **data**. Each datum refers to a single fact, statistic or code that exists without context. Data, in and of itself, is not information because it provides no ability to inform. It only becomes information when a context is added, either with circumstances or from other data. Data comes in any number of varieties and formats and can range from the binary code of a computer to the oscillations in a radio frequency wave. In tactical operations data may appear as a discrete event, fact, observation, message, or statement. In order to be useful, data must be collected, organized and interpreted.

Information may be best understood as a collection of facts or data from which conclusions may be drawn.[172] Information is the first step toward understanding and where meaning is attached. It is intended to provide substance and shape to a person's perspective and provide a basis for judgment. Unlike data, information is always enclosed in context and needs to be organized to be useful. Information that is jumbled, confusing, or ambiguous requires a decision maker to make a personal investment of effort and attention. Accordingly, the value of information is determined by the recipient. When the expected effort exceeds the perceived value the information is likely to be glossed over or ignored entirely.

Knowledge refers to a state of awareness of facts and circumstances accompanied with a personal assessment. Consequently, all knowledge is based on interpreted information. While data and information may be captured and stored on paper or a hard drive, knowledge belongs to people. While information is derived from data, knowledge is derived from information. The four most common ways that humans transform information to knowledge is through the use of:

- Comparison—how does one piece of information compare with another?
- Consequences—what are the implications of a particular piece of information in regards to forming a judgment?

- Connections—how does a particular piece of information relate to others?
- Conversation—what do other people think about a particular piece of information?[173]

Like information, knowledge can be shared. The knowledge belonging to a group is usually referred to as "corporate knowledge." **Corporate knowledge** is the collective knowledge of all participants in any plan or decision. It is invaluable in dealing with complex situations and is what makes units like explosive ordnance disposal, gang enforcement, SWAT, and narcotics teams so formidable.

The maneuver objective in cyberspace is gaining and applying understanding. **Understanding** identifies a person's thorough comprehension of the nature of something. It surpasses simply knowing something and provides insight for probabilities, expectations, opportunities, creativity and resourcefulness. True understanding enables intuition and so subtle factors and influences are more easily detected and reliable inferences can be formed. The difference between knowledge and understanding may seem subtle because they are so similar. The differentiating feature is that knowledge refers to a mental comprehension about something while understanding refers to the comprehension of something. As such, understanding includes an ability to interpret and extrapolate. That's why understanding, not knowledge or information, is the maneuver objective.

To better understand how these function and interact, imagine running a license plate while on patrol. The numbers and letters on the license plate are data. By themselves they have no meaning but when compared with other data, as that in the database of the department of motor vehicles, it provides the registered and legal owner of the vehicle, the vehicle description, the address, and even traffic accidents and offenses. Likewise, the officer notes that the license plate frame identifies a car sales agency from another state. The combined data is now information. The officer also remembers a briefing concerning guns being transferred to a local gang from the distant state and begins following the vehicle. He soon realizes it is headed toward a local gang hangout. His personal awareness of facts, coupled with the circumstances, has now transformed the data and information into knowledge. The officer is a seasoned veteran who has not only had much instruction on the nature of gangs but has personally had experience with this particular gang. He knows that when moving contraband gangs routinely use countersurveillance and support vehicles and quickly identifies a likely possibility. He rapidly formulates a plan and relays his instructions to responding units. Because of his understanding of the situation as a whole both vehicles are stopped well away from the gang area with sufficient support to ensure a decisive action should a confrontation occur. When guns are indeed discovered, the officer's increasing understanding provides even more insight and so everything from the identity of the recipients of the guns to information for obtaining a search warrant and even the expectation of a gang war can be reliably intuited.[174]

While the maneuver objective in cyberspace is understanding, maneuver is actually measured in knowledge. This is because while knowledge can exist without understanding, the reverse is not true. When seeking knowledge it is important to understand that it is not evenly distributed. In tactical operations it tends to accumulate according to two attractors. The first is by locale. There is more knowledge of the unfolding events at a crime or disaster scene, for instance, than at an emergency operations center. It also tends to be clumped by type. Experts are able to harvest more knowledge from the same information than are novices. Consequently, knowledge related to a particular event or activity is greater with technicians who specialize in that particular area. Furthermore, these specialists themselves tend to be grouped in specialized units like SWAT, canine, explosives ordnance disposal, narcotics, gangs, and so forth. With this in mind, some priorities begin to emerge in that efforts need to be made to make this knowledge available for decision makers. The extensive use of versatile and reliable communications is one the best methods of propagating knowledge from various locales. The use of liaisons and advisors for harvesting knowledge from subject matter experts is another.

FIGURE 17-3 CREATING UNDERSTANDING: Whether baking a cake, making an omelet or brewing coffee a process is involved. So it is with creating understanding. If one were to compare the process of gaining understanding with brewing coffee it might appear as the graphic above. The coffee beans represent the raw data and incapable of being used in their present form. After being ground and blended with other coffee beans they constitute a substance that provides a pleasant aroma but are still of no benefit. When placed in a coffee press with boiling water they create the first substance that would be readily recognizable as coffee. If the process were stopped here, however, the coffee is still undrinkable. Only after it is poured into a cup do the coffee beans fulfill their purpose. So it is with data, information, knowledge and understanding.

The process begins with the identification of facts, statistics or codes. These are called data and constitute the raw material from which understanding is ultimately drawn. As these data are gathered they create information. This is the first step in the process where meaning is attached. When information is gathered it can be analyzed to ascertain its relevance, reliability and accuracy. This is where knowledge is gained. Even so, only when a person uses knowledge to comprehend the nature of something does understanding result.

HUMANSPACE + CYBERSPACE = BATTLESPACE

Together, the dimensions of space and time make up that portion of battlespace occupied by humans, and as such, is called "humanspace." **Humanspace** is defined as that aspect of battlespace composed of the traditional dimensions of space and time in which humans, and their machines, move and fight.[175]

Until recently, humanspace has been the exclusive domain where combatants met and fought. When the dimension of cyberspace is added, however, combatants who remain in humanspace can be attacked with impunity from cyberspace. News reports of suspects captured because they were identified and located by someone with a cell phone, to include their photograph (and even video), are now commonplace. Moreover, fugitives are frequently captured when the authorities track a suspect's cell phone to a specific location.

What separates humanspace from cyberspace is a **human sensing dimensional barrier** beyond which a lack of knowledge prevents an adversary from being acquired and engaged. For example, the sanctuary of anonymity lies entirely in cyberspace as a void. As long as fugitives and terrorists are unable to be identified or located they are immune from attack. No amount of increased firepower is capable of defeating an adversary who, for all intents and purposes, is "invisible" even though he may be living and working right next door. Moreover, they remain free to maneuver through humanspace, even conducting their nefarious activities.

This barrier is a dynamic and contested frontier between opposing forces because terrorists and criminals will, quite understandably, take steps to avoid detection and thus remain in the safety of cyberspace. Humanspace is where a suspect will be arrested and taken into custody but cyberspace offers a refuge. This reveals one of the principle concepts when maneuvering in cyberspace which is that to prevail in five-dimensional battlespace we must either enter cyberspace or force the adversary into humanspace.

To force an adversary into human space will require enhancing human sensing capabilities to be able to "see" into cyberspace. Some technologies are already available and are being used. A suspect hiding in darkness, for one example, may be detected with the use of night vision goggles or thermal imaging devices. Likewise, a canine provides the same capabilities with a dog's increased abilities to see, hear and smell. An undetected terrorist presents more formidable, but not insurmountable, problems. Biometric technologies[176] are providing abilities to identify people with everything from fingerprints and retinal scans to facial recognition and handwriting. As the technologies continue to mature, movement through humanspace, especially through airports and border checkpoints, will be more and more troublesome for those attempting to remain anonymous.

Law enforcement has long been entering cyberspace in the form of undercover operations. In this manner, suspects are in law enforcement's battlespace but as long as the undercover officers remain undiscovered they are outside the suspects' battlespace. Undercover operations have proven to be one of the most, if not the most, effective method of gathering intelligence, which further reduces the sanctuary of anonymity. Even without knowing the location of a suspect or terrorist, their identification greatly reduces their freedom of movement and action and forces them to consider detection countermeasures, which can exacerbate their capabilities to the point of impotence.

Two aspects of the human sensing dimensional barrier are particularly advantageous to terrorists. The first is that, as long as they remain undetected they are immune from attack. Regardless of their particular location at any given time or how they are armed, an undetected terrorist is more dangerous than a known one. This renders the dimensions of time and space irrelevant for both defense and offense since the undetected terrorist is free to maneuver to strike at a time and place of his choosing. Second, it is cheap. In any prolonged engagement the most frugal side gains an advantage, sometimes even a decisive one. Searching in cyberspace can be horrendously expensive. Hiding in cyberspace costs nothing. This provides an asymmetric advantage to the adversary who chooses to avoid conventional conflicts by striking in stealth and compensates for the power, influence and wealth of a stronger adversary.

DOMINATING CYBERSPACE

Well over a century ago, American Civil War General Ulysses S. Grant said, "The laws of successful war in one generation would ensure defeat in another."[177] Whether it is the war on crime or the war on terrorism, the surest way to lose it is to fight it like the last one. Understanding that modern battlespace is five-dimensional fundamentally challenges thinking and planning for contemporary conflicts in at least five distinct areas.

First, recognizing that cyberspace is an inherent component of battlespace becomes a tactical imperative. Any commander who chooses to fight only in humanspace can expect to be "flanked" and attacked from cyberspace. This is particularly the case with terrorists who cannot win a "stand up fight" and must attack and return to the safety of cyberspace in order to survive, much less succeed. No amount of additional firepower will even the odds, because in cyberspace firepower is measured in gigabytes and terabytes.

Second, retooling and not rearming will be necessary. Sensors, not firearms will be required to identify and locate criminals and terrorists hiding outside human sensing capabilities. These will take on countless forms and provide any number of advantages. On the tactical level, devices that detect explosives and weapons will tremendously diminish a criminal's ability to commit robberies or a terrorist's ability to secrete and detonate bombs. On the strategic level, biometric devices will identify terrorists and criminals and remove them from the "sanctuary of anonymity." At all levels, devices that detect, intercept, capture, locate and interpret messages will be critically important.

Third, the rules of engagement in cyberspace are not based on the appropriateness of force but the invasion of privacy. Barriers already exist in cyberspace that prohibit viewing or listening in all but the most extraordinary circumstances. For example, some technologies provide an ability to search electronically for contraband and weapons without the knowledge of the person being searched. So, while a see-through-the-wall radar or audio interception device may be easy to justify during a hostage recovery operation, screams of protest erupt when biometric devices are suggested to scan and identify terrorists among passengers arriving from another country.

Fourth, the realm of cyberspace is far more expansive than the finite limitations of space and time that define humanspace. The volume of information is seemingly unfathomable. Consequently, tactics in cyberspace will not focus on the movement of personnel or equipment, but the ability to gain understanding and knowledge from a myriad of data. Information will need to be analyzed and appraised to determine meaning, relevance and significance before being incorporated into the decision making process. Accordingly, the most effective strategies will provide an ability to accumulate and distribute knowledge and to quickly sort the relevant from the volume.

Fifth, cherished methods and practices will be challenged. Nowhere will this be more prominent than in the command and control function. Currently, tactical decision making is accomplished by placing people with expertise and authority in a central location, generically referred to as a "command post," and then providing them information and knowledge to make decisions. The major problem with this method is that the authority and expertise to make effective decisions lies at the command post, while the greater situational awareness remains at the scene of the crime or disaster. Additionally, particularly complex tactical situations, such as those involving chemical, biological, or radiological threats, will require the advice of experts seldom affiliated with tactical organizations. Instead, college professors, scientists and engineers located at distant universities and research facilities will possess the essential knowledge. Incorporating their expertise into the decision making process becomes a compelling need for a satisfactory resolution.

These problems are greatly attenuated when a "cyber-command post" is created. Much like a teleconference, a cyber-command post does not rely on a physical location, but incorporates technology to immediately provide the insight of subject matter experts from wherever they are through the use of remote video viewing, the World Wide Web, email, cell phones, and the like. Thus, the tactical decision making process is immensely enriched with knowledge that far exceeds the capabilities of any tactical organization alone without the requirement of the participant to be physically present.

169. USMC General James E. Cartwright, Vice Chairman of the Joint Chiefs of Staff. General Cartwright is a pilot who, as he rose through the ranks, became known for his exceptional understanding of the changing nature of threats. The comment was made on March 21, 2007 as a statement to the House Armed Services Committee while General Cartwright was the Commander of the United States Strategic Command. He was not only explaining some of the challenges of cyberspace but why it was appealing to adversaries unable and unwilling to fight a conventional war. He also emphasized the need for an offensive capability in cyberspace. Even more poignant for the purposes of this chapter was a statement in which he pointed out that the principles of warfare also apply to cyberspace. "If we apply the principles of warfare to the cyber domain, as we do to sea, air, and land, we realize the defense of the nation is better served by capabilities enabling us to take the fight to our adversaries, when necessary to deter actions detrimental to our interests."
170. "Cyberspace" was coined by science fiction author William Gibson, in his book *Neuromancer*, published in 1984. The book is essentially a science fiction crime novel. While Gibson had used the term in a magazine article two years earlier, it wasn't until the book became popular that it gained widespread recognition.
171. The combination of two or more pieces of information to gain some new insight is called "information fusion" and is discussed in more detail in Chapter 9—Intelligence.
172. For a more thorough discussion of information, see Chapter 9—Intelligence.
173. Many of the ideas on generating knowledge and understanding for this chapter come from two seminal books on the subject. For further exploration and understanding see: *Working Knowledge: How Organizations Manage What They Know*, by Thomas H. Davenport and Laurence Prusak, Harvard Business School Press, Boston, MA, 2000 and *Information Anxiety 2*, by Richard Saul Wurman, Que Publishing, Indianapolis, IN, 2001
174. As the example illustrates, humans do not acquire understanding in a linear process but rather a highly complex and interactive process that includes gathering, organizing and testing data and assumptions, drawing inferences, making comparisons and mentally "explaining" the outcome. Experts are particular adept at making sense in situations where the available information is unreliable, confusing, incomplete and even conflicting because they have a larger repertoire of experiences for comparison. Moreover, they are just as likely to notice something

that should be present but is not as something that is present but out of place. They also engage in mental simulation of what has occurred and is transpiring, as well as what it means and what is likely to occur in the near future. One of the premier researchers in this area is Dr. Gary Klein (author of *Sources of Power, Power of Intuition, Intuition at Work* and *Streetlights and Shadows*) who coined the term "sensemaking" to describe this phenomenon.

175. Both the concept and the definition are taken from "Advanced Battlespace and Cybermaneuver Concepts: Implications for Force XXI," by Dr. Robert J. Bunker, published in *Parameters*, Autumn 1996, pp. 108-120. Dr. Bunker is a leading thinker and published author on multi-dimensional battlespace and future war. His research focus is on the influence of technology on warfare and political organization and on the national security implications of emerging forms of warfare. This article may be found at: http://www.carlisle.army.mil/usawc/parameters/Articles/96autumn/bunker.htm. Also see: "Higher Dimensional Warfighting." *Military Review*. Vol. 79. No. 5. September-October 1999: 53-62 and "Five-Dimensional (Cyber) Warfighting: Can the Army After Next be Defeated Through Complex Concepts and Technologies?" Carlisle, PA: US Army War College, Strategic Studies Institute. March 10, 1998: 1-42. http://www.strategicstudiesinstitute.army.mil/pubs/display.cfm?PubID=233.

176. Biometric technologies are those that identify and compare the physical characteristics and personal traits of people to distinguish them from others. Examples include facial recognition, retinal scans, fingerprints, voiceprints, DNA, and many others.

177. The quote by General Ulysses S. Grant was first noted in a biography published in 1879 entitled *Around the World With General Grant* by John Russell Young. After leaving the U.S. presidency, General Grant spent two years travelling abroad and was accompanied by Young, who was an accomplished journalist. Besides documenting the travels, Young added conversations he had with General Grant on questions regarding American history and politics. Numerous references attribute this particular quote to a discussion of the Battle of Vicksburg, Mississippi in July of 1863 and is thought to be one of the most brilliantly executed campaigns of the war. Vicksburg surrendered the day after the Battle of Gettysburg. Together they signaled a turning point in the Civil War from which the Confederacy never fully recovered.

SECTION 6

SECTION 6

ACTION BOOKENDS

In no other profession are the penalties for employing untrained personnel so appalling or so irrevocable. . .

—DOUGLAS MACARTHUR[178]

THE IMPORTANCE OF LEARNING FROM MISTAKES TO AVOID repeating them is so self-evident that it might seem superfluous to dedicate an entire chapter, much less a section, of this book to this issue. Nevertheless, even successful tactical operations and disaster responses are never completely error free. Mistakes can occur from neglect, ignorance, unpreparedness, overconfidence, misunderstandings, underestimations, carelessness and hundreds of other causes. The point is that, once recognized each of these causes is completely preventable. It would seem prudent then, to diligently and methodically identify them and make efforts to correct or avoid them in the future.

This last section has only two chapters; one dealing with efforts that can be taken before an action to make them safer and more effective and the other dealing with learning from the mistakes of previous actions to avoid repeating them. Hence the term "action bookends" is used to describe the focus of this section.

The first chapter begins by describing the nature and importance of operations intended to promote the accomplishment of operational objectives. These operations can often be done discreetly and with little opposition but can offer dramatic, even decisive, advantages for the follow-on operation. The chapter continues with an explanation of the concept of social forecasting and how it works to enhance preparedness and intervention tactics during potential social unrest. A discussion of the various ways of gaining knowledge through training and rehearsals follow with a description of the advantages and disadvantages of each. The chapter concludes by describing methods to gain insight and understanding in operations involving opposing forces by "gaming" an operation before it is actually implemented.

The last chapter provides an overview of the types of causes involved in failures as well as how to identify those that are apparent and relatively easy to fix as opposed to those that tend to be more subtle and pervasive but tend to be longer lasting and more harmful. The chapter concludes with proven methods of conducting postmortem analyses, both formal and informal, along with methods of identifying and recording problems and recommendations.

---

178. General of the Army Douglas MacArthur, Annual Report of the Chief of Staff, U.S. Army, 1933. Douglas MacArthur (1880-1964) was born and grew up on Army outposts after the American Civil War while his father, Arthur MacArthur, served in the U.S. Army. His father, who eventually became a Lieutenant General, had been awarded the Congressional Medal of Honor for heroism at the Battle of Chattanooga. In spite of Douglas MacArthur's top grades and the efforts of both his grandfather and famous father, he was twice refused for an appointment to the military academy at West Point. Undeterred, he passed an examination for an appointment through Congress and graduated at the top of his class. He commented on the experience by noting, "It was a lesson I never forgot. Preparedness is the key to success and victory." Throughout the remainder of his long and distinguished career his emphasis on training and preparedness distinguished not only himself but the units of which he was in charge. The entire quote reads "In no other profession are the penalties for employing untrained personnel so appalling or so irrevocable as in the military."

BEFORE THE ACTION

The Battle of Waterloo was won on the playing fields of Eton.
—ATTRIBUTED TO ARTHUR WELLESLEY[179]

ABOUT 400 YEARS AGO, MIGUEL DE CERVANTES WROTE IN HIS epic *Don Quixote*, "He who is prepared has his battle half fought."[180] This adage is as true today as when it was first written. While most law enforcement tactical operations cannot be predicted with any degree of certainty, many are capable of being foretold long in advance. Parades, political rallies, championship sporting events, protests, strikes, carnivals, festivals and parties are only a few of those that are commonly preceded by invitations, posters, notices, handbills, brochures, and even threats. These identify not only the type of occasion, but even the times and places they will occur. Other situations, like responses to natural disasters, are not quite so accommodating, but experienced experts can often identify likely locales and vulnerable times and effects, or at least eliminate those so improbable that they do not merit serious consideration. Once it becomes probable that some kind of intervention or response is likely, efforts can be made to maximize those factors and influences that will enhance success and degrade those that will interfere while at the same time avoiding the competing interests inherent in any ongoing operation. Some preparatory operations are so effective that the outcome is all but determined before the engagement.

SHAPING OPERATIONS

A **shaping operation** can be defined as any series of actions taken in anticipation of an engagement or tactical operation designed to promote accomplishment of strategic objectives. They enhance success by negating or mitigating potentially adverse effects while strengthening or increasing potentially favorable factors. Accordingly, they focus on any factor, or combination of factors that may influence the outcome and can involve any or all echelons of a tactical organization.

Perhaps the most easily understood shaping operation involves the conduct of the operation itself. Say, for example, that the control of a piece of terrain has been determined critical for success. The force that occupies and reinforces it before the onset of the operation gains a defensive advantage. Such actions can be decisive in nature.[181] In law enforcement such actions can be just as critical. It is commonplace, for example, to occupy stadiums, arenas, theaters and auditoriums hours before an event to "sterilize" the area by sweeping for bombs and removing unauthorized persons. Failing to take such actions early makes them nearly impossible to achieve after an event is underway. Likewise, evacuation of innocent persons inside a containment before attempting to arrest a barricaded suspect not only ensures their safety but enhances freedom of action for law enforcement personnel by removing concerns and distractions.

Some shaping operations may be taken months or years prior to actually employing them. This is especially important when governmental involvement is required. One excellent example is with emergency statutes. These are statutes that are crafted and approved by the local governmental authorities but not enacted. They remain "on the books" awaiting only a vote to make them law. One of the better known examples involves curfew laws. Curfews have proven one of the most effective tools for quelling and preventing escalation in civil disturbances. Notwithstanding, failing to anticipate and take the necessary steps to approve a curfew statute for future use negates its value because of the time-consuming legislative process. Similarly, other statues, not as critical, may involve building codes, and zoning or parking ordinances. These seemingly innocuous statutes can be used in support of all sorts of tactical and emergency response operations because they provide abilities to "shape the battlespace" by controlling such things as traffic routes and congestion, loitering, and more serious dangers. Consider the possibilities if a no parking zone had been in place beside the Murrah Federal Building in Oklahoma City prior to the bombing.

One of the most often overlooked aspects of a shaping operation involves information. Like other shaping operations, information operations are multi-faceted. The most well-known involves gaining an advantage by acquiring and verifying information of value for making informed decisions. Among other things, this involves scanning the environment for indications and clues for impending events of concern.[182] Indeed, vigilance is the most indispensable ingredient for preparedness. There is also a countermeasure factor inherent in information operations. Informing the public in advance of tactical operations, for instance, not only allows them to take personal measures to avoid inconveniences and adverse consequences but serves to "inoculate" them from exaggerations and propaganda from adversaries who seek to gain advantage with misinformation.

Shaping operations are nearly always in a supporting role,[183] but they do not always occur prior to other operations. In fact, shaping operations may continue through and even after the supported operation. A pending evacuation during a fire is an excellent example. Residents who are warned ahead of time not only tend to be more cooperative, but are also able to participate in their own displacement by gathering clothing, valuables and medicines, arranging shelter for pets and livestock, making notifications, fueling vehicles, and even arranging for their own transportation and shelter. Upon being released to return they often take it upon themselves in assisting one another, removing debris and accounting for missing persons, all of which aid the ongoing disaster response.

Law enforcement shaping operations are frequently multidisciplinary, and include functions and disciplines that are not strictly law enforcement in nature. Consequently, skills, knowledge, equipment and support from people working in parks and recreation, water and power, mass transit, public works, education, and others, are commonly needed for a comprehensive approach to shaping a time and place to make them more conducive for a successful operation. Other municipal departments assist in all kinds of ways, such as providing barricades for traffic control, buses for mass evacuations, or opening buildings and grounds for shelter, command centers and staging areas.

SOCIAL FORECASTING

Some types of shaping operations have proven so beneficial that they are used time and again. This is quite common when a jurisdiction has particular locales or recurring events that serve as venues and forums where trouble seems to reoccur. Depending on the circumstances, the size and type of response needed can vary dramatically. Clearly, an estimation of the expected nature and size of the problem is of great value. This is done with a forecast. A **forecast** is a calculation based upon the identification, observation and analysis of pertinent data coupled with an assessment of the likelihood of consequences. Understandably, the consequences are heavily influenced by the context. For example, the expected consequences for a protest can differ dramatically depending on whether it takes place among sympathizers or opponents.

A **social forecast** refers to an estimation of the potential, location, scope and volatility for societal events. Much like a weather forecast for which meteorologists use environmental factors such as humidity, wind, atmospheric pressure, temperature, and other factors to provide a range of probabilities for weather, it is possible to use sociological, cultural, economic and political factors for estimating social problems. Generically, these factors are referred to as "norms." A **norm** is a set of factors or influences that provide a model or pattern regarded as typical.

While a social forecast is more than a guess, it stops short of a prediction. A prediction implies a degree of precision that is simply not possible given the number of influences and possible permutations of social interactions. Even though it is not precise it still limits the possibilities to a range of likely outcomes. For instance, while societal events are not wholly predictable, there are precursor events that can identify a "window" of when they are likely to occur.

The greatest impediment to social forecasting seems to be a belief that because they can't be predicted precisely, they can't be predicted at all. Admittedly, certainty is impossible. Nevertheless, a forecast provides a means to reduce uncertainty even when it can't be completely eliminated. Developing a social forecast is not particularly complex, but does benefit from the training, experience and education of subject matter experts. This is because subtle influences may have substantial importance but are easily overlooked by a novice. Consequently, the opinions of these experts should be sought early and often.

While there is no standard procedure, a social forecast is usually conducted in three phases; vigilance, alert and threat. The process begins with an understanding that *vigilance* is the default mode. No extraordinary effort is required. This phase simply attempts to identify conditions that could signal problems if not appropriately and timely handled. An irony exists in that they are always present but tend to go unrecognized until hindsight makes them both conspicuous and irrefutable.

One of the most useful methods for identifying those factors and influences that can be used to develop a social forecast is with a technique known as **environmental scanning**. An environmental scan attempts to detect and identify potential threats by systematically examining factors and influences in a particular social setting. The combination of environmental, social, economic, cultural and political conditions at a particular place and time provide an abundance of clues concerning the likelihood of an event and how it will appear. The data and information necessary to begin the analysis can be gleaned from everything from letters to the editor in the local papers to posters on telephone poles and kiosks near school campuses, shopping and civic centers. Fliers, brochures and advertisements have proven particularly useful because they provide a time, place, and often a point of contact. For the same reasons, web sites of involved organizations have also proven fruitful, and are generally more comprehensive and timely.

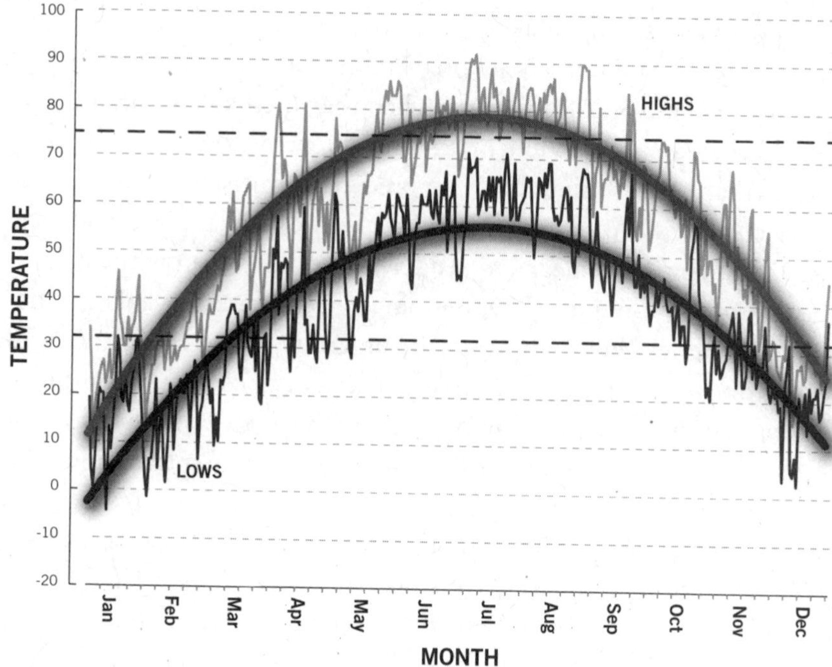

FIGURE 18-1 NORMS CHART: People commonly use weather forecasts to plan for recreational and other activities.

The chart above plots the daily temperatures for a small city in the Midwest. While they fluctuate greatly and may be impossible to predict on any given day, some reliable generalizations can be made. For example, the temperatures are highest in the months of June, July and August and lowest in the months of January, February and December. The darker lines identify the statistical "norms" of the temperatures and serve to provide a reliable estimation of the expected temperatures in future years. If, for example, a minimum temperature of 75 degrees is necessary to enjoy water skiing it would be prudent to plan it during the summer months. Conversely, temperatures around freezing are necessary for winter sports like ice skating, sledding and skiing. One other obvious conclusion is that the data shows periods of time where it would be impossible to conduct some activities. Thus, these norms help to define the limits of what is possible and what is not.

While social factors are not as easily identified or measured as those for weather, they still provide strong clues to estimate things like the probability of occurrence, approximate time, likely location and potential for violence. A lack of ability to be precise must not be an excuse for a lack of foresight.

Consider the implications of being able to forecast civil unrest, as one example. Many acts of civil unrest take law enforcement agencies by surprise not because they missed precursor events and signals, but because they weren't even looking! Large "rave" parties, block parties, "frat" parties, and the like are well-known for their propensity for getting out of hand and yet the most common method of attracting attendees is with fliers, posters, websites and social media. Likewise, some groups have a history for disruptive acts, civil disobedience or violent protests. Thus, a knowledge of the history and stated objectives of groups likely to be involved or attending a function can provide a wealth of knowledge before problems are encountered.

When attempting to identify and isolate factors that might provide clues for forecasting civil disorder and assessing the impact, two factors are particularly useful. These are trends and potentials. A **trend** is a combination of measurement and prediction used to identify a general tendency, inclination, predisposition or frequency. Trends are discerned by identifying and measuring events and provide value for both measurement and prediction. An **event** is a single, discrete one-time occurrence which has an impact on a given issue. Events may be specifically related to the issue at hand or drawn from similar situations that have occurred in the past. When two or more events can be identified as being related to an issue, an estimate can be made as to another. The more events and the greater precision that they can be measured, the more accurate and reliable becomes the forecast. When time permits, this might be done statistically with spreadsheets or databases and presented with graphs and charts. Because of the harsh time constraints inherent in tactical operations, however, they are more often based on appraisals and rough estimates.

The second category is potentials. **Potentials** describe the ability or capacity of something. Because the second, and most important, part of a trend is the prediction, potentials are always an approximation. Potentials set limits on the possibilities. These are often defined using a best case scenario, worst case scenario and most-likely scenario. The best case scenario takes all factors into account but assumes favorable influences and effective actions. Similarly, the worst case scenario assumes that there will be unfavorable influences and actions will be minimally effective and describes the worst possible outcome. The most-likely scenario describes that outcome which, based upon all the known factors, is most likely to occur. Since potentials delineate possibilities, they are used to assess the impact of trends. Thus, trends and potentials are inseparable and inter-related.[184]

Once a developing situation is identified, the forecast becomes more focused and attempts to delimit the range of possibilities even further. This begins the *alert* phase of the process. To a greater or lesser degree, events, groups, issues, spokespersons, critical dates and locations, alliances and allegiances, all provide clues to make an accurate and reliable forecast as to the likelihood and extent of a civil disorder disrupting the community. This step simply increases the state of vigilance and provides both a focus and lead time for more comprehensive planning and better preparations. Of particular importance during this step, is the information received by personnel closer to the problem. One of the best sources of information is from the people actually involved. Many protest leaders are eager to meet with law enforcement to avoid problems with counter-protestors or even the more radical elements of their own groups. In some cases negotiations can provide rules of engagement so that protestors have a clear understanding of what types of conduct will result in interventions. This tactic has proven particularly beneficial in that it often results in "self-policing" when group members restrain others conducting provocative acts.

Like the vigilance phase, the alert phase benefits by distilling the available information into two categories. These are capabilities and intentions. **Capabilities** describe the ability of a specific opposing interest to successfully accomplish an action. They provide a measure of ability in terms of logistical support or operational sophistication as well as providing a calculation of the degree of impact on a region, function or organization. It is important to understand that capabilities identify not only what an agent can do, but what it cannot do, because both are essential for planning and conduct of operations. In many respects, capabilities are related to trends, but where trends are used to identify a pattern or class of antagonist, capabilities are specifically applied to a discrete, identifiable opposing force.

Intentions is the second category and refers to the actual or potential activities of an opposing force. They identify their aims and likely courses of action by answering questions like what is likely to happen, and who is likely to be involved? Once an opposing force can be identified, capabilities provide the possibilities and intentions identify the probabilities. Consequently, capabilities and intentions are also inseparable and inter-related.

The last step in the process is an appraisal of the *threat*. When observing civil disorders in the past, three interrelated factors have always been present. These are the size of the crowd, the amount of commitment to an issue and the amount of emotion likely to be present. The term **critical mass** is used to describe the point at which these three factors, alone or in combination, could result in some type of civil disorder. For example, a very small crowd, but comprised of members highly committed to a cause, has proven more than capable of causing considerable disruption to a community by blocking traffic, obstructing sidewalks, preventing access or egress to and from buildings, stopping construction or demolition, as well as acts of vandalism and violence. Likewise, a relatively small, but emotionally charged crowd and with nearly no commitment to an issue, has demonstrated on more than one occasion an ability and willingness for lawlessness with acts of vandalism, looting and arson. In fact, this is the most common type of situation in the case of celebration riots after championship games, tournaments and other sporting events.

Even without a high degree of commitment and little or no emotion, a very large crowd can grow impatient with traffic signals, restricted pedestrian access, and crowd control measures such as fences and barricades. These situations are ripe for pandemonium and escalating acts of lawlessness. Using these three factors, a prognosis can be formulated and preventative measures can be identified and implemented.

TRAINING AND REHEARSALS

Of all the forms a shaping operation may take, training is not only the most common but the most likely to be taken for granted. While no one disputes the importance of training it is not normally thought of as a shaping operation. Nevertheless, the more tightly the training is focused on a specific set of circumstances the more beneficial it is when those same conditions are part of an actual situation. Some operations are so complex that rehearsals are considered an absolute necessity. This is especially the case with hostage recovery operations.[185] Training provides a safe method for identifying problems, testing solutions and increasing cooperation. In fact, training has been called the "grease" of tactical organizations in that it is one of the best methods for reducing the friction inherent in collaboration of personnel with disparate skills and knowledge.

The two most essential characteristics of a good tactical response organization are that it be well-trained and well-disciplined. These characteristics are manifested in every organizational achievement. Discipline derives and flows from training. Good training instills confidence when circumstances encourage fear. In complex situations it provides guidance. In dangerous assignments it provides assurance. It fosters pride and cohesiveness. It is indicative of the readiness of a unit. It is no accident that the best response teams are also the best trained.

Training needs to be comprehensive. It relates to everything a unit does or may be expected to do. The ability of team members to work together depends largely upon the knowledge and insight of the responsibilities and assignments of the other team members. This can only be gained by training and experience. The key to successful training is to raise the skill level of every individual and every component of a response organization. This emphasizes the importance of cross-training. **Cross-training** refers to the efforts focused on increasing the proficiency and understanding of different (but usually related), skills and tasks. Cross-training maximizes the benefits provided by subject matter experts by allowing less-skilled personnel to work under their guidance. Moreover, some preliminary and rudimentary tasks can be fulfilled by personnel with only a basic understanding of what is needed to release the experts to concentrate on the more complex. A unit that practices cross-training tends to be more versatile and adaptable.

Two factors are inherent in all effective training. These are the amount of realism desired and the amount of time and resources available. Generally, the more closely training simulates actual conditions the more time and resources are required, and accordingly, the more complex the training is to develop and conduct. There are no limits on how training is conducted but some approaches have been so productive that they merit mention. The "training realism curve" provides a graphic display of the various approaches according to an estimation of the degree of realism compared with the amount of resources and difficulty to conduct. It might also be compared with a learning curve in that the more training simulates real life the more relevant it becomes.

- Think about task—Merely thinking about the task at hand is training in and of itself. It provides a means to organize thoughts and identify promising options. Numerous studies have confirmed that people who have only thought about a particular problem have already identified and considered prospective solutions and discarded unlikely actions. As such, when confronted with an actual situation they don't start from the beginning but rather pick up where they left off in their thinking. This method is especially fruitful for people with training and experience related to the problem because they tend to detect and consider subtle influences that might be overlooked in the "heat of battle." As shown in the diagram, (Figure 18-2) it is the simplest to set up but the least realistic.
- Chalk Talk—A chalk talk is a little bit more trouble than just thinking about a problem but not much. A chalk talk is usually conducted with two or more people and can be as simple as drawing lines in the dirt or as complicated as annotating printed photographs, drawing maps or making diagrams. A chalk talk has two advantages over just thinking about a problem. The first is that the more durable format allows contemplation by more than one person and over longer periods of time. Second is that more details can be displayed than are easily held in working memory and so subtleties and permutations are more easily recognized and likely to be grasped.
- Situational Training—This type of training isolates a technique or procedure and examines it in minute detail. A procedure for a crisis entry may be evaluated step by step,

for instance, or a hostage recovery technique might be polished. It is still not very realistic but has the advantage of focusing attention on just one aspect of an operation. This is particularly advantageous to new personnel who are often overwhelmed by the amount of new information they must absorb.

- Scenario Review—A scenario review examines a completed operation and provides insight and understanding by examining the actions of others in a particular context. It is important to understand that the scenario reviewed need not have been successful to benefit from it. Blunders often serve to isolate and highlight training points that are otherwise lost in the glory of a successful operation.
- Debriefings—Similar to a scenario review, a debriefing has the advantage of the student having actually been involved in the operation. Because this is more relevant than a scenario review more learning may be expected.[186] In fact, debriefings are so productive that many agencies require them as a matter of policy.
- Field Training—This type of training describes a training assignment which is monitored. It differs from a scenario review and debriefing in that the student is actually participating in the problem solving. The monitors are experts who observe for this very purpose or are, as is more often the case, the supervisors and mentors of the students.
- Free Play—Free play refers to a type of training in which two or more opponents face off on a given assignment and compete against each other. This adversary relationship simulates real life and employs an opposing will. In order to encourage the maximum amount of creativity and ingenuity, free play exercises normally have only two sets of rules; those that relate to personal safety and those required for the protection of the training site. The players are free to solve the problem in any manner which suits them. This type of training is more difficult to set up but closely resembles real life situations in that the assignments are usually modeled after actual opera-

tions. Examples include problems such as a sniper with the high ground, a barricaded suspect with hostages, evacuations under fire, urban movement, and so forth.

- Live Fire Entries—Easily the most dangerous and complex of all types of special operations training, it is also one of the most relevant. Only free play exercises come close to simulating the actual problems encountered in real operations.[187] Little things taken for granted during a dry entry have profound significance during live fire. The lessons learned in live fire exercises are deeply ingrained and highly durable.
- Actual Operations—You will notice that there is a break in the line between live fire entries and actual operations. This is to signify that, unlike the other areas discussed, an actual assault is not intended for training, even though training will occur. Experience is a great teacher but it is a ruthless schoolmaster.

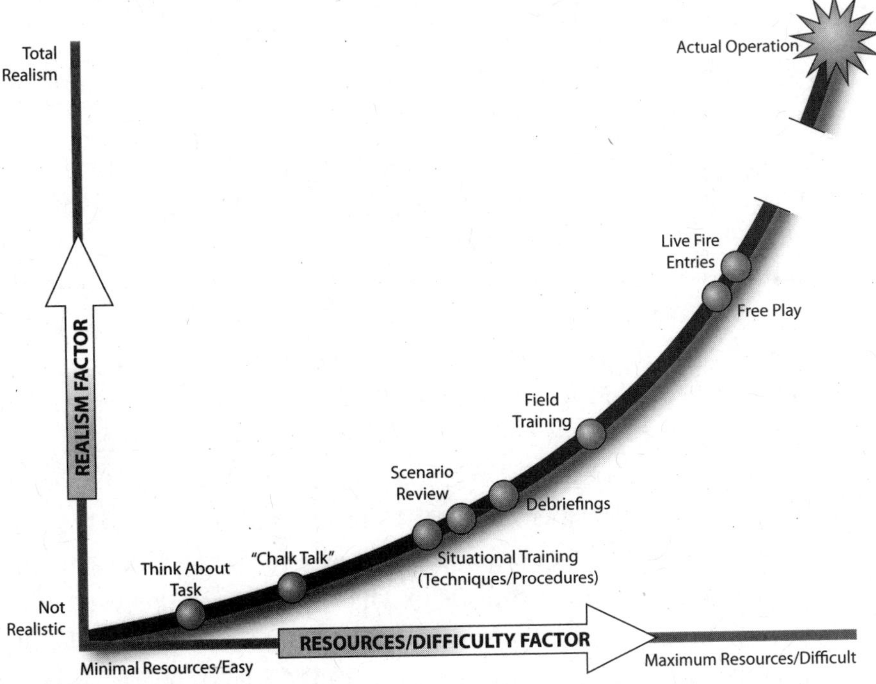

FIGURE 18-2 TRAINING REALISM CURVE

OPFOR GAMING

During the First Peloponnesian War nearly 2,500 years ago, Pericles was giving a speech to the Athenians when he stated that "I am more afraid of our own mistakes than our enemies' designs."[188] In truth, most tactical operations and disaster responses fail not because of overwhelming resistance or a more cunning scheme but because of mistakes made by the people and agencies assigned to handle the situation. Ironically, and sadly, these mistakes are often apparent to nearly everyone afterwards. Needless to say, the true value in identifying mistakes is to avoid them. While debriefings and after action reviews serve to identify mistakes to avoid their repetition, measures taken to identify and correct them before they are encountered are far more important. One of the best methods to accomplish this is through the use of "OpFor gaming." OpFor is a military acronym which stands for "opposing forces." **OpFor gaming** involves two or more opposing forces competing in an exercise in which all relevant factors, such as knowledge, strategy, skills, endurance, timing, and even chance, are critical for success. Aside from the obvious objective of "winning," the true value of OpFor gaming is in identifying and correcting unsuspected vulnerabilities.

OpFor games are often identified as "red teaming," "threat exercises," "force on force" or "aggressor operations." While these terms refer specifically to tactical operations, the concept is long-known and well-established in the business community. It is not uncommon, for example, to assign a "devil's advocate" to examine plans during meetings, conferences and the like. A **devil's advocate** is a person who is called upon to adopt and defend opposing views, as well as identifying weaknesses and attacking those being presented. In fact, this is the most simplistic method of OpFor gaming and is often used by law enforcement tactical teams as well. Likewise, "reverse engineering" might also be considered as a form of OpFor gaming. **Reverse engineering** is a process in which an assembled device, often a competitor's, is taken apart to learn how it works and identify parts and processes that can be improved. OpFor gaming attempts to disassemble carefully laid plans and procedures to expose defects. A variation of this reverse engineering method is called a **Pre-mortem**

Exercise. A pre-mortem exercise assumes the planned operation has failed and challenges participants to discover how. In this manner, planners delve into the plan seeking weak points.

Generally, OpFor gaming involves "free play" exercises. **Free play exercises** are those in which two or more opponents face off on a given assignment and compete against each other. To the maximum extent possible, this adversary relationship simulates real life operations and creativity and ingenuity are encouraged. Typically, the only rules are those which relate to the protection of the training site and personal safety. The players are "free" to solve the problems in any manner that suits them. While this type of exercise is more difficult to prepare and coordinate, it provides nearly unlimited opportunities to experiment with new equipment and tactics. Likewise, players are equipped as realistically as possible as if the exercise was an actual operation.

One of the greatest advantages of using scenario based exercises is the incorporation of stakeholders and decision makers who would be participating in actual operations but who are often unavailable for more conventional training activities. This is especially the case with agency executives and politicians. An ability to gain insight and understanding in the factors and influences involved in complex tactical operations and emergency responses without the stress and anxiety of being in the glare of the public eye encourages experimentation and risk taking. In fact, the more closely the scenario can approximate an actual event, real or anticipated, the more the decision maker gains experience and understanding without the devastating consequences of a mistake.[189]

Besides the more comprehensive scenario based exercises, OpFor gaming can also be used to experiment with and test a single tactic, technique, weapon or piece of equipment. When used in this manner the exercise is tightly focused on a single process or activity. Two of the most common for tactical teams are movements and entries in which an opposing force attempts to compromise an approach or thwart efforts to gain a maneuver advantage. These types of activities are, in and of themselves complex, and OpFor gaming not only provides a realism that is conspicuously lacking without an adversary but serves to make weaknesses far more conspicuous.

One of the greatest values in OpFor gaming, however, are the lessons learned that would not be discovered by other methods, particularly those actions that might lead to surprise. Surprise, by definition, involves the unexpected. A worthy adversary actively seeks areas of vulnerability that are otherwise unforeseen or neglected. Once identified, these areas of vulnerability can be reinforced or eliminated entirely.

Another major advantage of OpFor gaming is revealing friction. Even a small tactical operation or disaster response has many "moving parts" all of which need to work well together. Friction is a force that resists all action and is inevitable in these types of situations. Nevertheless, it is essential that efforts be made to reduce it. Friction usually occurs between processes and people. Friction with processes, like briefings, staging, movements, entries, actions on the objective, and so forth, are the most frequently cited reasons for less than perfect operations. Sometimes the simplest things cited as failures in vital processes could have been easily avoided had they only been anticipated. In much the same manner, friction occurs between people. The personal stress and anxiety of performing well in adverse circumstances frequently makes compromise difficult and accommodation less likely. For whatever reasons, some people are unwilling or incapable of working together. Second only to actual operations, OpFor gaming is the best method for revealing these points of friction and emphasizes the necessity of alleviating or avoiding them altogether. Like a sparring partner working with a boxer, OpFor gaming sharpens the skills and wits of all concerned and is a mainstay in training and preparing tactical teams and disaster response agencies for actual operations.

---

179. For more than a 150 years this quote has been attributed to Arthur Wellesley, the 1st Duke of Wellington and the British general who, once and for all, ended Napoleon's reign when he defeated him at the Battle of Waterloo. Wellesley was educated at Eton College but without distinction. The citation was first recorded in a book in 1856 by Charles de Montalembert, *De l'Aveni politique de l'Angleterre* (*The Political Future of England*), and then restated by a number of books and news-

paper accounts. The phrase became popular both for the emphasis on preparation and training necessary for success and the prestige that accompanied it from the huge popularity and esteem of Wellesley. While there is no doubt of Wellesley's understanding and emphasis on planning and preparation, history has cast serious doubt that Wellesley ever uttered anything remotely familiar in that he apparently held little fondness for Eton. Notwithstanding, it remains popular today and encapsulates the critical importance of preparation for success.

180. Miguel de Cervantes, *Don Quixote*, Chapter XVII, 1615. Cervantes spent time as a soldier and fought bravely in the Spanish Naval Corps. He was wounded three times and eventually captured, spending five years in captivity in Algiers. Although it is virtually impossible that Cervantes was aware of it, the concept was expressed even earlier by Sun Tzu in *The Art of War* (circa 500 BC., translated by Samuel B. Griffith) when he stated ". . .to be prepared beforehand for any contingency is the greatest of virtues."

181. As just one notable historical example, the Union's early occupation and resolute defense of Cemetery Ridge during the Battle of Gettysburg is often cited as the decisive action that ensured the Union victory. For a law enforcement example, consider the implications of who controlled the "Texas Tower" at the University of Texas, Austin during the shooting attacks on August 1, 1966. The control of that piece of terrain was so crucial for success that in order to deprive Charles Whitman of the use of it, it had to be physically taken to end the engagement.

182. It should go without saying that in this day and age, the "environment" includes all dimensions, especially the information available on the World Wide Web.

183. On exceptionally rare occasions, a shaping operation can be designated as the principal operation. In law enforcement, this may occur when factors like favorable public opinion are deemed more important than prevailing in a civil disturbance.

184. Trends, potentials, capabilities and intentions are discussed earlier in this book. For more information see Chapter 5—Envisioning and Achieving an End State

185. Hostage recovery operations are among the most dangerous and complex of all domestic law enforcement activities and are usually developed according to a five-phase sequence. These are planning, rehearsal, movement, assault and withdrawal. Each phase focuses on a different aspect of the operation. The rehearsal phase emphasizes the need to seamlessly integrate a number of disparate skills and abilities and is specific to the conditions expected during the assault phase.

186. For more information on debriefings see Chapter 19—After the Action

187. The use of simmunitions, or other safe methods of determining hits and casualties, has the advantage over live fire training of allowing adversarial actions—tactical "actors" are forced to deal with people actually shooting back. Thus, nearly all aspects of an actual situation can be incorporated into a free play exercise without the danger of live munitions. The single exception is the stress inherent in life and death actions. Consequently, nearly all of the more progressive special operations teams incorporate at least some form of live fire exercise into their training regimen.
188. Pericles, 432 BC, as quoted in Thucydides, *History of the Peloponnesian War*, circa 404 BC. Pericles was not only a general but a statesman and had a major influence on ancient Athenian society during the "Golden Age," sometimes known as "The Age of Pericles" (between the Persian and Peloponnesian wars). It is largely believed that the war was not so much won by Sparta as lost by Athens, making the fear of Pericles all the more poignant.
189. The obvious next step in this process is computer-based simulation such as that used by pilots. Such simulation is currently extraordinarily expensive but allows these professionals to make life-and-death mistakes, safely, and to learn from them. As computers become more powerful and various tactical roles more complex, simulators will certainly fill this critical gap in other disciplines, roles and specialties.

AFTER THE ACTION

Errors and defeats are more obviously illustrative of principles than successes are . . . Defeat cries aloud for explanation; whereas success, like charity, covers a multitude of sins.

—ALFRED THAYER MAHAN[190]

SUCCESS IN TACTICAL OPERATIONS AND DISASTER RESPONSES is never an absolute. Compromises are always necessary. Sometimes a building must be left to burn because firefighters are fully engaged in preventing a toxic cloud from spreading or a suspect must be killed in order to save a hostage. Perfection is a goal not a standard. Nevertheless, the clarity of hindsight makes it easy to cast blame and nearly always overshadows the chaotic and confusing conditions under which the situation actually unfolded. Even those with no expertise in tactical operations are able to assuredly identify shortcomings after an event. With hindsight, even imbeciles can be geniuses. Somewhat ironically, one of the most valuable methods for achieving success in tactical operations is by analyzing failures.[191] The harmonious resolution of the factors and influences involved in successful operations make them all but indistinguishable from each other but they are frequently patently obvious in failures.

Analyzing failure is not peculiar to tactical operations. A story is told of the inventor, Thomas Edison, who after thousands of unsuccessful attempts to construct a usable light bulb was chided for having failed so many times. His reply was that he had not failed because he alone knew of thousands of ways in which it couldn't be done. Those without that knowledge are prone to follow the same failed pathways. So it is with tactical operations. It seems prudent then, to make a strong effort in understanding how failures occur to avoid repeating them.

FAILURE ANALYSIS

Failures in tactical operations can be attributed to one of two types of causes; proximate causes and root causes. A **proximate cause** is a factor or influence that appears clearly apparent and directly connected to the outcome. Proximate causes tend to be conspicuous, especially in failure, because they are so closely connected to the actual problem. They are usually relatively easy to fix but tend to be short lasting because deeper problems often still remain. They are also the most commonly cited cause for injury in civil cases.

A **root cause** is one that begins a causal chain that eventually leads to an outcome. Root causes are not as apparent as proximate causes and require more effort to identify and correct. Furthermore, root causes have wider reaching effects than proximate causes and they tend to be more difficult to correct. While it is not uncommon to have a single proximate cause, more often than not, root causes occur in groups.

To understand the distinctions between a proximate cause and a root cause, consider an investigation into a series of accidental discharges. The fact that the shooters' fingers were on the triggers would be a proximate cause and can easily be corrected by prohibiting that behavior. Upon closer examination, however, the investigation reveals that the shooters had never been trained to keep their fingers off the trigger. The lack of training then, becomes a root cause. As the investigation continues it also reveals that a cutback on training several years earlier had resulted because of funding shortfalls and had never been reinstated when monies became available. A lack of administrative oversight then becomes another root cause.[192]

While there are a multitude of reasons that failures occur during tactical operations two occur so often that they merit special

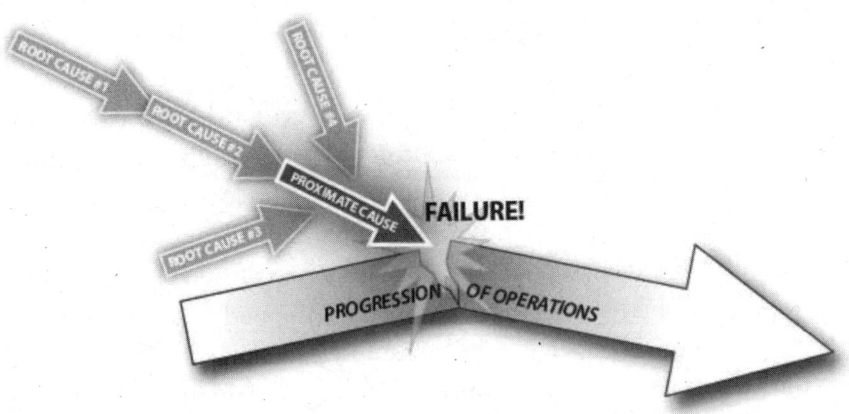

FIGURE 19-1 FAILURE ANALYSIS: While mistakes are inevitable, catastrophic failures never result from a single factor. The most obvious shortcoming is called the proximate cause because it is directly connected to the failure. Understandably, proximate causes are the most often cited in civil suits. Root causes are not only more subtle but have longer-lasting impact and wider reaching effects. Failure to identify and remediate root causes ensures that the same proximate cause will reoccur or morph into some other form of failure. As depicted in the graphic, root causes may appear as an antecedent to a proximate cause, as with root causes number 2, 3 and 4, or as part of a causal chain, as with root cause 1 and 2.

To better understand the significance of root and proximate causes, imagine the sinking of the Titanic. It would be easy to blame the iceberg for the heavy loss of life but if the analysis stopped there the solutions would be limited to avoiding ice-filled waters, sailing only during the daylight hours or with empty ships. Digging even a little deeper reveals that incidents involving ships far less modern than the Titanic had been navigating iceberg filled waters for centuries, some even colliding with them without sinking. Moreover, even when they sank they hardly ever suffered such horrendous loss of life. Some of the root causes were that the Titanic was considered unsinkable and supported a mindset that many safeguards were superfluous, not the least of which was having enough lifeboats for all the passengers. Other root causes include the delay in abandoning the ship while evaluating the damage, presumably because of the overconfidence that it could not sink. Still others were the design of the watertight compartments that allowed water to flow over them, the brittleness of the ship's hull from the freezing water and high sulphur content and failure of the rivets; all of which led to better materials and design for future ships.

attention. The first is misplaced confidence. **Misplaced, or overconfidence,** occurs when those involved underestimate the abilities of the adversary[193] or overestimate their own capabilities. Clues that this is a problem are expressions like, "It can't happen here;" "It won't happen to me;" "The odds are in our favor;" or "We can handle it."[194] Two common manners in which this occurs are with creeping missions or drifting standards.

Mission creep occurs when a mission is changed or expanded without compensating for the shortcomings of equipment or capabilities. It is usually insidious and barely noticeable and follows the path of least resistance until some calamity makes it painfully apparent. Mission creep usually occurs by one of two methods. The first way is when a unit is not properly equipped or trained and a higher headquarters shifts the mission. The second way is when a unit itself attempts to do more than was originally intended or assigned. Somewhat ironically, mission creep is more likely to happen with success since successful missions invite expansion. After all, if it worked once why won't it work again? Or, if it worked here why won't it work there? While these questions seem benign on the surface, without more careful scrutiny they invite failure, since the same tactics, tools, training, and the like, will simply be reapplied in new situations until they eventually prove unsuccessful. Each success invites a more ambitious attempt and/or broader scope.

Arguably, the most common example of mission creep with law enforcement tactical teams is when a team feels underutilized. Because of the expense in equipping and training a competent team, a "return on investment" is seen as a justification for maintaining them over the years. When a lack of activity leaves them languishing, other assignments that have not historically required such attention become appealing. Thus, a team formed for handling armed and barricaded suspects or high risk warrants begins handling assignments not rising to the same degree of risk. Initially at least, the shifts are minor and nearly unnoticeable but, left unexamined and unchecked, the next shift moves the focus still further from the mission as originally planned. Lacking further examination the emphasis gradually moves toward even more routine assignments. Eventually, the mission of the team has been expanded to be so broad in scope that it encroaches on those without demonstrable need for such a specialized team.

Conversely, a team that has succeeded in one area, especially one where it gains credibility and recognition, encourages an expansion to more dangerous assignments. What has succeeded in the past makes it far more difficult to make a case for more training or better equipment. Success then, becomes its own impetus. Equipped and trained for one mission can still leave a team deficient for another.

Drifting standards is a condition that results from a lack of enforcement of minimum standards. Regardless of whether it is marksmanship, physical fitness, or some other perishable skill, once an exception is made, even a small or temporary one, a new minimum has been established and so the standard begins to drift and diminishes in value. Avoiding drifting standards requires constant vigilance since the reasons that exceptions are seen as necessary may be strong and reasonable in the present situation but a new set of circumstances can appear equally persuasive and once there is a precedent it makes the next exception even harder to refuse. And so, it begins. While there are a multitude of examples, some of the more common include making exceptions, extending deadlines and granting exemptions.

Both drifting standards and mission creep are dangerous. But while a failure resulting from drifting standards can be troublesome, failures from mission creep are often catastrophes. The unforeseen difficulties are only discovered after some conspicuous, and often tragic, event. Mature teams understand and manage their own limitations and will readily admit when reinforcements are necessary, equipment is deficient or training is inappropriate or substandard. Only when there is a clear and compelling need for an exception or extension of a deadline should requirements or deadlines be waived and only when accompanied by a comprehensive mission analysis should missions be changed or expanded. Drifting standards are generally the responsibility of the commander of the concerned unit but mission creep is always the responsibility of the commander of the authorizing authority.

A second common failure is when the people in charge are unfit for command.[195] This generally occurs for one or more of three reasons; a failure to learn, a failure to adapt or a failure to anticipate. A **failure to learn** can usually be attributed to either ignoring or not recognizing contributory factors and influences. These are especially egregious when they are obvious, such as those that have occurred in previous operations. They reoccur most commonly as a result of failing to objectively critique and correct them. Only through a careful examination of what went right and wrong in previous operations can the favorable factors and influences be encouraged while restraining those that are not. Moreover, critiquing operations of others is just as valuable. As one adage states, "Learn from the mistakes of others because you'll never live long enough to make them all yourself."

A **failure to adapt** occurs when a commander fails to adjust to changing circumstances. One common cause is when tactics are practiced as a skill set rather than an intuitive application of tried and true principles. This is most commonly a result of a shallow understanding of the doctrine which comprises tactical science. Another frequent cause is when a plan is used as a "script" rather than as a flexible design capable of accepting change while remaining focused on the outcome.

A **failure to anticipate** occurs when a commander fails to plan and prepare for those factors and influences that can be reasonably expected. A lack of adequate planning is one common cause and is often unjustly blamed on the inability to precisely determine future events. While it may be impossible to precisely predict future events, it is no excuse for a lack of foresight. Even when planning is adequate, some actions require specialized equipment and skills. Failing to organize and have them available is almost always attributed to a lack of preparation. Too often, the extra costs in time, money and effort are used as excuses for not having adequate equipment and proper skills available when needed.

Another common cause for failing to anticipate is from incremental decision making. In the simplest terms, incremental decision making occurs when decisions are made and actions taken in solving an immediate problem without concern for the ultimate objective. This can easily lead to disorientation and disarray because it lacks the ability to progressively promote the accomplishment of strategic objectives.

COOPERATION FAILURES

Regardless of the amount of preparation or the quality of planning and leadership, potentially severe consequences are inherent in crises and can never be completely eliminated. To the extent possible then, it becomes essential to reduce the adverse influences. Once an operation is underway this responsibility falls squarely on the response organization. Each response organization involves a temporary alliance of people with varying degrees of skill, knowledge and experience and specialized units with skills and knowledge as disparate as explosive ordnance disposal to searching with dogs to tracking logistical supplies with computer databases.

It is said that complex systems that work evolve from simple systems that work. The number of critical functions involved can be staggering and the failure of any one can result in a debacle. In some circles this is called the "Anna Karenina Effect," taking its name from the opening of the classic book of the same name by Leo Tolstoy, which opens with, "Happy families are all alike; every unhappy family is unhappy in its own way." The deduction drawn is that each unhappy family is a result of its own unique difficulty but in order to be happy everything has to work. So it is in tactical operations and the **Anna Karenina Effect**[196] can be described as the absolute necessity for all critical components of any response organization to function. Failure of any one can be devastating in and of itself or by adversely affecting others.

When the failure of one function results in the failure of others it is called the "Cascade Effect." The **Cascade Effect** is defined as any failure or succession of failures resulting from a preceding failure. Consequently, even seemingly trivial failures may lead to severely adverse outcomes. Nearly all tactical fiascoes are a result of an aggregate of failures leading to the cascading effect. Debacles resulting from a single failure, of any kind, are exceedingly rare.

While it is impossible to discuss every potential adverse influence the fact that those previously mentioned have names should speak for itself. Anytime a mistake is repeated often enough to have been given its own name is worth minding. Even the most rudimentary understanding of those influences forearms a commander. Failing to learn from experience results in the lesson being repeated and while experience may be the best teacher it is a harsh schoolmaster. The best commanders learn from the mistakes of others.

DEBRIEFINGS AND AFTER ACTION REVIEWS

Successful or not, every tactical operation yields fruit in the form of lessons learned. Accordingly, some effort needs to be made to "harvest" knowledge that can be used in bettering future operations. While methods may vary, they usually take the form of a debriefing or after action review. While slightly different in style and methodology, they share many similarities. For example, both are done after an operation or training exercise, they both include a careful examination of the components, actions and junctures of an operation and they are both focused on improving performance.

The simplest and most informal method is a debriefing. A **debriefing** is a moderated discussion focused on gaining understanding and insight regarding a specific operation or exercise and involving those people who were personally involved. Debriefings can occur with all echelons of an organization but are predominately done at the lowest levels and include only those persons personally involved in a given operation or exercise. Most debriefings are conducted by a person of authority or a subject matter expert, and usually, but not always, without an agenda. The moderator normally opens the discussion with a short overview of the situation, mission and outcome before opening the topic for general discussion. The principal job of the moderator is to keep the discussion tightly focused on the specific subject at hand while capturing the lessons learned as they become apparent. This often requires someone to act as a scribe to encapsulate the ideas and proposals in the form of bullets or short comments. Debriefings are typically of short duration, normally lasting from a few minutes to a few hours.

While there are no rules for conducting debriefings, three conventions tend to be universal. The first is that the focus of a debriefing is on fact-finding not fault-finding. While mild criticism is to be expected, allegations of malfeasance, dereliction or negligence are reserved for more formal investigations. Secondly, open discussion is nearly unlimited in scope as long as the focus remains on the operation or exercise. Consequently, any person is allowed to introduce any subject for discussion and recommendations. Lastly, when concluding a debriefing the moderator often solicits input from subject matter experts and those who have not actively participated. The military often calls these comments "saved rounds"[197] in that they were frequently overlooked or seemed less important while discussing other matters. When this occurs, the junior and newest members of the organization are called upon before the senior members. This encourages them to speak freely without being intimidated by ranking officers, more experienced members or subject matter experts. Perhaps because of the limited scope of most debriefings, resulting reports, if any, are usually short; commonly only a few pages or even paragraphs.

An **After Action Review** is a structured process for analyzing a particular operation or exercise, and usually includes subject matter experts or superiors specifically tasked with identifying areas for improvement. After Action Reviews, oft times just referred to by the initials "AAR," can be either informal or formal and may be convened either before an exercise or after an operation. When convened before an exercise the members are often referred to as a "Tactical Exercise Control Group" or just "TECG," and the ranking member is designated as the "Tactical Exercise Coordinator" or just "TEC." When convened after an operation they tend to take the form of a commission, panel or board and the ranking member has often been appointed by an organizational or governmental authority for the specific purpose of conducting an investigation.

Informal AARs are normally reserved for small units and when there is no specific need or resources to conduct a more formal review. They share many of the same advantages and methods of a debriefing, especially because they are conducted by the people involved and everyone participates. Nevertheless, they are more structured than a debriefing and often have specific objectives. Consequently, they examine issues more thoroughly and may extend over several days or weeks.

Formal AARs are reserved for larger organizations in examining complex training exercises or operations resulting in calamities and may take several months. They routinely have both an agenda and a schedule. Furthermore, they are tightly focused and are often limited in scope. They more closely resemble an investigation than any of the other methods and are the most comprehensive. Accordingly, and nearly without exception, a formal AAR requires a written report.

There is no standard format for recording lessons learned but one format is so commonly used that it is nearly universal, especially for debriefings and informal AARs. It is popular because it is simple, clear and easy to understand. It originated with the military services, and like many military terms is often referred to by its initials, "IDR," which stand for Item, Discussion and Recommendation. The **IDR format** is a simple, three-step process for identifying and describing issues, items or ideas with their related recommendations after a training exercise or tactical operation. The IDR format works well even when the report is lengthy. When a large number of items, issues or ideas are identified they are often grouped according to function, subject, area, clientele or time.

The *item, issue or idea step* identifies the particular subject and provides a brief but precise description of the concern. It also serves as the title of the subject[198] and as such is normally just a few words and never longer than a single sentence. The idea is to descriptively but succinctly encapsulate the essence of what is to follow in as few words as possible. This provides both an ability to group similar subjects in lengthy reports as well as to quickly identify a particular subject when seeking information afterwards.

The *discussion is the second step* and is a short summary explaining why the concern is relevant. It is intended to provide sufficient information to convince an uninformed reader of how the problem was manifested and in what circumstances and context. When more than one contributory cause is identified they are all listed only if they can be rectified by a single recommendation. The discussion component may be several paragraphs to as long as a single page. Those items that require longer explanations and descriptions are normally reserved for more formal reports. When a number of factors are noted it is common to simply list them as bullets.

The *recommendation is the last step* and is a short statement suggesting a corrective course of action, countermeasure or remedy. It is not uncommon to have each contributor author their own suggestions which are then collected into a single report. When this occurs the author's name and contact information are usually provided at the end of this section.

In spite of the value of debriefings and AAR, there are still administrators who see them as a waste of time. From their perspective, unless something went drastically wrong there is nothing more to be gained by talking about it. Worth repeating is that experience may be the best teacher but it is a harsh schoolmaster and failing to correct mistakes ensures they will be repeated. Do not confuse good luck with good fortune.[199] Tactical shortcomings are measured in lives!

---

190. Rear Admiral Alfred Thayer Mahan, *Naval Strategy*, 1911. Rear Admiral Mahan was not only a naval officer but a teacher, historian and strategic theorist. He based many of his beliefs on the writings of Antoine-Henri Jomini and pointed out that control of terrain features along the boundaries of the seas provided strategic advantages, especially choke points, refueling stations and so forth. His writings were exceptionally clear and widely accepted and influenced naval strategy and thought throughout the world, especially in Germany and Japan, who would become enemies of the United States during World War II. In fact, he is considered by many to be the most important American strategist of his time. He is credited with coining the term "middle east" to describe the region where so much contemporary conflict exists. There is little doubt that his historical studies led to the insightful quote.
191. USMC General James N. Mattis, currently the commanding general of U.S. Central Command, has summarized this concept by stating that "Success yields a warm afterglow in which lessons are often glossed over; failure leads to soul-searching and a far more effective decision analysis."
192. One useful technique to identify root causes was developed in the 1970s by Sakichi Tayoda for the Toyota Corporation and is called the "5 Whys Analysis." The technique works by starting with the observed

failure and to ask "Why?" When the question is answered the process is repeated again and again with each succeeding answer challenged with the same question until the layers of symptoms obscuring the root causes are removed. The analysis is elegant in that it is extremely simple to learn and apply while revealing the true nature of the failure.

193. In natural and mechanical disasters, this occurs when the magnitude or scope of the consequences are underestimated.
194. This last expression is particularly difficult to accept in elite units of highly competent members with specialized skills. These people are accustomed to succeeding in the most trying situations and can be averse to admitting weaknesses and shortcomings. A "can do" attitude must be tempered with the practical realism of the totality of the circumstances.
195. The concepts described in this section are largely taken from two outstanding books on the subject, both of which are focused primarily on military operations but easily adaptable to those in law enforcement. *Military Blunders: The How and Why of Military Failure* by Saul David and *Military Misfortunes: The Anatomy of Failure in War* by Eliot A. Cohen and John Gooch are well worth the effort to read and understand.
196. This concept was coined by Jared Diamond and is described in more detail in his Pulitzer prize-winning book, *Guns, Germs and Steel*, W.W. Norton & Company, Inc., New York, New York, 1999, p. 157
197. In the military services a "saved round" refers to an unfired round that, for one reason or another, was legitimately not fired and the shooter is allowed to fire it for qualification. In a briefing or debriefing, it refers to items and issues that were not part of the agenda but that need to be brought up for consideration or notice.
198. Because it serves as a title, it is sometimes referred to as the "Identification" or "ID" step.
199. This is a favorite saying of Lt. Ken Hubbs, San Diego Police Department and President of the California Tactical Officers Association.

APPENDIX A

CONCEPT GLOSSARY

THIS CONCEPT GLOSSARY IS PROVIDED TO FACILITATE A QUICK review. The concepts are arranged alphabetically without regard to where they were introduced in the book but because many of them interact with one another are also cross-indexed to others. Additionally, some are most relevant as part of a process, system or category and so are arranged together. Consequently, there may be more than one entry for the same concept.

2/3 Rule A planning principle that states that two-thirds of available planning time always belongs to the next subordinate unit. This increases participation, enhances trouble-shooting and ensures subordinates have time for preparation and implementation.

Active Intelligence An intelligence strategy that assigns intelligence missions to personnel and units whose primary responsibility is to obtain the information and relay it to a command post. Gathering intelligence is not a subordinate task, but the primary mission. (See also *Passive Intelligence*)

Administrative Control A command relationship that gives authority to a commander for controlling all things of an administrative nature. Sometimes referred to by the acronym ADCON. (See also *Operational Control* and *Tactical Control*)

After Action Review A structured process for analyzing a particular operation or exercise and usually includes subject matter experts or superiors specifically tasked with identifying areas for improvement. After Action Reviews can be either informal or formal and may be convened either before an exercise or after an operation. (See also *Debriefing*)

Alert Order An order that is used to initiate a heightened state of vigilance or preparation for some action. It signals individuals or units that they may be assigned a mission concerning a developing situation. (See also *Four Types of Orders*)

Analysis A mental process that breaks a problem into its component parts to determine the essential features and relationships. (See also *Synthesis*)

Anna Karenina Effect A concept that describes the absolute necessity for all critical components of any response organization to function. A failure of a single component within a disaster response or tactical intervention may cause collapse but success requires that every one of them work as designed. (See also *Cascade Effect*)

Annex An extension to a written plan that contains information that provides specific and detailed instructions related to a single aspect or function of a plan. An annex often deals with a specific function like logistics, communications, intelligence, or a particular problem, evacuations, traffic control, investigations, etc. (See also *Appendix* and *Enclosure*)

Appendix An extension to a written plan that contains detailed supplemental information that adds clarity or precision to an overall plan. An appendix is usually added when further information or explanation is necessary, often in the form of checklists, charts, tables, or schedules. (See also *Annex* and *Enclosure*)

Archival information Any information that seldom, if ever, changes. For example, all historical data is archival in nature. (See also *Four Types of Information*)

Area of Influence A geographical region in which a commander may influence an operation, even indirectly, without being in command. (See also *Zone of Action*)

Area of Interest A geographical region of concern to a commander, either because of the impact on current operations or those that are planned, but that are unable to be controlled. (See also *Zone of Action*)

Area of Operations (AO)

The geographical area associated within a single command where the commander has the authority to plan and conduct operations. (See also *Zone of Action*)

Arranging Information

(See also *Four Types of Information*)

Category means to group it by type or variety; fruits and vegetables, cats and dogs or apples and oranges, for example

Time means to arrange it in chronological order in which events occurred.

Location refers to a physical place where information is stored.

Alphabetical means to arrange it in the order of the alphabet but it also includes numerical progression.

Continuum. Continuums are used when there is a continuous succession of which no part is readily distinguishable from another except by arbitrary division; smallest to largest, darkest to lightest, weakest to strongest, slowest to fastest, most to least, and so forth.

Assets

A term used to describe the equipment, tools, weapons, personnel and the like, that are owned by an organization. (See also *Resources*)

Assumptions Anything that is taken for granted or accepted as true without proof. To be useful, an assumption must be valid, that is a logical inference or deduction based upon all the facts available, (even though incomplete). An assumption is used when an EEI or OIR cannot be obtained in time to be incorporated into the decision-making process. (See also *Essential Elements of Information* and *Other Intelligence Requirements*)

Asymmetric Strategy A strategy that attempts to apply strength against weakness. This may mean using dissimilar techniques, technologies or other capabilities to maximize our strength while exploiting weaknesses in an adversary. (See also *Symmetric Strategy*)

Asynchronous System Refers to a method of communicating that provides communications but does not require all participants to be involved at the same time. (See also *Synchronous System*)

Azimuth An angle of deviation measured clockwise from north, nearly always given in degrees.

Barrier Obstacles that are so formidable as to prevent movement. (See also *Obstacle*)

Battlespace The area, dimension or environment determined by the maximum capabilities to acquire and engage an adversary.

Bond Relationship Targeting

A method of targeting that focuses an attack on the association, connection or cohesion that binds two or more people or organizations. This is often a particularly desirable target because once the relationship is broken other vulnerabilities are ripe for exploitation.

Boyd's Cycle or the OODA Loop

A notional tool used to understand how events unfold in time as a series of four overlapping steps.

Observation scans the environment and includes all aspects, such as the physical surroundings, lighting conditions, weather, terrain, the adversary and even themselves. This is the first step in identifying those factors and influences that are relevant to the specific situation from the volume of information available. Understandably, the better the observation the clearer will be the perspective gained by the observer.

Orientation identifies the need to gain perspective and provides a foundation for understanding. The experience, insight and understanding of the decision maker weigh heavily on the clarity and comprehension gained.

Decisions must be made to influence the outcome. Based upon the decision maker's understanding of the situation, hypotheses are developed and conclusions are drawn.

Actions are always necessary to affect those factors that influence a favorable outcome, whether by making adverse influences less likely to occur or less damaging when they do, or conversely, to encourage those that are favorable.

Branches Courses of action that may be necessary, dependent upon the changing circumstances. Branches answer questions of "what if?" All contingency plans are branches of the deliberate plan. (See also *Sequels*)

Broadcast Any means of simultaneously communicating to a wide audience. The main advantage of broadcasting is that it gets the information to the widest audience in the shortest amount of time with the least effort. (See also *Narrowcast*)

C^2 An abbreviation used to identify and describe the inseparable and interacting nature of "command" and "control."

C^3 An abbreviation used to identify and describe the inseparable and interacting nature of "command," "control" and "communications."

Capabilities

Describes the ability of a specific opposing agent to successfully accomplish an action. When the agent is an adversary, capabilities provide a measure of ability in terms of logistical support or operational sophistication. When the agent is a natural or mechanical disaster, capabilities provide a calculation of the degree of impact on a region, function or organization. (See also *Trends*, *Potentials* and *Intentions*)

Cardinal Directions

A system of navigation that uses the cardinal points of a compass for steering. Directions are given with one of the four cardinal points of a compass; north, south, east and west. When more precision is necessary the intermediate points of northwest, northeast, southwest and southeast are provided. (See also *Navigation Methods*)

Cascade Effect

Any failure or succession of failures resulting from a preceding failure. A cascade of failures can often be attributed to a seemingly trivial action upon which other functions and actions were dependent. (See also *Anna Karenina Effect*)

Center Of Gravity (COG) A concept that identifies something a suspect is dependent upon for success, and which, if eliminated, damaged, diminished or destroyed, will severely impact his opportunities for success. In natural or mechanical types of crises, a center of gravity identifies the major factor that attenuates the adverse consequences of a calamity. (See also *Critical Vulnerability*)

Centralized Distribution A logistical strategy that employs supply dumps, staging areas and issue points where individuals and deployed units are expected to provide their own transportation to collect their supplies. (See also *Decentralized Distribution*)

Chain of Command The line of authority along which information and instructions are passed between superiors and subordinates. It is also referred to as a command channel. (See also *Command and Control Architecture, Command Channel* and *Table of Organization*)

Chance Turns of events that cannot reasonably be foreseen and over which neither opponent has any control. Chance is a major contributor to both fog and friction.

Characteristics of Good Intelligence **Objective** intelligence is as free as possible from personal prejudices, distortions, feelings or interpretations.

Thorough intelligence is sufficient to allow a decision maker to draw reliable conclusions.

Accuracy means that the information is factually correct. Because it is impossible to be exhaustive, accuracy becomes all the more important since decisions will need to be made on whatever information is available.

Timeliness means that the information is available when needed. The best intelligence is rendered useless if it arrives too late to be of use.

Usable requires that the intelligence is provided in such a manner that it can be used "as is" without additional effort by a decision maker.

Relevant means that the intelligence supports decisions for the issues at hand. Thus, the same information may be relevant at one location or echelon of command and be completely useless at another location or echelon.

Available means that the intelligence must be accessible and in a usable format to provide understanding for planners and decision makers. While it is necessary to keep some intelligence secret, it must also be understood that secrecy is that antithesis to availability.

Cloud Swarm A swarming tactic that forms after the maneuver elements have massed at a staging area or from another formation and then disperse to simultaneously attack from multiple directions. It is also called a "massed swarm."(See also *Vapor Swarm*)

Collaborative System A communications system that requires compatible equipment or software for both the sender and recipients. (See also *Communication Systems*, and *Noncollaborative System*)

Collective Planning A planning process that involves the combined efforts of a more than one person. Collective planning reduces the impact of personal prejudices, enhances perception and provides a more accurate assessment of risk. (See also *Individual Planning*)

Command and Control Architecture A design or system to provide for the interaction of the essential components and assures that all efforts are directed toward achieving a common goal. It is necessary to effectively define lines of authority, distribute power and allocate resources and is also called a table of organization. (See also *Chain of Command*)

Command Channel The line of authority along which information and instructions are passed between superiors and subordinates. It is sometimes referred to as a chain of command. (See also *Chain of Command, Command and Control Architecture* and *Table of Organization*)

Command Element The function in a tactical organization responsible for identifying and stating the ultimate objectives to be accomplished as well as providing essential planning guidance to achieve the necessary cooperation and coordination among the other functions. All other functions are subordinate to this one. An implied responsibility for this component requires the monitoring of all activities within the tactical organization, especially concerning the other three functions of intelligence, operations and logistics. (See also *Intelligence*, *Logistics* and *Operations*)

Command Relationship Any formal association between two or more people that establishes a connection through which command is exercised. Of necessity, both superior and subordinate roles will be designated. (See also *Chain of Command* and *Command Channel*)

Command The power one holds because of their position in an organization. Command involves delegated authority; that is authority that a person possesses by virtue of their position within an organization. (See also *Control*)

Commander's Intent A commander's concise expression of the purpose of the operation and the desired end state. It provides the essential focus to concentrate activities and facilitate coordination. Accordingly, it serves as the initial impetus and provides a foundation for the planning process to follow.

Commanding Terrain

Any terrain that offers a decisive advantage. The control of commanding terrain (sometimes called decisive terrain) is so influential that it often determines the outcome. (See also *Key Terrain*)

Common Operational Picture

The shared knowledge and understanding between individuals, teams or groups. (See also *Situational Awareness*)

Communication Forms

Signal describes anything that serves to indicate, warn or direct some event or action. Signals come in all forms but the most common include sounds, lights and gestures.

Numbers refer to the concept of quantity. Numbers have the advantage of conveying precision more than any other method or combination of methods because they impart a precise value.

Graphics are images of all types. Images can be actual representations of objects or scenes or, just as useful, abstract expressions and ideas.

Language used for communicating includes all its forms but primarily expressions provided either as text or verbally.

Communication Requirements

Reliability assures that communications will function when needed and relies heavily on careful planning and dependable equipment.

Security refers to the precautions taken to deny unauthorized persons information of value that could be used to adversely affect an operation. Security measures are all encompassing and include anything that might expose information to unauthorized parties.

Speed describes the time it takes to move a message from a sender to a recipient.

Flexibility refers to the ability to both support a wide dispersion of units as well as adapt to adverse and varying conditions.

Communications Channel

Refers to the route and medium that links two or more stations. Stations may share more than one channel, for example, it is not unusual to have multiple command posts linked by radio, telephone, email and messengers, each of which constitutes a separate communications channel. (See also *Communications Network*)

Communications Network

A term used to describe a group of communication stations linked by a common means of communicating. (See also *Communications System and Communications Channel*)

Communications System

A group of independent but interrelated elements necessary for establishing, maintaining and operating communications that make up a unified whole. They include the various methods for transmitting information and the myriad configurations these take on and are limited only by the imagination and resourcefulness of the planner. (See also *Communications Network*)

Collaborative System is a communication system that requires compatible equipment or software for both the sender and recipients.

Noncollaborative System is a communications system that allows communication without requiring compatible equipment. Noncollaborative systems are especially useful when impromptu communications are required.

Synchronous System is one that requires all participants to communicate at the same time and with compatible equipment. Radios and telephones are examples of synchronous systems.

Asynchronous System is one that provides an ability to communicate without the necessity of participants to be involved at the same time, or even the same equipment. Email and text messages are examples of asynchronous systems.

Communications Any method of conveying information from one person or place to another to improve understanding. The term is exhaustive and includes everything from speech and writing to signals and gestures.

Competing Interest Anything that engages the attention and results in a division of attention or resources. (See also *Conflicting Interest*)

Concept of Operations A series of actions designed to progressively promote the accomplishment of strategic objectives. A concept of operations may be understood as a scheme for orienting activity without precisely prescribing what must be done. It always involves a number of missions, which necessarily includes a multitude of tasks.

Conflict A type of crisis in which there is an irreconcilable clash between opposing wills. While a crisis may result from whims of nature, such as fires, floods, or earthquakes or mishaps from traffic accidents and airplane crashes, conflicts always involve an adversary who is actively engaged in thwarting the will of the tactical commander.

Conflicting Interest Anything that results in incompatibility to the extent that two or more actions are mutually exclusive. (See also *Competing Interest*)

Constraints Controls that demand some action. Constraints may be imposed by law, policy or a plan. (See also *Restraints*)

Contemporaneously One of the three ways of implementing a plan. This method reacts to a developing situation and is the most common for both fire and law enforcement in that they are the two most common disciplines called upon to intervene in deteriorating circumstances. (See also *Four Types of Orders, On Order* and *Time or Sequence*)

Contingency Plan An alternate plan that focuses thought and effort on anticipated problems that may arise during the conduct of an operation. Because a contingency plan is a branch from the deliberate plan, it is often referred to as "Plan B." Contingency plans allow for operational deviation while maintaining continuity with the preferred course of action and guard against operations being stymied by confusion caused by a sudden change in the situation. (See also *Deliberate Plan* and *Hasty Plan*)

Control The influence exerted by personal expertise, persuasion or charisma. Control involves perceived authority, which is authority bestowed upon a person by those they seek to direct. (See also *Command*)

Corporate Knowledge The collective knowledge of all participants in any plan or decision.

Coup d'Oeil Concept A French expression which loosely translated means the "strike of the eye" or the "vision behind the eye." The closest English concept would be that of intuition. Intuition is defined as "perceptive insight" or "the power to discern the true nature of a situation."

Couplings A relative term used to describe how two or more components in a plan interact.

Creeping Missions A gradual and barely noticeable change or expansion of missions without a conscious decision. Because of the lack of intent, a creeping mission fails to compensate for the shortcomings of equipment or capabilities necessary for the new mission. This is sometimes referred to as a "mission creep."(See also *Drifting Standards*)

Crisis An emotionally stressful event or situation involving an impending, abrupt and decisive change. While there is a natural tendency to view a crisis as bad it is more precisely defined as a situation that can turn out bad. Thus, more descriptively, a crisis is a form of threat.

Crisis Decision Making The mental process of reaching a conclusion during a time of instability and danger relevant to resolving the situation.

Critical Capabilities Describes those inherent abilities that enable a center of gravity to function. Critical capabilities answer questions as to what are the ways of attaining the end state?(See also *Critical Requirements*)

Critical Mass A concept used to describe the point at which the size of a crowd, the amount of commitment to a cause and the amount of emotion present, alone or in combination, could result in some type of civil disorder.

Critical Requirements Describes those conditions, means and resources that enable a critical capability. More simply put, critical requirements are inherent preconditions for critical capabilities and answer questions as to what are necessary to enable the identified critical capabilities?(See also *Critical Capabilities*)

Critical Vulnerability (CV) A concept that identifies a weakness which, if exploited, will create failure. (See also *Center of Gravity*)

Cross-training The efforts focused on increasing the proficiency and understanding of different (but usually related), skills and tasks. Cross-training maximizes the benefits provided by subject matter experts by allowing less-skilled personnel to work under their guidance.

Current information

Any information that is time sensitive and pertains to details, events or actions occurring in the present or very near past. Dynamic information is a subset of current information that is in a near constant state of change. (See also *Four Types of Information*)

Cyberspace

An intangible information space where people interact with one another and machines. Cyberspace is distinguished from space and time because knowledge can be in more than one place at the same time. (See also *Humanspace, Space* and *Time*)

Debriefing

A moderated discussion focused on gaining understanding and insight regarding a specific operation or exercise and involving those people who were personally involved. Debriefings can occur with all echelons of an organization but are predominately done at the lowest levels and include only those persons specifically involved in a given operation or exercise. (See also *After Action Review*)

Decentralized Distribution

A logistical strategy where equipment is issued directly to an individual and/or a deployed unit. (See also *Centralized Distribution*)

Decision Point

A technique that is incorporated into a tactical plan to call attention to the need to make a decision. It identifies an event, time or sequence at which further guidance is necessary to proceed. (See also *Tripwire*)

Decision

A conclusion reached through deduction or inference. Decisions involve three separate, but interrelated, factors

Reason or Judgment involves an objective and rational comparison and selection between alternatives.

Emotions are subjective feelings and influences that occur without conscious effort and are affected by such things as anxiety, fatigue, hunger and pain. Emotions also influence decisions from personal dispositions, biases, and prejudices.

Perceptions refers to how the mind interprets a sensory stimulus. How humans interpret information and determine its importance is a complex and interrelated process of culture, values and experience, embedded in context.

Deconfliction

A term used to identify those steps taken to reconcile potential conflicts. Deconfliction measures encompass everything designed to reduce friction and increase cooperation and collaboration.

Defilade Terrain Any terrain that is used so that it provides increased protection from observation or hazard. No terrain feature is inherently defilade and the protection exists only because of a temporary position of personnel or equipment relative to the terrain. (See also *Enfilade Terrain*)

Deliberate Plan A comprehensive and detailed method for accomplishing an objective. A deliberate plan is the preferred course of action and is as comprehensive as time will permit. It is frequently referred to as the "master plan," since it serves as a baseline for all related plans and operations and describes the preferred course of action. (See also *Contingency Plan* and *Hasty Plan*)

Demand-Pull System A logistical strategy that places responsibility on the supported unit for requesting logistical support. This means that all resupplies, maintenance, calibration, reliefs, and so forth, are "pulled" by requesting them as needed. It is sometimes referred to as a logistical pull system. (See also *Supply Push System*)

Density The quantity of activities per unit of time. In space, density refers to the quantity of objects in a given region. (See also *Initiative* and *Tempo*)

Devil's Advocate A person who is called upon to adopt and defend opposing views, as well as identifying weaknesses and attacking those being presented.

Dimension An environment, realm or domain which defines the state and conditions of the predominate influences. The rules that govern one dimension are completely irrelevant for another.

Direct Order An order that is precisely and clearly expressed directly from a superior to a subordinate. Direct orders may be verbal or written and are the norm when supervisors and subordinates are collocated or connected directly through some type of communications device. (See also *Indirect Order*)

Direct Support The command relationship for a unit whose actions support a specific component of the overall operation. Reinforcing units are assigned direct support missions by the command authority of the entire operation. (See also *General Support*)

Dispersed Swarm A swarming tactic that involves maneuver elements that are already dispersed and converge on a target from many directions. It is also called a "vapor swarm."(See also *Massed Swarm*)

Distribution Identifies the logistical need to disperse equipment and personnel to where they are most needed and when. Distribution is one of the four principal roles in the logistical process. (See also *Logistical Process*, *Procurement*, *Recovery*, and *Sustainment*)

Division of Labor — Refers to the categorization and assignments of specific knowledge and skills in the performance of roles within an organization. For example, police agencies have specialists in patrol, investigations, custody, and so forth.

Drifting standards — A condition that results from a lack of enforcement of minimum standards. Drifting standards nearly always begin with an exception of some kind that sets a precedent for future exceptions. (See also *Creeping Missions*)

Dynamic information — A subset of current information that is in a near constant state of change. (See also *Four Types of Information* and *Current Information*)

Echelon of Command — The term used to describe a layer of an organization of which all members have equal decision making authority. Generally, the higher the echelon the greater the responsibility, and understandably, greater authority. While an echelon is usually composed of equal ranks, the definitive criterion is not rank but authority. (See also *Table of Organization*)

Economy of Force — One of the nine principles of war that refers to the preservation of personnel and/or equipment at a given time and place to ensure readiness for both sustainment and achieve superiority at a decisive place and time. It is the reciprocal of mass. (See also *Nine Principles of War* and *Mass*)

Emerging Multi-Organizational Network (EMON) A self-evolving organization that is specifically designed for resolving a crisis. Because EMONs evolve in response to situations that are always somewhat unique they take on different forms, sizes, and configurations depending on the circumstances presented. They are also referred to as Emergent Multi-Organizational Networks.

EMON (Splitting) All events requiring a tactical intervention tend to evolve from a simpler form to one that is more complex. When it becomes necessary to divide a tactical organization to make it more manageable there are five common methods.

Time—the most common method of splitting a response organization is with time and is almost always according to shifts and/or "operational periods."

Geographical Area—this division groups people by where they are physically located and working. This allows closer coordination and supervision.

Purpose—when EMONs are separated by purpose they are almost always by functions, such as traffic control, containment, communications, evacuations, and so forth.

Process—this division occurs according to the methodology or ongoing series of actions to accomplish some activity. Separating an EMON by process is useful when knowledge of a process is a major contributing factor in accomplishing a similar, but not identical activity.

Clientele—division by clientele refers to a grouping of people, regardless of how they are identified or assembled, and for whom some service is required.

EMON — An acronym commonly used as a substitute for the longer term, "Emerging Multi-Organizational Network." An EMON is a self-evolving organization that is specifically designed for handling a crisis. (See also *Emerging Multi-Organizational Network*)

Enclosure — An extension to a written plan that contains specific information on a single subject that is used for reference. An enclosure is often a separate document prepared for a different purpose but that provides clarity and understanding in the new context. Common examples of enclosures include photographs, maps, sketches, and the like. (See also *Appendix* and *Annex*)

Encyclopedic information — Any information that is durable, but not everlasting. Examples include such things as home telephone numbers, work assignments, or special skills.
(See also Four Types of Information)

End State Those required conditions that define achievement of the commander's objectives. In the simplest terms, the end state describes the desired result, or final outcome, of a tactical operation. (See also *Objective*)

Enfilade Terrain Any terrain that increases the vulnerability of personnel and equipment because it exposes them to observation or hazard. No terrain feature is inherently enfilade and the vulnerability exists only because of a temporary position of personnel or equipment relative to the terrain. (See also *Defilade Terrain*)

Envelopment A tactic that works by attempting to fix an adversary's attention on one area while the main force exploits a weakness in another. It avoids the "front," which is usually more heavily guarded, and strikes from one of the flanks. Thus, envelopments are more easily understood as flanking maneuvers. (See also *Pincer*)

Environmental Scanning A systematic examination that attempts to detect and identify potential threats by detecting factors and influences in a particular social setting.

Essential Elements of Information (EEI) Essential elements of information are those critical facts that a decision maker must have to reach a conclusion. (See also *Assumptions* and *Other Intelligence Requirements*)

Event Horizon That portion of the future in which decision makers can reasonably anticipate the consequences of their actions. It is the far threshold of a range in time called the foreseeable future. (See also *Foreseeable Future* and *Manageable Future*)

Event Matrix A chart designed to identify what units have been assigned to which tasks. This ensures that valuable resources are appropriately assigned and that critical functions are not overlooked.

Event A single, discrete, one-time occurrence that has an effect on a given issue. When two or more events can be identified as being related to an issue a prediction can be made as to another. (See also *Trends*)

Excessive Force Any force that is deemed to be more severe than is necessary in either kind or duration. Excessive force by kind is that which inflicts more pain, suffering or injury than is deemed proper to accomplish the tactical objective. Excessive force by duration is when force is applied longer than is necessary.

Execute Order An order that is used to implement or carry out some action in accordance with a plan. (See also *Four Types of Orders*)

Experience Practical wisdom comprised of knowledge and skills attained through personal participation or observation.

Expertise The advanced skills and knowledge people use for decisions and actions. All expertise is contextual in that it is limited to a specific discipline, subject or field of study.

Exploitation Window A period of time in which an individual or unit is at some sort of disadvantage as a result of an intentional action by their opponent. (See also *Opportunity*)

Expressed Threat A threat where the consequences of defiance are made known. (See also *Implied Threat*)

Fast Transient The capability of rapidly changing from one maneuver state to another. The four most common methods are changing speed, direction, location or attitude.

Field of Fire The area that a weapon can cover effectively from a given position. (See also *Sector of Fire*)

First Common Senior Rule A rule that establishes the authority to decide (resolve conflicts) with the first superior in charge of all disputants. (See also *Chain of Command* and *Command Channel*)

Fixed Time A method of dividing time that is definitively and unequivocally set and not dependent upon external factors. Examples include deadlines and curfews. (See also *Periodic Time* and *Relative Time*)

Focus of Effort (FOE)	The predominant activity or assignment that a commander identifies that must be accomplished to achieve a successful resolution. All other assignments and missions are subordinate. Focus of effort answers the questions of what is to be done?(See also *Main Effort*)
Fog	The condition that prohibits a tactical commander from obtaining accurate information in a timely manner.
Follow-on Actions	Those intended procedures and activities that follow others. Follow-on actions are often contributory to a desirable end state but are not necessarily prerequisites. They are typically preparatory in nature in that they anticipate and prepare for additional requirements.
Force	The exercise of strength, energy or power in order to impose one's will. It can be focused on a person or a thing, as in using force to push a car. In resolving a conflict, however, it is always focused on one or more people.
Force Continuum	A tool used to describe a succession of force options from minimal to maximum.
Force Multiplier	Any capability or advantage that, when added to and appropriately employed, significantly increases the potential of an individual or group. Force multipliers are very diverse and can be as complex as a superior weapon or as simple as a better idea.

Forecast

A calculation based upon the identification, observation and analysis of pertinent data coupled with an assessment of the likelihood of consequences. While a forecast is not precise, it does limit the possibilities to a range of likely outcomes.

Foreseeable Future

That portion of the future in which the consequences of actions can be reliably inferred and estimated. (See also *Event Horizon*)

Four Types of Information

Archival information is that which seldom, if ever, changes. For example, all historical data is archival in nature.

Encyclopedic information is durable, but not everlasting. Examples include such things as home telephone numbers, work assignments, or special skills.

Current information is that which is time sensitive and pertains to details, events or actions occurring in the present or very near past.

Dynamic information is a subset of current information that is in a near constant state of change.

Future information is that information that can be confidently derived by forecast or projection. (See also *Arranging Information*)

Four Types of Orders

Alert Order is an order used to initiate a heightened state of vigilance or preparation for some action. It signals individuals or units that they may be assigned a mission concerning a developing situation.

Warning Order is an order used when it appears certain that an individual or unit will be required, but is not immediately needed. It can also be used to advise that some type of action may be required. This is particularly valuable if the action requires unusual resources or extraordinary preparation.

Execute Order is an order that is used to implement or carry out some action in accordance with a plan.

Fragmentary (frag) Order is an order that is used to modify or rescind any existing order by providing additional details to a situation or by adding to, changing or countermanding a previous order. Because it is only used for changing an existing order, nothing except essential information is provided. Thus, it is incomplete, or "fragmentary," without the preexisting order.

Fragmentary (frag) Order Fragmentary (frag) Order is an order that is used to modify or rescind any existing order by providing additional details to a situation or by adding to, changing or countermanding a previous order. Because it is only used for changing an existing order, nothing except essential information is provided. Thus, it is incomplete, or "fragmentary," without the preexisting order. (See also *Four Types of Orders*)

Free Play Exercises Any exercise in which two or more opponents face off on a given assignment and compete against each other. To the maximum extent possible, this adversary relationship simulates real life operations and creativity and ingenuity are encouraged. (See also *OpFor Gaming*)

Friction The force that resists all action. It makes the simple difficult and the difficult seemingly impossible. It may be psychological, self-induced or physical.

Future Information Any information that can be confidently derived by forecast or projection. (See also *Four Types of Information*)

General Support The command relationship for a unit whose actions support the organization as a whole rather than any particular component. When in general support, lines of command and control are essentially the same, with the exception that the portion of the unit actually deployed is under the authority of the incident commander. (See also *Direct Support*)

Graphics A means of communication which includes images of all types. Images can be actual representations of objects or scenes or, just as useful, abstract expressions and ideas. (See also *Communication Forms, Language, Numbers* and *Signal*)

Grid System A navigation system that utilizes a map, diagram or aerial photograph superimposed with straight lines intersecting at right angles over it. The squares formed by the lines are called "grid squares" and the lines are assigned either numbers or letters to identify a particular square. (See also *Navigation Methods*)

Hammer and Anvil A tactic that works by using two forces, one stationary and one mobile. The stationary force "fixes" the adversary and prevents escape while the mobile force moves toward it with the adversary caught between.

Hasty Plan

A plan that is used to provide an organized response for spontaneous or unintentional events and which are so impromptu that detailed planning is not possible or so remote that comprehensive planning is not justified. In simpler terms, hasty plans provide an organized response to surprise. (See also *Contingency Plan* and *Deliberate Plan*)

Heuristic

A procedure or technique that increases the probability of finding solutions with less time and effort than that required by a random or exhaustive search. (See also *Rule of Thumb and Similarity Heuristic*)

Human Sensing Dimensional Barrier

A barrier that separates humanspace from cyberspace beyond which a lack of knowledge prevents adversaries from being acquired and engaged because of an inability to determine their identity and/or location. This barrier is a dynamic and contested frontier between opposing forces because terrorists and criminals will take steps to avoid detection and thus remain in the safety of cyberspace. (See also *Humanspace* and *Cyberspace*)

Humanspace

That aspect of battlespace composed of the traditional dimensions of space and time in which humans, and their machines, move and fight. (See also *Cyberspace, Space* and *Time*)

IDR Format
An acronym describing a simple, three-step process for identifying and recording lessons learned. The acronym takes its name from the three components, Item (or Issue or Idea), Discussion and Recommendations. (See also *After Action Review* and *Debriefing*)

Implied Threat
A threat where the consequences of defiance are left to the imagination of the adversary. Because even absurd and bizarre options are possible in our imaginations, the implied threat is far more powerful than an expressed threat. (See also *Expressed Threat*)

Incremental Decision
A decision that offers a partial solution and involves little risk but with the expectation that subsequent decisions will progressively promote a satisfactory resolution

Indirect Order
An order that is issued through an intermediary. While it is not uncommon for an indirect order to be issued verbally, they are most commonly written, especially in the form of a plan, policy or instruction. Indirect orders are the norm when a commander issues an order to an entire unit and requires the same degree of compliance as a direct order. (See also *Direct Order*)

Individual Planning A planning process that involves the efforts of only one person, or in some instances, a very few. Because individual planning is faster than collective planning it is used when speed is more important than precision. (See also *Collective Planning*)

Information The knowledge or news of an event or situation gained through collection of facts or data. Information is best understood as "raw data" while intelligence is "processed data."(See also *Intelligence*)

Information Fusion The combination of two or more pieces of information to gain some new insight.

Initiative The power or ability to begin and follow through with some plan or task. Initiative lies entirely in the dimension of time. It is not action, per se, but rather the freedom of action; the ability to choose when and how to act, or in some cases, not to act. (See also *Density* and *Tempo*)

Intelligence Axiom An intelligence principle that states that anything that decreases the effort in obtaining information automatically increases its value. (See also *Intelligence Paradox*)

Intelligence Function The function in a tactical organization responsible for the gathering, recording, evaluating and disseminating of all pertinent information relating to an incident. An implied responsibility with this component requires the continual assessment of all information to determine its relevance, accuracy and timeliness in forecasting the impact on the overall operation. (See also *Command Element*, *Logistics Function* and *Operations Function*)

Intelligence Paradox A concept that describes a paradox in that the better the intelligence predicting an undesirable event, the less likely it is to occur if properly acted upon. Thus, good intelligence appears flawed. (See also *Intelligence Axiom*)

Intelligence Process Those procedures designed to identify, collect, process and disseminate information to be used for planning and decision making.

Direction stems straight from the operational mission and identifies both the nature of the intelligence sought and the means to attain it.

Collection refers to those efforts made at obtaining the information and making it available.

Processing and production is the step where loose data is analyzed and organized into a usable form.

Dissemination ensures that the varying organizational components get the needed intelligence in an appropriate form and in a timely manner.

Intelligence The specific information related to a situation at hand. Information is best understood as "raw data" while intelligence is "processed data."(See also *Information*)

Intentions Refers to the actual or potential activities of an opposing force. Intentions answer the question, "What is likely to happen?" When applied to an adversary, they generally identify their aims and likely courses of action and when applied to natural or technological disasters, intentions identify probable behaviors and consequences. (See also *Trends*, *Potentials* and *Capabilities*)

Intuition The thoughts and preferences that come to mind quickly and without much reflection. Intuition allows a decision maker to quickly grasp the essence of a situation, sort through a vast amount of ambiguous and uncertain information and find an acceptable solution.

Isolation Effect A human mental trait describing the fact that the more information stands out the more likely it is to be remembered. It is also called the "Von Restorff Effect" after the German psychologist who first reported it.

Issue Owner The person most accountable for performing a specific function or solving a particular problem. The closer a person is to a problem the more likely they are to be familiar with the specific factors and influences in play.

Joint Command A command relationship between two or more agencies working together in which all internal command channels remain the same with the senior commander of the supporting unit subordinate to the original incident commander. Generally, the supporting (reinforcing) unit or agency reports to the incident commander of the supported (reinforced) unit and is attached to the existing tactical organization as a separate component. (See also *Unified Command*)

KOCOA An acronym used to identify the five most commonly used steps in conducting a terrain analysis. These are "Key terrain features," "Observation and fields of fire," "Cover and concealment," "Obstacles," and "Avenues of approach and escape." The first component is sometimes identified as "Critical terrain features."(See also *Terrain Analysis* and *Terrain Analysis Steps*)

Language A means of communication which includes all its forms but primarily expressions provided either as text or verbally. (See also *Communication Forms, Graphics, Numbers* and *Signal*)

Legitimacy A principle of war that is often called the "10th Principle of War." It identifies the absolute necessity of maintaining the confidence of the community of the lawfulness and morality of actions. (See also *Nine Principles of War*)

Leverage Point A critical time, place, step or event in a system where force can be applied to make a change. (See also Decision Point and Tripwire)

Logistical Process Those procedures designed to procure, distribute and recover all materiel necessary to sustain operations.

Procurement identifies the need to obtain the essential equipment, weapons, supplies, consumables and personnel.

Distribution involves the dispersing of equipment and personnel to where they are most needed and when.

Sustainment is the third logistical role and ensures that the maintenance, replenishment and/or replacement of equipment, consumables and personnel are accomplished to ensure uninterrupted operations.

Recovery and identifies those efforts focusing on the return of all equipment and personnel to their proper place and condition at the conclusion of the operation.

Logistical Pull System

A logistical strategy that places responsibility on the supported unit for requesting logistical support. This means that all resupplies, maintenance, calibration, reliefs, and so forth, are "pulled" by requesting them as needed. It is sometimes referred to as a "demand-pull system."(See also *Logistical Push System*)

Logistical Push System

A logistical strategy that places responsibility on the logistics section for providing all necessary support to a deployed unit. Supplies and personnel reliefs are usually assigned, moved and distributed according to a schedule based upon an estimate of need by the logistics component. It is sometimes called a "supply push system."(See also *Logistical Pull System*)

Logistical Tasks

Manning is directly supportive of activities involved with personnel. In the simplest terms, manning refers to the posting of people at the right place and time with the right equipment.

Arming refers to providing appropriate weapons, ammunition and related equipment.

Fueling is necessary for all engines and is often referred to in the military as P-O-L, which stands for Petroleum, Oils and Lubricants.

Fixing is necessary to ensure that all equipment remains operational. Besides repairs, some types of equipment need calibration and maintenance to ensure continued operations.

Moving is a logistics task that refers to the necessity of moving personnel and equipment to where they are needed.

Protecting is a comprehensive logistical task that refers to safeguarding, shielding and preserving all materiel and personnel.

Logistics Function The function in a tactical organization responsible for the acquisition, identification, tracking, staging and recovery of all personnel, assets and resources. An implied responsibility is sustaining operations. (See also *Command Element*, *Intelligence Function*, and *Operations Function*)

Loosely Coupled Plan Plans in which the interactions between the various components do not require close coordination. Loosely coupled plans tend to be more flexible but less efficient that tightly coupled plans. (See also *Tightly Coupled Plan*)

Main Effort (ME) The agency, unit or component which has been assigned as the primary means to accomplish the interest or activity defined by the focus of effort. Main effort answers questions of who is to do something?(See also *Focus of Effort*)

Manageable Future That portion of the future that lies between the best and worst case scenarios, with the highest confidence nearest the most likely scenario and oriented closest to the present. The manageable future identifies that portion of the future in which efforts are focused in order to achieve a more favorable outcome. (See also *Event Horizon* and *Foreseeable Future*)

Maneuver Element A component of a tactical formation capable of changing position in order to gain a position of advantage.

Maneuver One of the nine principles of war that refers to the movement of troops and equipment to gain an advantage. (See also *Nine Principles of War*)

Map Reconnaissance An inspection of one or more maps of an area in question to gain a general perspective.

Mass One of the nine principles of war that identifies the importance of the concentration of personnel and/or equipment at a decisive time and place. It is the reciprocal of economy of force. (See also *Nine Principles of War* and *Economy of Force*)

Massed Swarm A swarming tactic that forms after the maneuver elements have massed at a staging area or from another formation and then disperse to simultaneously attack from multiple directions. It is also called a "cloud swarm."(See also *Dispersed Swarm*)

Materiel A term used to describe the aggregate of all things needed in a venture, especially tactical and military operations. (See also *Logistics Function*)

Memorandum of Understanding (MOU) An understanding between agencies that assigns responsibility and/or allocates resources according to an agreement. MOUs identify potential resources not ordinarily or readily available and greatly simplify and expedite the means to make them available.

METT-T An acronym that identifies the five most commonly used steps in conducting an operational analysis. These are "Mission," "Enemy," "Terrain and weather," "Troops and support available," and "Time available." In domestic law enforcement applications the second component is more often adapted by substituting "Obstacle" for enemy. (See also *Operational Analysis* and *Operational Analysis Steps*)

Micro-terrain Terrain that is tactically significant because it will have an impact on an operation but is too small or insignificant to be depicted on a map.

Misplaced Confidence A failure that occurs when those involved underestimate the abilities of the adversary or overestimate their own capabilities. In natural and mechanical disasters, this occurs when the magnitude or scope of the consequences are underestimated. (See also *Overconfidence*)

Mission Creep A gradual and barely noticeable change or expansion of missions without a conscious decision. Because of the lack of intent mission creep fails to compensate for the shortcomings of equipment or capabilities necessary for the new mission. This is sometimes referred to as a "creeping mission."(See also *Drifting Standards*)

Mission Tasking A method of assigning tasks and missions that works by recognizing that each mission actually consists of two parts; the task to be accomplished and the reason or intent it is necessary.

Mitigation The phase in emergency management that involves those activities designed to prevent and/or reduce losses from disaster. Mitigation efforts almost always involve long-term actions such as reinforcing structures, installing backup power sources for critical installations, educating the community and sanctioning strict building codes and zoning ordinances. (See also *Phases of Emergency Management*)

Mnemonic

Any technique that aids memory. Mnemonics often take the form of verses, acronyms, stories, and anecdotes. They work by linking the information with other information so that is easier to retain.

MOOSEMUSS

The acronym used to remember the nine principles of war. Each of the letters identifies a principle and keeps them mentally available for review. While no particular order is implied, the letters generally stand for "Maneuver," "Objective," "Offense," "Simplicity," "Economy of Force," "Mass," "Unity of command," "Surprise" and "Security." (See also *Nine Principles of War*)

MOU and MOA

An acronym that is used to identify a formal understanding between agencies. They stand for, "Memorandum Of Understanding," and "Memorandum Of Agreement." While there may be subtle legal differences that distinguish them from one another, they are most commonly used in law enforcement applications as synonyms. (See also *Memorandum of Understanding (MOU)*

Multi-disciplinary

Any function or factor that pertains to more than one discipline, such as a combination of law enforcement and medical, fire or rescue disciplines.

Mutual Aid

The reciprocal support that different agencies, disciplines and jurisdictions provide each other in times of need. (See also *Reinforcement*)

Narrowcast

Any means of communicating that is sent to specific users who have a need for it. Narrowcasting has the advantage of focusing communications to a particular person or group. (See also *Broadcast*)

Nature of Knowledge

Data refers to facts, statistics or codes that exist without context. Data, in and of itself, is not information because it provides no ability to inform.

Information may be best understood as a collection of facts or data from which conclusions may be drawn. Information is the first step toward understanding and where meaning is attached.

Knowledge refers to a state of awareness of facts and circumstances accompanied with a personal assessment. Consequently, all knowledge is based on interpreted information.

Understanding identifies a person's thorough comprehension of the nature of something. It surpasses simply knowing something and provides insight for probabilities, expectations, opportunities, creativity and resourcefulness. True understanding enables intuition and so subtle factors and influences are more easily detected and reliable inferences can be formed.

Navigation Methods

Cardinal directions is a system of navigation that uses the cardinal points of a compass for steering. Directions are given with one of the four cardinal points of a compass; north, south, east and west. When more precision is necessary the intermediate points of northwest, northeast, southwest and southeast are provided.

Shift from a Known Point is a navigation system that calls attention to an easily identifiable terrain feature or man-made object and then provides a direction and distance from it.

Grid System consists of a map, diagram or aerial photograph superimposed with straight lines intersecting at right angles over it. The squares formed by the lines are called "grid squares" and the lines are assigned either numbers or letters to identify a particular square. The grids can be mentally divided into even small grids for more precision.

Numbering System assigns a number or letter to each side of a building to enable clear and precise directions with a minimum of confusion or conversation.

Nine Principles of War

Refers to nine tried and true principles that provide guidance, understanding and insight for developing plans, determining courses of action and making decisions in tactical operations and disaster responses. While originally identified and described for military operations, they have equal applicability in crises, especially conflicts.

Maneuver refers to the movement of troops and equipment to gain an advantage.

Objective is called the master or controlling principle. This is because it is the basis for which all planning must necessarily follow. In the simplest terms, objective means purpose.

Offense refers to active attempts to gain an advantage and force a favorable outcome. While defense is valuable, it cannot, in and of itself, be decisive because the initiative cannot be gained or maintained and so the best that can be hoped for is a stalemate.

Simplicity refers to the freedom of complexity, intricacy or pretentiousness. A plan that cannot be understood cannot be implemented.

Economy of Force is the preservation of personnel and/or equipment at a given time and place to ensure readiness for both sustainment and achieve superiority at a decisive place and time. It is the reciprocal of mass.

Mass is a concentration of personnel and/or equipment at a decisive time and place. It is the reciprocal of economy of force.

Unity of Command ensures that all efforts are focused on a common goal. Unity of command is achieved by vesting a single commander with the requisite authority to direct, coordinate and control the actions of all forces employed in reaching the objective.

Surprise results from striking an adversary at an unexpected time or place, or in an unanticipated manner. It is not necessary that an adversary be taken completely unaware, only that he becomes aware too late to effectively react.

Security refers to the precautions necessary to deny an adversary any unexpected advantage. The principle of security encompasses far more than just secrecy, however, and may be better described as protectiveness.

Legitimacy is often called the "10th Principle of War." It identifies the absolute necessity of maintaining the confidence of the community of the lawfulness and morality of actions.

Noncollaborative System A communications system that allows communication without requiring compatible equipment. Noncollaborative systems are especially useful when impromptu communications are required. (See also *Communication Systems, and Collaborative System*)

Norm A set of factors or influences that provide a model or pattern regarded as typical. Even when precision is not possible, norms provide an ability to make reliable estimates and approximations for planning and decision making. (See also *Trends*)

Numbering System A navigation and/or orientation system that assigns a number or letter to each side of a building to enable clear and precise directions with a minimum of confusion or conversation. (See also *Navigation Methods*)

Numbers A means of communication which refers to the concept of quantity. Numbers have the advantage of conveying precision more than any other method or combination of methods because they impart a precise value. (See also *Communication Forms, Graphics, Language* and *Signal*)

Objective

One of the nine principles of war that identifies the goal to be attained. It is often identified as the master or controlling principle because it provides the basis for which all planning must necessarily follow. In the simplest terms, objective means purpose. (See also *Nine Principles of War*)

Offense

One of the nine principles of war that refers to the active attempts to gain an advantage and force a favorable outcome. While defense is valuable, it cannot, in and of itself, be decisive because the initiative cannot be gained or maintained and so the best that can be hoped for is a stalemate. (See also *Nine Principles of War*)

On Order

One of the three ways of implementing a plan. A plan that is implemented in this manner is upon receipt of a command. Plans that are implemented in this manner have been prepared but not yet carried out and await only the order to put them into action. (See also *Four Types of Orders, Contemporaneously* and *Time or Sequence*)

OODA

An acronym that identifies the four steps in the Boyd Cycle. These are, "Observation," "Orientation," "Decision," and "Action." This acronym is so popular that it is just as often used as a substitute for the concept. (See also *Boyd's Cycle or the OODA Loop*)

Operational Analysis

A method for developing a plan. It is a fundamental, but sometimes complex, prerequisite for any commander to gain the necessary understanding to formulate an effective strategy. Accordingly, it is a first step in gaining true situational awareness and is a valuable tool for translating operational requirements into tactical guidance. (See also *METT-T and Operational Analysis Steps*)

Operational Analysis Steps

A most useful method for conducting an operational analysis is outlined with a mnemonic called **METT-T** that identifies the five essential factors of Mission, Enemy (or obstacle), Terrain and weather, Troops and support available, and Time available.

Mission refers the absolute necessity of developing and providing a clear, concise statement of what is to be done and for what purpose. It provides the basis for all future planning.

Enemy (or obstacle) is the second factor and identifies the threat, which is whatever needs to be defeated, removed, circumvented or surmounted to achieve a satisfactory resolution to the problem.

Terrain and Weather Identifies the environmental factors involved in an operation. Both terrain and weather will impact operations, most commonly in the form of trafficability, visibility and sustainability. Trafficability refers to the condition of the soil or terrain with regard to being travelled over and is both terrain and weather dependent. Trafficability will impact everything from suitable modes of transportation to where they can go. While visibility can be terrain dependent, as with terrain shielding, it is most often affected by weather and lighting conditions. Sustainability identifies the need to maintain or endure. Weather effects like extreme heat or cold, rain, hail, or humidity will all affect how well and how long both equipment and personnel can operate effectively.

Troops and Support identifies the personnel and equipment available for estimating the effectiveness, efficiency and sustainability of operations.

Time is always a factor in tactical operations and disaster responses and imposes prioritization requirements, especially when the time available and the time required may be irreconcilable.

Operational Control A command relationship that gives a commander authority to assign tasks, organize and employ the supporting unit's assets and give direction throughout the accomplishment of the mission. Sometimes referred to by the acronym OPCON. (See also *Administrative Control* and *Tactical Control*)

Operations Function The function in a tactical organization responsible for the actions focused on reducing the immediate hazard and safeguarding life and property. Accordingly, this is where actions are organized, staffed, coordinated and directed toward a common objective. In the simplest terms, this function is responsible for ensuring that the end state, as defined by the command element, is efficiently and effectively accomplished. (See also *Command Element*, *Intelligence Function*, and *Logistics Function*)

OpFor Gaming An exercise that involves two or more opposing forces and which involves all relevant factors, such as knowledge, strategy, skills, endurance, timing, and even chance. Most OpFor exercises are "free play," in that constraints are kept to an absolute minimum to encourage ingenuity and creativity. It is often referred to as "red teaming."(See also *Free Play Exercises*)

Opportunity A brief interval in time in which circumstances are temporarily favorable. Opportunities are the maneuver objective when maneuvering in time. In tactical settings, opportunities tend to be elusive, sporadic and fleeting. (See also *Exploitation Window*)

Order A command given by a superior requiring the immediate and full obedience in the execution of some task. Orders differ from similar terms, such as "instructions" or "directives," because they require immediate and strict compliance.

Other Intelligence Requirements (OIR) Information that is not absolutely essential but is "nice to have." OIRs complement the more critical EEIs by "filling in the blanks" and providing a more complete picture of the situation. (See also *Assumptions* and *Essential Elements of Information*)

Overcome By Events (OBE) A condition in which decision makers lose the ability to efficiently prioritize between competing interests when they become overwhelmed with their magnitude and complexity. It is also referred to as "Overwhelmed by Events."(See also *Tempo*)

Overconfidence A failure that occurs when those involved underestimate the abilities of the adversary or overestimate their own capabilities. In natural and mechanical disasters, this occurs when the magnitude or scope of the consequences are underestimated. (See also *Misplaced Confidence*)

Overwhelmed By Events (OBE) A condition in which decision makers lose the ability to efficiently prioritize between competing interests when they become overwhelmed with their magnitude and complexity. It is also referred to as "Overcome By Events."(See also *Tempo*)

Passive Intelligence An intelligence strategy which advocates methods that rely on deployed personnel with the belief that, because they are already in the field, and in many cases personally involved with the incident, they are the most able to provide the necessary information. In the law enforcement community, this strategy is sometimes referred to as a "windshield survey."(See also *Active Intelligence*)

Periodic Time A method of dividing time that refers to a specified division, portion or interval identified by a distinctive characteristic. Examples include hours, days and weeks or daytime, nighttime, afternoon, evening, etc. (See also *Fixed Time and Relative Time*)

Phases of Emergency Management

Mitigation refers to those activities designed to prevent and/or reduce losses from disaster. Mitigation efforts almost always involve long-term actions such as reinforcing structures, installing backup power sources for critical installations, educating the community and sanctioning strict building codes and zoning ordinances.

Preparedness is focused on planning and preparing for an effective response. Of necessity, this includes establishing priorities and organizing, equipping and training personnel for their expected roles when they are needed.

Response involves the mobilization and deployment of personnel and equipment to respond to an anticipated or unfolding situation. Actions in the response phase are tightly focused on preserving life and property.

Recovery refers to activities focused on quickly restoring an affected area and people to their former state. This phase often overlaps the response phase and begins as soon as the threat to human life has subsided.

Physical Force

Any force that is perceptible to the senses and subject to the laws of physics. Physical force is tangible and can be measured. (See also *Psychological Force*)

Pincer

A tactic that works by employing two moving forces closing toward each other with the adversary caught between them; hence it is sometimes referred to as a "double envelopment."(See also *Envelopment*)

Plan Implementation

On Order is one method of implementing a plan that is executed upon receipt of a command. Plans that are implemented in this manner have been prepared but not yet carried out and await only the order to put them into action.

Time or Sequence is a method of implementing a plan that awaits a scheduled event or when one event is a precursor for another.

Contemporaneously is a method of implementing a plan when reacting to a developing situation. This method is the most common for both fire and law enforcement in that they are the two most common disciplines called upon to intervene in deteriorating circumstances.

Plan

A structured configuration of actions in time and space envisioned for the future. The focus of every plan is as a design to change the future to something better than anticipated.

Planning

The art and science of envisioning a desired future and laying out effective ways of bringing it about.

Potentials Describes the ability or capacity of something. Potentials set limits on possibilities. (See also *Trends*, *Capabilities* and *Intentions*)

Pre-mortem Exercise Assumes the planned operation has failed and challenges participants to discover how. This requires planners delve into the plan seeking weak points before it is executed.

Preparedness The phase in emergency management that is focused on planning and preparing for an effective response. Of necessity, this includes establishing priorities and organizing, equipping and training personnel for their expected roles when they are needed. (See also *Phases of Emergency Management*)

Principle of Repetition Refers to any series of drills, exercises or practices intended to increase proficiency in preparation for an actual event. Repetition reduces unfamiliarity, increases confidence, and enhances the speed necessary for surprise.

Principle of Speed Refers to the rapidity and quickness of actions. It includes all functions and operations involved in a tactical operation but is especially critical in a conflict.

Procurement — Identifies the logistical need to obtain essential equipment, weapons, supplies, consumables and personnel. Procurement is one of the four principal roles in the logistical process. (See also *Logistical Process*, *Distribution*, *Recovery*, and *Sustainment*)

Prominent Terrain — Any terrain feature that can be easily identified and is displayed on a map. Prominent terrain is especially useful for orientation and navigation.

Proximate Cause — A factor or influence that appears clearly apparent and directly connected. Proximate causes tend to be conspicuous, especially in failure, because they are so closely connected to the actual problem. (See also *Root Cause*)

Psychological Force — Any force that is focused on the mind or will of a person. The effects of psychological force are imperceptible and unable to be measured. (See also *Physical Force*)

Pull Strategy — An intelligence strategy that places information in a central repository where it is available for subordinate units to access as desired. In this manner, local commanders are provided an ability to build their own intelligence picture (OIR) by augmenting what they have been given with whatever else they want to know. (See also *Push Strategy*)

Push Strategy. An intelligence strategy that uses higher headquarters to decide who needs to know what, and then "push" it to subordinate units in the form of intelligence updates and summaries. (See also *Pull Strategy*)

Ramp-Up Strategy A deployment strategy in which the size and type of units needed to adequately handle a situation are estimated and dispatched. (See also *Surge Strategy*)

Reachback A term used to describe the process of obtaining products, services, forces and equipment from people or organizations that are not deployed and may not even be otherwise involved in the operation or response.

Reactions Responses to some treatment, situation, or stimulus. Unlike decisions, mental reactions are processed in a more primitive portion of the brain that is incapable of conscious thought.

Reconstitution A logistical term that describes the necessity to reconstitute tactical units when degraded by injuries, fatigue, and the like.

Recovery In the logistical function, recovery identifies those efforts focused on the return of all equipment and personnel to their proper place and condition at the conclusion of the operation. Recovery is one of the four principal roles in the logistical process (not to be confused with the recovery phase of emergency management).

Recovery The phase in emergency management that involves those activities focused on quickly restoring an affected area and people to their former state. This phase often overlaps the response phase and begins as soon as the threat to human life has subsided. (See also *Phases of Emergency Management* and *Response*)

Reinforcement The augmentation of a tactical organization with additional troops or equipment. Reinforcements are commonly required to counter unforeseen threats, or to prolong or renew some action and are provided in either general support or direct support. (See also *Mutual Aid*)

Relative Superiority That temporary advantage gained by a smaller force over a larger one or a well-defended opponent.

Relative Time A method of dividing time that is a point or period of time having significance only in relation to something else. Examples include "now," "before," "again," as well as consecutive, continual, temporary, subsequent, and so forth. (See also *Fixed Time and Periodic Time*)

Repetition Describes any series of drills, exercises or practices intended to increase proficiency in preparation for an actual event. Repetition is critical in special operations missions because it increases confidence, reduces unfamiliarity and enhances the speed necessary for surprise.

Replacement A logistical term that refers to providing substitutes for damaged or destroyed equipment, vehicles and so forth.

Replenishment A logistical term which refers to refilling or resupplying what is lacking.

Reserve Designated personnel or equipment retained or set aside for future use or a special purpose.

Resource Driven Tasks Tasks that are largely dependent upon the amount and type of resources that can be dedicated to them are called resource driven. A resource driven task can be expedited by adding resources. (See also *Time Driven Tasks*)

Resources A term used to describe the equipment, tools, weapons, personnel and so forth, that are available but not owned by the organization. (See also *Assets*)

Response The phase in emergency management that involves the mobilization and deployment of personnel and equipment to respond to an anticipated or unfolding situation. Actions in the response phase are tightly focused on preserving life and property. (See also *Phases of Emergency Management* and *Recovery*)

Restraints Controls which prohibit some action. Restraints may be imposed by law, policy or a plan. (See also *Constraints*)

Reverse Engineering A process in which an assembled device, often a competitor's, is taken apart to learn how it works and identify parts and processes that can be improved.

Root Cause A causal chain that eventually leads to an outcome. Root causes are not as apparent as proximate causes and require more effort to identify and correct. Root causes have wider reaching effects than proximate causes and they tend to be more difficult to correct. (See also *Proximate Cause*)

Rule of Thumb A mental principle with broad application that gets a decision maker close to a solution. It is not precise enough to identify a solution but it helps provide a focus to avoid pitfalls and unproductive efforts. (See also *Heuristic*)

Rules of Engagement (ROE)

Controls that describe the circumstances, and set forth the conditions, under which law enforcement officers may initiate and/or continue actions against adversaries. They are crafted to address the specific situation for a particular operation, and are usually, but not always, more restrictive than existing policies generally permit.

SALUTE Report

A field intelligence report that provides information about a specific occurrence in a standardized format. There are six steps that describe the observation and are always given and recorded in the exact order.

Size refers to the size, extent or magnitude of the event.

Activity provides a description of the particular observation.

Location refers to the precise location where the activity is occurring. If the incident is dynamic, the direction and approximate speed it is moving is also be provided.

Unit or uniform describes who or what is involved and what they look like. Whenever possible, precise identification is preferred but when that is not possible a detailed description is substituted.

Time and duration identifies the time that an observer first noticed the event, or if it is concluded, the time that it was observed. When an event is ongoing or continued for a period of time, the time it first was first noticed is provided with the duration of the observation.

Equipment or weapons describes any equipment or weapons involved.

Sanctuary of Anonymity A refuge provided by an inability to determine the identity of an adversary. Unknown adversaries not only present a threat but are able to move and act with impunity.

Satisficing A method for making decisions that opts for a prompt search for adequacy over a prolonged one for the optimal.

Scenario Review A method that identifies likely probabilities from boundless possibilities. It identifies realistic probabilities with a best and worst case scenario, as well as the presumptive with a most likely scenario.

Sector of Fire A designated zone to be protected by an individual, team, or unit. Any target within a sector of fire is the responsibility of the person or unit assigned, and conversely, no individual is allowed to shoot outside their assigned sector of fire. (See also *Field of Fire*)

Security One of the nine principles of war that identifies the importance of taking precautions to deny an adversary any unexpected advantage. The principle of security encompasses far more than just secrecy, however, and may be better described as protectiveness. (See also *Nine Principles of War*)

Sequels Courses of actions that follow other actions. Sequels answer questions of "what next?"(See also *Branches*)

Shaping Operation Any series of actions taken in anticipation of an engagement or tactical operation designed to promote accomplishment of strategic objectives. Shaping operations enhance success by negating or mitigating potentially adverse effects while strengthening or increasing potentially favorable factors.

Shift from a Known Point A navigation system that calls attention to an easily identifiable terrain feature or man-made object and then provides a direction and distance from it. (See also *Navigation Methods*)

Signal to Noise Ratio A metric used to compare the amount of useful information with the amount of useless information. The higher the ratio the more difficult it is to comprehend.

Signal A means of communication which includes anything that serves to indicate, warn or direct some event or action. Signals come in all forms but the most common include sounds, lights and gestures. (See also *Communication Forms, Graphics, Numbers* and *Language*)

Similarity Heuristic A procedure or technique that provides clues to solutions based upon what has worked in the past in similar situations. Similarity heuristics rely on pattern recognition in that the decision maker is able to classify the current problem as fundamentally the same as one in memory, either from training and education or from personal experience.

Simplicity One of the nine principles of war that identifies the freedom from unnecessary complexity, intricacy or pretentiousness. A plan that cannot be understood cannot be implemented. (See also *Nine Principles of War*)

Situation Assessment Any analysis that attempts to identify the various elements and dynamics at play in an unfolding situation, especially those that may influence a favorable outcome. (See also *Analysis* and *Synthesis*)

Situational Awareness

A concept that describes a person's knowledge and understanding of the circumstances, surroundings, and influences with regard to an unfolding situation. It also includes everything that is known about the situation leading up to the current episode, as well as the impact it might have on other incidents. (See also *Common Operational Picture*)

Six Principles of Special Operations refers to six principles which are crucial to the success of special operations. These are simplicity, security, repetition, surprise, speed and purpose. (See also *Nine Principles of War*)

SMEAC—Five Paragraph Planning and Briefing Format

Situation is the first component and provides a brief summary of all that has transpired and any mitigating or aggravating circumstances that can affect the operation.

Mission is the second component and precisely identifies the objective to be accomplished. This is the most important component because it provides the basis for which all planning must eventually follow.

Execution is the component is that is usually the most voluminous and time consuming because it not only assigns missions to each unit, but also describes how they are expected to be achieved.

Administrative and Logistics is the fourth component and is often referred to as the "beans, bandages and bullets" section. This component provides instructions for logistical support, such as how personnel are to be fed, equipped, transported and relieved. (also referred to as the Service and Support or Service and Supply component)

Command and Signal. This component identifies and describes the critical command and control personnel and facilities and provides information on how the various units will communicate.

Social Forecast An estimation of the potential, location, scope and volatility for social events. While a social forecast is more than a guess, it stops short of a prediction.

Space A three-dimensional realm in which matter exists. Space is comprised of length, width and height and maneuver can be in any direction. (See also *Cyberspace, Humanspace and Time*)

Span of Control Refers to the number of subordinates that are under the direct supervision of a single superior. (See also *Table of Organization*)

Speed Refers to the rapidity and quickness of actions. It includes all functions and operations involved in a tactical operation, but is especially critical in a conflict. (See also *Tempo*)

Standing Operating Procedures (SOP) A formal policy that standardizes methods and routines within an agency according to established procedures. This provides an ability to quickly and easily incorporate units with complex functions without extensive elaboration. They are also referred to as "standard" operating procedures and may be written or unwritten.

Steering Mark Any well-defined object on the ground that can be used for orientation. (See also *Prominent Terrain*)

Stockholm Syndrome An emotional attachment between hostages and hostage-takers that develops when a hostage is threatened with death and unable to escape.

Strategy The planning and development of large-scale and/or long-range operations to ensure a satisfactory end state. Strategies employ a broad perspective and look at the problem as a whole. They treat problems in a holistic manner rather than simply a collection of the component parts. (See also *Tactics* and *Techniques*)

Supply Push System

A logistical strategy that places responsibility on the logistics section for providing all necessary support to a deployed unit. Supplies and personnel reliefs are usually assigned, moved and distributed according to a schedule based upon an estimate of need by the logistics component. It is sometimes called a "logistical push system."(See also *Demand-Pull System*)

Surge Strategy

A deployment strategy that intentionally overestimates the immediate need and attempts to quickly provide a decisive intervention to avoid potentially devastating consequences. (See also *Ramp-up Strategy*)

Surprise

One of the nine principles of war that emphasizes the advantages that result from striking an adversary at an unexpected time or place, or in an unanticipated manner. It is not necessary that an adversary be taken completely unaware, only that he becomes aware too late to effectively react. (See also *Nine Principles of War*)

Sustainability

An ability to maintain or endure. Sustainability is heavily influenced by environmental conditions. (See also *Trafficability* and *Visibility*)

Sustainment Identifies the need to maintain or endure. While sustainability includes many aspects it is especially susceptible to weather conditions. Weather effects like extreme heat or cold, sleet, dust, or humidity will all affect how well and how long both equipment and personnel can operate effectively. Sustainment is one of the four principal roles in the logistical process. (See also *Logistical Process*, *Procurement, Distribution,* and *Recovery*)

Swarming Tactic A tactic in which the scheme of maneuver involves multiple semi-autonomous units that converge on a single target from many directions.

SWOT Technique A method of analysis that integrates four factors that make up the acronym; *strengths*, *weaknesses*, *opportunities* and *threats*. Strengths and weaknesses are inward looking and normally focused on the response organization itself. Opportunities and threats are outward looking and attempt to identify factors, influences and opportunities that result from environmental factors and adversary errors. (See also *Situation Assessment*)

Symmetric Strategy A strategy in which one force attempts to match—or rather, to overmatch—an adversary's strengths. (See also *Asymmetric Strategy*)

Synchronous System — Refers to a method of communicating that requires all participants to communicate at the same time. (See also *Asynchronous System*)

Synthesis — A mental process that involves integrating the various components and activities of an intervention into a cohesive whole so that the plan is both effective and efficient. It is of great value for estimating the impact of the various dynamics and identifying intermediate objectives. (See also *Analysis*)

Table of Organization — A table of organization, sometimes called an "organizational chart," is a chart-like "picture" of an organization that reveals the formal relationships within it. It is used to depict lines of authority, spans of control, echelons of command, and other factors. It is also called the command and control architecture. (See also *Command and Control Architecture, Chain of Command and Command Channel*)

Tactical Control — A command relationship that gives a commander authority for assignments limited to objectives necessary to accomplish specific missions. Sometimes referred to by the acronym TACON. (See also *Administrative Control* and *Operational Control*)

Tactical Science — The systematized body of knowledge covering the principles and doctrines associated with tactical operations and emergency responses. It reconciles scientific knowledge with practical ends.

Tactics The methods and concepts used to accomplish particular missions. (See also *Strategy* and *Techniques*)

Technique A procedure or process for performing a specific task or function. Techniques almost always involve the employment or utilization of a weapon or piece of equipment. (See also *Strategy* and *Tactics*)

Tempo The speed, rhythm or rate of movement of something. In a tactical operation it describes the rapidity at which events are unfolding. (See also *Density* and *Initiative*)

Terrain Analysis Steps **Key Terrain** is any locality or area, the control of which affords a marked advantage to either the suspect or police. A subset of key terrain is *commanding terrain*, which is any terrain that offers a decisive advantage

Observation refers to the ability to view an area or other feature. **Field of fire** refers to the area that a weapon can cover effectively from a given position. (See also *Sectors of Fire*)

Cover is anything that protects against weapons fire and their effects. In order for something to be considered as cover it must not only protect from projectiles but any of their effects. **Concealment** refers to anything that prevents observation.

Obstacle is any object that stops, impedes or diverts the movement of forces. When an obstacle is so formidable that it completely prevents movement it is called a *barrier*, and is a subset of this component.

Avenue of Approach is simply a route by which friendly forces can reach an objective. **Avenue of Escape** is simply a route by which a suspect can maneuver to a better position or evade attempts to capture him.

Terrain Analysis The process by which important terrain features are identified and evaluated for their impact on a tactical operation. A terrain analysis may be as simple as a mental survey of the likely influence of various terrain features or as sophisticated as a written, comprehensive and detailed analysis that includes the effects of lighting and weather. (See also *Weather Analysis*)

Terrain Appreciation The process used to glean insight from how terrain will affect an operation. Because the use of terrain is also heavily influenced by weather conditions, weather and lighting factors are also part of the process.

Terrain Shielding The utilization of terrain, including the vegetation and structures on it, as protection from a threat. (See also *Cover* and *Concealment*)

Tightly Coupled Plans A plan that requires close coordination and has more time-dependent processes. While no plan is exclusively tightly coupled, those that rely on scarce resources or resources not controlled by the incident commander benefit from tight couplings. Tightly coupled plans tend to be more efficient than loosely coupled plans but are not very flexible and are easily damaged. (See also *Loosely Coupled Plans*)

Time A non-space continuum where events occur in an irreversible succession from the past through the present to the future. Because time is a succession, maneuver is always linear and moves only forward in time. (See also *Cyberspace, Humanspace and Space*)

Time Divisions **Fixed Time** is definitively and unequivocally set and not dependent upon external factors. (See also *Time*)

Periodic Time refers to a specified division, portion or interval identified by a distinctive characteristic. (See also *Time*)

Relative Time is a point or period of time having significance only in relation to something else. (See also *Time*)

Time Driven Tasks Tasks that have fixed durations are time dependent. A time driven task cannot be expedited by adding resources. Sometimes referred to as "time dependent" tasks. (See also *Resource Driven Tasks*)

Time or Sequence — One of the three ways of implementing a plan. This method awaits a scheduled or anticipated event or when one event is a precursor for another. (See also *Four Types of Orders, Contemporaneously* and *On Order*)

Trafficability — The ability of moving something from one place to another, especially in a conveyance of some sort. Trafficability depends on a combination of the conditions and the mode of transportation. (See also *Sustainability* and *Visibility*)

Trends — A trend is a combination of measurement and prediction used to identify a general tendency, inclination or predisposition. Trends are identified by measuring events. (See also *Potentials*, *Capabilities* and *Intentions*)

Tripwire — A technique used to automatically implement a plan, procedure or series of actions. Tripwires afford instant action within predetermined guidelines without burdening a busy commander with needless concern over decisions which are so apparent that they can be "defaulted." (See also *Decision Point*)

Unfit for Command — A common cause of failure of tactical operations and disaster responses which, generally, can be attributed to one or more of three factors.

Failure to Learn can usually be attributed to either ignoring or not recognizing contributory factors and influences, often because of failing to objectively critique and correct past mistakes.

Failure to Adapt occurs when a commander fails to adjust to changing circumstances.

Failure to Anticipate occurs when a commander fails to plan and prepare for those factors and influences that can be reasonably expected.

Unified Command A command relationship between two or more agencies working together which incorporates the senior commanders from supporting units into a single command module where command is shared. Unified command is commonly used when the reinforcing unit is larger than the one reinforced. (See also *Joint Command*)

Unity of Command One of the nine principles of war that ensures that all efforts are focused on a common goal. Unity of command is achieved by vesting a single commander with the requisite authority to direct, coordinate and control the actions of all forces employed in reaching the objective. (See also *Nine Principles of War*)

Unity of Effort Refers to the collaboration of all forces toward a common objective even though they may have different supervisors and report through different chains of command.

Unreasonable Force The use of any force when it is unjustified. The most common mistake associated with complaints of unnecessary force is lack of urgency. (See also *Excessive Force*)

Vapor Swarm A swarming tactic that involves maneuver elements that are already dispersed and converge on a target from many directions. It is also called a "dispersed swarm."(See also *Cloud Swarm*)

Visibility The clarity and distance something can be seen with or without visual aids. (See also *Trafficability* and *Sustainability*)

Warning Order An order that is used when it appears certain that an individual or unit will be required, but is not immediately needed. It can also be used to advise that some type of action may be required. This is particularly valuable if the action requires unusual resources or extraordinary preparation. (See also *Four Types of Orders*)

War of Attrition A conflict which is resolved through the gradual diminution of forces and/or resistance by constant stress, exhaustion or casualties.

Weather Analysis The process by which atmospheric conditions are identified and evaluated for their impact on a tactical operation. (See also *Terrain Analysis*)

Weather The state of the atmosphere at any given time and place with respect to such things as temperature, wind speed and direction, humidity, precipitation, and so forth.

Will A desire, purpose or determination held by one or more people. Thus, a single will can represent an opposing position from any number of suspects or terrorists.

Window of Vulnerability A period of time when conditions exist that place a tactical team at a disadvantage.

Windows of Opportunity Intervals in time which provide temporary advantages.

Exploitation Window is a period of time in which an individual or unit is at some sort of disadvantage as a result of an intentional action by their opponent.

Window of Vulnerability occurs when conditions exist that place a tactical team at a disadvantage.

Zone of Action Any geographical region where a commander is actively attempting to influence the outcome of an operation or disaster response. Zones of action are typically comprised of areas of operation and areas of influence. (See also *Area of Operation*, *Area of Interest* and *Area of Influence*)

INDEX

ABOUT THE PUBLISHER

2011

LANTERN BOOKS was founded in 1999 on the principle of living with a greater depth and commitment to the preservation of the natural world. In addition to publishing books on animal advocacy, vegetarianism, religion, and environmentalism, Lantern is dedicated to printing books in the U.S. on recycled paper and saving resources in day-to-day operations. Lantern is honored to be a recipient of the highest standard in environmentally responsible publishing from the Green Press Initiative.

www.lanternbooks.com